Talking Dirty on *Sex and the City*

Talking Dirty on *Sex and the City*

Romance, Intimacy, Friendship

Beatriz Oria

ROWMAN & LITTLEFIELD
Lanham • Boulder • New York • Toronto • Plymouth, UK

Published by Rowman & Littlefield
4501 Forbes Boulevard, Suite 200, Lanham, Maryland 20706
www.rowman.com

10 Thornbury Road, Plymouth PL6 7PP, United Kingdom

British Library Cataloguing in Publication Information Available

Library of Congress Cataloging-in-Publication Data

Oria, Beatriz, 1981–
Talking dirty on Sex and the city : romance, intimacy, friendship / Beatriz Oria.
p. cm.
Includes bibliographical references and index.
ISBN 978-1-4422-3580-9 (cloth : alk. paper) — ISBN 978-1-4422-3581-6 (ebook) 1. Sex and the
city (Television program) 2. Sex on television. I. Title.
PN1992.77.S465O75 2014
791.45'72—dc23
2014005810

Printed in the United States of America

To my mother, Ana

Contents

Acknowledgments

Research for this book was funded by the Spanish Ministerio de Ciencia e Innovación (research project nos. HUM2007-61183 and FFI2010-15263) and the Diputación General de Aragón (re. H12). Part of this research was carried out at the libraries of the British Film Institute, Senate House Library (London), Bobst University Library (New York), University of Illinois at Chicago, and Columbia College (Chicago). I would like to thank all the members of the Cinema, Culture and Society research group. My participation in this group has helped me shape my own ideas about film genre, and its influence is palpable in my work. More specifically, I am hugely indebted to Professor Celestino Deleyto, who has been involved in this project since its inception. His influence is written all over this book and I am deeply thankful for his generosity, both in academic and personal terms.

Finally, I owe most to Daniel, my partner in life, for bearing with me— and my work—through all these years; to my father Alejandro, who would have been so proud to have this book in his hands; and to my mother Ana, whose unconditional love and support have literally brought me where I am today. This book is dedicated to her.

Introduction

Welcome to the Age of Un-Innocence

"Once upon a time, an English journalist came to New York . . ." She met her Prince Charming, and just when she thought they were headed for the altar, he simply stopped calling her: "No one had told her about the end of love in Manhattan." These are the opening words in *Sex and the City*'s pilot episode. *SATC* kicks off in fairy tale mode, but the mood changes quickly, as the show has little to do with the hopeful mood of fairy tales and its happily-ever-afters:

> Welcome to the age of "un-innocence." No one has breakfast at Tiffany's, and no one has affairs to remember. Instead, we have breakfast at 7:00 a.m. . . . and affairs we try to forget as quickly as possible. Self-protection and closing the deal are paramount. Cupid has flown the co-op. How the hell did we get into this mess?

Carrie Bradshaw's (Sarah Jessica Parker) voiceover introduces us in this frank manner to a glossy world of art gallery openings and trendy Manhattan clubs populated by "toxic bachelors," "modelizers," "gay straight men," "straight gay men," "frenemies," and a wide array of picturesque social types whose complex mating behavior will be closely scrutinized by the series. The show offers a quasi-anthropologic analysis of turn-of-the-century social and sexual relationships through the experiences of its protagonist, Carrie, a thirty-something journalist working for the (fictional) *New York Star*. She writes a weekly column called "Sex and the City" that attempts to make sense of contemporary New York's sociosexual mores. Every week she researches a different topic, frequently related to her busy love life. The best way to do this is to share her experiences and doubts with her group of close friends.

Thus, in each episode, a central issue is discussed by the protagonists and subsequently explored through their actual romantic lives: "Are threesomes the new sexual frontier?"; "How often is normal?"; "Are relationships the religion of the nineties?"; "What are the breakup rules?"; "Is it still possible to believe in love at first sight?"; "Is it better to 'fake it' than be alone?"; "Can you change a man?"; "Can you be friends with an ex?" These are just some of the topics dealt with in the series in the course of its six seasons, comprising ninety-four episodes. The questions posed by the show are manifold, but they always have to do with the social and sexual habits of a socially specific group of New Yorkers who are taken as representative of modern sociosexual protocols. These questions, which were considered to be remarkably daring for mainstream television in the show's heyday, do not seem to have lost momentum a decade after its final episode was aired, and only a handful of shows have reached *SATC*'s quotas of boldness and popularity. Quite the contrary, *SATC* remains arguably unmatched to date in the successful combination of both.

In the pilot episode, the big question of the night is "Can women have sex like a man?" which actually implies a more intriguing issue: "Were women in New York really giving up on love and throttling up on power?" Carrie discusses the matter with her friends: Miranda Hobbes (Cynthia Nixon), a relationship-cynic corporate lawyer; Charlotte York (Kristin Davis), a hopelessly romantic art gallery manager; and Samantha Jones (Kim Cattrall), a PR executive for whom the "sexually liberated" qualification falls short. This is the first of a very long list of "chat-and-chew"[1] scenes in which a puzzling dating enigma is explored. This scene serves to introduce the characters and to establish their positions as far as sex and relationships are concerned. The series offers a variety of female types in order to facilitate identification: first, we are introduced to Samantha, a commitment-phobic forty-something highflier with an extremely "progressive" attitude toward sexual matters. In this scene, she defends a woman's right (and even need) to treat men as sexual objects. On the opposite side of the "femininity spectrum" is Charlotte, who prudishly despises the idea of sex without feeling and is a firm believer in romance. Miranda represents a more ambivalent stand, which encapsulates the high degree of complexity relationships have attained at the turn of the millennium: "[men] don't want to be in a relationship with you . . . but as soon as you only want them for sex, they don't like it." This scene is representative of the "roles" these characters are going to play throughout the rest of the series, thus establishing a dynamic of counterbalancing opinions about whatever topic is tackled. Within the group, Carrie occupies a "moderate" position as well, but she also fulfills the role of semi-detached observer, constantly asking questions and leading the conversation toward the points that may help her untangle her weekly conundrum. She is a much better defined character, and we are consistently invited to identify with her: unlike the other characters, we are routinely provided full access to her thoughts and inner feelings.[2]

The episode thus proceeds to explore the question of whether it is possible for women to have sex like men, that is, without feeling. However, it also hints at other recurrent topics throughout the series, thus introducing the viewer to what *SATC* is going to be about: the fear of remaining single forever, the need to play "by the rules" if you want to get a man, the difference between settling and settling down, or the end of romance in contemporary society. The episode chooses to focus on the latter, setting a romantic view of sex against a more cynical one. With the purpose of researching the question, Carrie goes to bed with an ex-boyfriend who repeatedly broke her heart in the past. Without any trace of feeling left for him, she leaves him after climaxing, disregarding the rules of sexual reciprocity. This makes her feel powerful at first, but the episode ends on a rather ambiguous note when she meets him again and realizes that she does not really feel so much in control as she thought. The realization that she is not really as cool with the situation as he appears to be makes her question the idea that the episode seemed to have initially endorsed, namely, that "this is the first time in the history of Manhattan that women have had as much money and power as men, plus the equal luxury of treating men like sex objects." However, the option of "playing by the rules" and behaving according to traditional female protocols is also dismissed, as Charlotte is left feeling equally dissatisfied with her date, who ends up having casual sex with Samantha. In this way, the episode offers no clear-cut answers to the question initially posed. The pilot, which will be later analyzed in this book, is a good example of the structure usually followed by the series: the issue that is raised at the beginning of the episode is subsequently explored and explicitly reflected on, only to be partially resolved by its denouement. In the end, a loose moral conclusion is usually reached, but one that tends to acknowledge the different viewpoints exposed throughout the episode, leaving it open-ended in many occasions.

By means of this "polyphonic" narrative structure, from one episode to the next, *SATC* explores a different weekly dilemma. The dilemma in question is invariably related to issues of interpersonal relationships and sociosexual protocols in a culturally specific context. The aim of this book is to analyze the discourses on intimacy and relationships proposed by the series from a generic point of view. Thus, I will examine *SATC*'s approach to issues like singleness, romance, sex, sexual identity, monogamy, marriage, or friendship in connection with the series' deployment of the conventions of romantic comedy. This book will discuss the ways in which the serial structure interacts with this particular genre, while also taking into account the program's context. Social theory on love, romance, intimacy, sexuality, the family, and friendship will be used in order to explore *SATC*'s engagement with these topics. The two films that have been made following on the series' success will be left out of this book, since I consider them to be entirely different texts in terms of content, form, and ideology.

This book has five chapters and a conclusion. Chapter 1 situates *SATC* within the television and film context in which it was produced. Regarding the former, the show is inextricably linked to the industrial changes brought about by the advent of the "Quality TV" phenomenon, which was led by cable channels like HBO. As far as the film context is concerned, it should be pointed out that the critical literature on the show has taken a great variety of approaches, but nothing has been written about this series from a film studies perspective so far. Since one of my main aims is to focus on the interaction of one particular genre—romantic comedy—with the cultural context in which the series is inscribed, it is necessary to contextualize the show within the history of romantic comedy.

The following chapters examine *SATC*'s attitude toward contemporary intimate discourses and how they are articulated through specific formal and generic conventions. For practical reasons, and due to the length of the series, only a representative selection of episodes is analyzed in depth. *SATC* tackles a great variety of topics, but I only focus on questions related to intimacy and interpersonal relationships. Thus, each of the four following chapters examine one of the main topics that the show revolves around, namely, "romance," "heterosexual love," "sex and sexuality," and "friendship." The analysis combines genre theory and social theory.

Thus, chapter 2, "Have We Become Romance Intolerant? Romancing Consumption," uses Eva Illouz's theories to analyze the representation of romance in *SATC* in connection with the ethos of the capitalist society in which it is inserted. In the show the idea of "true romance" seems to be clearly linked with the world of manufactured consumption. However, this chapter shows how, despite appearances, *SATC* is more prone to the romanticization of middlebrow commodities that symbolize the "ordinary." As a result, it manages to endorse an "accessible" kind of romance while fully reinforcing the legitimacy of consumption and reinventing romantic comedy's conventions for a media-savvy audience.

Chapter 3, "What's the Harm in Believing? Romantic versus Democratic Love," is concerned with the representation of heterosexual love in the series. Two main trends can be generally identified in contemporary definitions of intimacy. On the one hand, there are those who propose the norms of friendship as the model to follow for contemporary intimacy (Giddens; Pahl; Evans). This trend argues in favor of the democratization—and in its most extreme stand—the rationalization of love. On the other hand, other authors support the idea that romantic love is better equipped to cater to the individual's needs today (Luhmann; Levinas; Beck and Beck-Gernsheim, *The Normal Chaos of Love*; Nehring), since it is more in tune with the individualistic ethos of our times and it encompasses an element of passion generally overlooked by the "friendship model." With these ideas in mind, I analyze how *SATC* deploys romantic comedy conventions to represent one of its main obsessions: the permanent struggle between single life and coupledom. One of the main preoccupations in the show is the way in which women's wish for intimacy clashes with the limitations that love paradoxically imposes on the self. I analyze this double bind in the light of two of the main contemporary theories on relationships and intimacy: the romanticization of love versus its rationalization.

Chapter 4, "What's Love Got to Do with It? The Representation of Female Sexuality," analyzes *SATC*'s depiction of sex. It explores changing social attitudes toward female sexuality as reflected by the series, as well as the show's contribution to the construction of new meanings about sex and sexual identity at the turn of the century. The chapter uses Giddens's notion of "plastic sexuality" and Foucault's concept of confession in order to unravel the connection established by the show between sexuality and self-identity and how this is filtered through the comic perspective of romantic comedy.

Chapter 5, "With a Little Help from My Friends: New Family Models in *Sex and the City*," looks at the changes experienced by means of the concept of "family relationships" and the increasingly important role played by friendship in the organization of the individual's "personal community" (Pahl and Spencer). I analyze the ways in which the series both reflects and helps normalize the major modifications the traditional family unit has undergone in recent years. The individual's increased preference for the company of a close circle of friends as a substitute for the traditional family unit constitutes a remarkable sociological trend that forms part of the radical refashioning the family has experienced in recent decades (Silver; Jamieson; Pahl and Spencer; Beck and Beck-Gernsheim, *The Normal Chaos of Love*; Watters). The valuing of urban networks of friendship as an alternative to conventional family formations in the series is considered: not only is female solidarity privileged over traditional family models in the show, it is potentially perceived as a preferable option to the heterosexual romantic union, thus providing an alternative meaning for romantic comedy's happy ending.

By focusing on these four aspects, and combining a film and TV studies approach to the show with social theory, I hope to offer a new perspective on one of the most cherished programs in recent television history, one that, more than a TV show, has become a cultural touchstone in its own right at the turn of the millennium.

NOTES

1. This is a term coined by the series crew in order to describe the frequent scenes in which the girls gather around cocktails, coffee, or brunch in order to discuss the week's central

dilemma (Sohn 102). Together with the "think-and-type" scenes (Sohn 103), they form the show's narrative backbone.

2. During the first season, Carrie would speak to the camera directly in order to communicate to the viewer her thoughts and feelings, but this device was dropped in the second season. However, the spectator still has free access to her consciousness thanks to the voice-over that accompanies a great part of the action.

Chapter One

Sex and the City in Context

SATC was first aired on June 6, 1998, on U.S. premier subscription–only cable channel HBO. It did not receive much attention at first, being more of a cult show, but during the second season its popularity started to grow and it became a hit. The result was unparalleled audience figures for a cable channel: an average of six to ten million people were estimated to follow the girls each week in their adventures, occasionally surpassing the ratings of the four major networks (ABC, NBC, CBS, and FOX) among female viewers between the ages of eighteen and thirty-four (Associated Press). This is a remarkable feat, especially if we take into account that, at the time of *SATC*'s first broadcasting (1998–2004), HBO only reached thirty-two million homes, in contrast with the networks' access to at least one hundred million. Unlike most TV programs, for which ratings tend to decrease with time, *SATC* drew more and more viewers with every new episode.

The show was not only supported by audience figures. It also received a great deal of critical acclaim and an unprecedented number of awards for a program on a cable channel. During its six seasons, it was nominated for twenty-four Golden Globes, winning eight times. It was also nominated for fifty Emmys, winning seven times and becoming the first cable show to win the Emmy for an outstanding comedy series in 2001. *SATC* is thus generally credited (together with *The Sopranos*, *Six Feet Under*, and *The Wire*) as one of the key shows for HBO's transformation into a powerhouse for original series (Braxton, "*Sex and the City* Gets Set to Call It a Night").

The most striking fact, however, is that *SATC*'s popularity did not diminish when it ended. On the contrary, its fame experienced a remarkable growth since its conclusion in 2004, crossing boundaries thanks to syndication and DVD releases. Its fan base extends through Latin America, Europe, the Middle East, Oceania, and Asia, where the show was reported to be "a

1

smash among young professionals" in cities like Bangkok, Manila, Taipei, and Hong Kong (Tang). Even in places like Singapore and mainland China, where the series was not broadcast by any channel due to official regulations, the show became a huge success thanks to pirated DVD copies passed around among young people (Jones). In the United States, an average of 2.5 million viewers kept watching the show in reruns every day until 2010 on TBS, which reportedly paid $750,000 an episode for the syndication rights. Since its debut in June 2004, it quickly became "the No. 1 comedy in ad-supported cable among adults 18 to 34 and 18 to 49" (Moss, n.p.). Today, reruns of the series are still regularly broadcast in countries all over the world, including United Kingdom, United States, Russia, Spain, India, Australia, and Turkey.

Another proof of the show's good health more than fifteen years since its debut is the enduring popularity of the "SATC Hotspots Bus Tour" organized in New York by "On Location Tours." It is estimated that an average of fifty thousand people from all over the world travel every year to the Big Apple to ride this bus (Baird), which takes fans of the series to its best-known locations. Surprisingly, instead of waning, the tour's demand since the show's end seemed to surge (McGrath). The release of *SATC*'s two cinematic sequels is another sign of its lasting popularity. Surrounded by controversy and speculation since the possibility of its making was first rumored, *Sex and the City: The Movie* (2008) created so much anticipation that it was joyously hailed by some overexcited critics as "the most important movie ever shot in New York" (Hayes 8). Even though this claim is clearly excessive, the film opened with $56.8 million in box-office returns in its first weekend, thus becoming the highest-grossing debut ever for a movie starring women only. It is also the first tent-pole blockbuster to rest squarely on a female demographic—85 percent of the audience on opening night (Setoodeh). By the end of its theatrical run the film grossed more than $415 million worldwide, becoming the eleventh-highest-grossing film of 2008. Its success encouraged a follow-up, *Sex and the City 2* (2010), which grossed $288 million with a $100 million budget.

However, apart from audience ratings, awards, and cinematic sequels, *SATC*'s relevance can be best measured by its "legacy." The number of TV series that have been influenced by *SATC* in one way or another is certainly outstanding. *SATC*'s producer, Darren Star, tried (and failed) to repeat his previous success with *Miss Match*. Other failed shows arguably influenced by *SATC* are *Leap of Faith*, *Watching Ellie*, and *The Mind of the Married Man*, which was said to be a male version of *SATC* but did not succeed with the critics or the audience (Brownsfield). The show is also credited as precursor of more successful and "edgy" series like *Queer as Folk*, *Desperate Housewives*, and *The L Word*. However, *SATC* did not only "inspire" subsequent shows—it also prompted straightforward imitations that tried to cash in on its success unashamedly. Such was the case with *Lipstick Jungle* and *Cashmere Mafia.*[1] Similarly, *SATC* generated a number of local "replicas" in countries all over the world, such as *Mistresses* in the United Kingdom, *The Marrying Type* in South Korea, *The Balzac Age, or All Men Are Bast . . .*in Russia, and *Hot Ladies* in China.[2] More than a decade after its conclusion, the show's influence is still clearly discernible in successful women-centered shows such as *Secret Diary of a Call Girl, Girls, The Mindy Project, Gossip Girl, Two Broke Girls, Don't Trust the B in Apartment 23, City Girl Diaries,* and of course, *The Carrie Diaries,* the prequel to *SATC* based on the Candace Bushnell novel that deals with Carrie's adolescence.

SATC's huge success is especially outstanding if we take into account the remarkable amount of controversy it generated in its heyday. The intensity of this debate seems to be unparalleled in recent TV history: since the show first saw the light, it became the subject of a heated debate between those who hated[3] and loved[4] the show. Most of the literature on *SATC* has focused on its ideology. The favorite task of critics since the show was first broadcast has been trying to decide whether it is revolutionary[5] or conservative[6] in its representation of gender, class, race, and female sexuality. Most of all, though, *SATC* scholarship has wrestled with the series' stance vis-à-vis feminism, an issue that provokes a striking degree of disagreement. On the one hand, there are those who, broadly speaking, regard the show as anti-feminist (Raven; Bignell, *An Introduction to Television Studies*; D'Erasmo; Coren; Roberts; Gill), describing it in terms that range from "feminism lite" (Bunting) to "surprisingly retrograde" (Orenstein). Many other scholars, however, praise its feminist commitment to empowering female viewers and to supporting a model of female friendship which not only presents singleness as a legitimate way of life for women, but also contributes to the development of an alternative vision of the contemporary family (Wolf; Sayeau, "Carrying On"; Jermyn, "In Love with Sarah Jessica Parker"; A. Nelson, "Miss Bradshaw Goes to Washington"; A. Nelson, "Sister Carrie Meets Carrie Bradshaw"; Gerhard; Henry; Kohli).

Despite the great controversy generated by the show (or maybe because of it), *SATC*'s figures are certainly noteworthy. Not many series in recent TV history have managed to achieve its status. How can this popularity be explained? Why did a program broadcast to a very limited number of homes and addressing such a specific niche audience manage to become such a television touchstone? The reasons for this are manifold and go from the show's edgy scripts and outstanding performances to its impeccable attention to costume and cinema-like production values. However, many other TV shows meet these criteria and do not attain the same quotas of success. The key to *SATC*'s unmatched popularity lies not only in its quality as a media product, but more importantly, in its ability to tap into the zeitgeist of its age. *SATC* clearly struck a cultural chord, asking the right questions at the right time, directly interpolating its audience with relevant identificatory models. In its weekly exploration of a contemporary dilemma, the show did not necessarily provide satisfactory answers, but at least made millions of perplexed viewers feel that they were not alone in their daily struggles. For some critics, *SATC*'s cultural resonance became so evident that it arguably stopped reflecting reality in order to have a palpable influence on it, especially on contemporary sexual scripts (Jensen and Jensen; Markle). Reportedly, a new type of woman who tried to resemble the show's protagonists in her way of life and attitude toward relationships started to become visible (Chaplin; Skov Anderson et al.; Hymowitz, "The New Girl Order"; Marikar).[7] This is just one of the most noticeable examples of the show's far-reaching impact on the social context in which it is inscribed. In light of everything that has been said here, it seems safe to suggest that *SATC*'s legitimacy as object of study lies not simply in its status as a TV landmark, but more importantly, in its significance as cultural marker of the premillennial zeitgeist.

SOMETHING SPECIAL'S ON: THE TV CONTEXT

The aim of this chapter is to situate *SATC* within the cinematic and TV context in which it was produced. Concerning the latter, the show is indebted to a long tradition of women-centered shows that have been a regular feature on the small screen since the 1950s. Apart from this, it is also inextricably linked to the industrial changes brought about by the advent of the third era of television and the "Quality TV" phenomenon, which has its clearest proponent in HBO.

Before *Sex and the City*

During the 1950s and early 1960s, most women on television were married. *I Love Lucy* was one of the first successful female-centered shows. This series, which is credited with establishing the basic formula of the sitcom format (Mills, "I Love Lucy"), dramatized the struggle between the status quo's will to position women within the domestic sphere and its protagonist's determination to break free from her frustrating life as a housewife. Although the general tendency was to depict women as devoted wives, some shows like *Our Miss Brooks* and *The Ann Sothern Show* started to portray single professional women. Despite this, the women in these shows usually held traditionally "feminine" jobs and their ultimate goal was always marriage and children.

In contrast, the late 1960s and 1970s witnessed the advance of the sexual revolution and second-wave feminism, ushering in a new kind of female: the proud single working woman. This "new woman" was greatly influenced by the publication of the groundbreaking 1962 book, *Sex and the Single Girl* by

Helen Gurley Brown (Luckett). During this time, some women's priorities began to change as they started to reject marriage as their ultimate life goal in favor of professional fulfillment and economic independence. Social changes affecting women going on at the time—such as the legalization of abortion, the no-fault divorce, or the newly acquired rights to credit (Rosen)—also started to make their way into TV. Series like *That Girl, The Mary Tyler Moore Show,* and *Rhoda* depicted the lives of single women—by choice—living in the city.[8] In this sense, they constitute the clearest early precursors of *SATC.* Shows like *Maude* and *One Day at a Time* followed the same pattern, but featured more explicit, self-identified feminist characters.

The feminist militancy of the 1970s was replaced in the 1980s by a conservative media backlash against female emancipation. However, feminist advances could not be simply ignored. As a result, during this decade television tended to depict women who had both a family and a career, but stressed domestic life and rarely showed these presumably successful professionals at work or having to negotiate both aspects of their lives. Such was the case of the women depicted in *The Cosby Show, Family Ties,* or *Growing Pains.* Due to the scarcity of series emphasizing the joys of single life for women during this period, the greatest signs of "progress" in the representation of women at the time can be seen in those shows which did not focus on traditional home life, but chose to represent female solidarity and friendship instead. Such was the case of *Cagney and Lacey, The Facts of Life, Kate & Allie,* and *Designing Women.* Some of these shows featured single working women, but the stress was laid on the relationship between their female characters, which frequently functioned as a surrogate family, thus representing an alternative to the nuclear family promoted by the Reagan administration. The most successful of these series, *The Golden Girls,* is the most significant precursor to *SATC.* The similarities between the two sets of characters are obvious, as each "golden girl" seems to find her match in *SATC* (Griffin and Bolonik; Macey; Jermyn, *Sex and the City*). Nevertheless, the most important resemblance between both shows lies in their message: male lovers may come and go, but female friendship is forever.

The late 1980s witnessed the appearance of a highly influential show for the representation of single professional women: *Murphy Brown.* This series showed Candice Bergen—also featured in several episodes of *SATC*—as Murphy, a single news anchor. The show was a remarkable success: it ran for ten seasons—from 1988 to 1998—and won numerous awards, but it acquired an unprecedented political relevance when Murphy had a child out of wedlock. This was pointed out by Vice President Dan Quayle, a Republican, during the 1992 presidential election, in what has become known as the "Murphy Brown speech" (May 19, 1992). In it, Quayle attacked the series for mocking the importance of the nuclear family, and "calling it just another lifestyle choice" (quoted in Fiske 69). This sparked a great deal of controversy and a public discussion on family values. In September 1992 the show incorporated this debate into the actual plot of the series by including Quayle's speech and having Murphy respond to him in her news show. Ashley Sayeau argues that it was this controversy that "set off a string of series in the 1990s about non-traditional families, especially ones about older single friends living together, as in *Friends* and *Sex and the City*" ("As Seen on TV" 59). It is unlikely that an isolated occurrence like this might have triggered a whole new television trend. Rather, the proliferation of this kind of show is probably related to larger sociological trends, such as the disintegration of the traditional family unit with the increase of divorce, nonheterosexual lifestyles, and women's reluctance to give up their single status and professional careers for marriage and motherhood. On the other hand, the public resonance of the Quayle controversy is, no doubt, a symptom of a society trying to assimilate these changes.

Another show that can be seen as *SATC*'s precursor during the late 1980s and early 1990s is *The Days and Nights of Molly Dodd*. For Amanda D. Lotz, this series constitutes *SATC*'s clearest antecedent, not only for its subject matter—a divorced woman facing the vicissitudes of single life in New York—but, more importantly, because of its formal style. *The Days and Nights of Molly Dodd* was one of the first shows to mix comedy and drama, which allowed for more sophisticated plots and more complex characters. The series also featured a self-conscious style that drew attention to the text as a construction (Lotz). Shows like this introduced new elements that would become common during the 1990s, such as the abandonment of the realist tradition of storytelling, the emergence of the postfeminist heroine, and the proliferation of the "dramedy" genre.

It is in this context that *SATC* was born. Running from 1998 to 2004, the series was shaped by third-wave feminism and its inherent ideological ambivalence. Together with *Ally McBeal*, another prominent contemporaneous show, it built on the tradition of the "new woman" series and participated in the 1990s fondness for representing singleness. Formally, both shows expand the form of the "new woman" show through the use of narrative conventions such as these: a mixture of episodic and serial plots; a blend of comedy and drama; the use of self-conscious devices, such as first-person narration and parody; an emphasis on characterization rather than on plot development; and the construction of narratives around a multiplicity of female characters, which allows for different points of identification (Lotz). Ideologically, both shows feature postfeminist characters who have mixed feelings about marriage and independence. These contradictory feelings are a direct result of the conflicting messages that characterize the postfeminist agenda. The final outcome is a more realistic and complex rendering of womanhood than representations of previous decades had offered.

SATC and *Ally McBeal* are by no means alone as examples of female-centered series at the turn of the millennium. Lotz noted an unprecedented proliferation of this kind of drama from the mid-1990s to the mid-2000s. By female-centered drama, she understands this as series that "construct their narratives around one or more female protagonists, regardless of whether the audience—intended or hailed—is predominantly female" (30). Examples include *Living Single, Xena: Warrior Princess, La Femme Nikita, Buffy the Vampire Slayer, Any Day Now, Charmed, Providence, Judging Amy, Once and Again, Strong Medicine, That's Life, The Huntress, Dark Angel, Gilmore Girls, The Division, Kate Brasher, Witchblade, Crossing Jordan, Philly, Alias, The American Embassy, The Court, Birds of Prey, Presidio Med, Girls Club, MISSING, Wildcard, Joan of Arcadia, Tru Calling, Cold Case, Karen Sisco, Wonderfalls, The L Word, Veronica Mars, Desperate Housewives, Medium, Grey's Anatomy, The Inside,* or *The Closer*. As this list shows, the proliferation of programming focused on women in U.S. television at the turn of the century was extraordinary—particularly taking into account its past scarcity. This phenomenon was also accompanied by a significant rise in the number of female-targeted cable networks. This increased attention to female audiences may be attributed to significant changes in the competitive environment of the TV industry: factors such as the multichannel transition, the increase in viewer control thanks to new technologies, the reduction of regulations, the rise in multi-set homes, and the decrease in family viewing created the need to address specific niche groups rather than mass audiences. At the end of the twentieth century, this strategy expanded from cable to broadcast networks (Lotz). Thus, it can be said that the advent of the post-network era was partly responsible for increasing women's visibility in the TV environment. This is a positive occurrence, as TV has always functioned as a public arena for women to discuss the issues that affected them. Maybe because they have traditionally lacked access to positions of political and social power, Ashley Sayeau believes that "it is often through television . . . that women's issues have been most delicately and persuasively addressed" ("As Seen on TV" 59). If this is so, this book hopes to show that *SATC* has been a key player in the debate.

The Quality TV Phenomenon

HBO is frequently quoted as one of the main exponents of "Quality TV." However, what does Quality TV mean exactly? This term is generally assumed to have been coined by Robert J. Thompson in his 1996 volume *Television's Second Golden Age: From* Hill Street Blues *to* ER. In this work, Thompson argued that "quality TV is best defined by what is not. It is not 'regular' TV. . . . In a medium long considered artless, the only artful TV is that which isn't like all the rest of it" (13). Thompson's provocative claim was accompanied by twelve criteria of definition: U.S. Quality TV breaks the rules of established television; it has a "quality pedigree" in the sense that it is produced by people coming from "classier media"; it addresses a blue-chip audience; it does not usually participate in the commercialist values of regular television; it features a large ensemble cast which allows for a variety of viewpoints; it has a "memory" in the sense that shows tend to refer back to previous episodes; it creates a new genre by combining existing ones; it is literary and writer-based; it is self-conscious, controversial, and with aspirations of "realism"; and last, but not least, it enjoys critical acclaim.

For Thompson, the first phase of this new kind of TV fiction stretches from the debut of *Hill Street Blues* in 1981 to the cancellation of *Twin Peaks* in 1991, and includes shows like *St. Elsewhere, thirtysomething, Moonlighting, Northern Exposure, Cagney & Lacey, L.A. Law,* and *China Beach.* In the early 1990s, the success of *NYPD Blue* and *ER* green-lighted a new style of drama that consolidated itself as a genre throughout the 1990s, becoming the norm in television fiction by the end of the decade and during the 2000s with series like *The Practice, Ally McBeal, Boston Public, Buffy the Vampire Slayer, Angel, The X-Files, Once and Again, Judging Amy, Providence, Law & Order, The West Wing, Oz, The Sopranos, Sex and the City, The Wire, Curb Your Enthusiasm, Six Feet Under, Deadwood, Carnivàle, The Shield, Nip/Tuck, Rescue Me, Over There, CSI, Lost, Californication, Mad Men, 30 Rock, Damages, Weeds, Desperate Housewives, Entourage, House M.D., Grey's Anatomy, Studio 60, True Blood, Flight of the Conchords, Rome, Firefly, Battlestar Galactica, The Office, Fringe, Band of Brothers, Dexter, Generation Kill,* and *The Pacific.* This list is by no means exhaustive; it simply aims to illustrate how Quality TV as a genre has flooded the small screen in the last twenty years or so.

Janet McCabe and Kim Akass have lately reformulated the chronology of the genre. For them, the first phase goes from 1981 to 1996. The latter date coincides with the publication of Thompson's book and inaugurates the postnetwork era: a highly competitive market characterized by multi-channel TV and the cable revolution, in which consumer demand gains relevance thanks to the assistance of digital technologies and new ways of distribution (*Quality TV* 3–5). This second golden age for TV fiction, the age of *SATC,* goes roughly from 1996—the year of publication of Thompson's book—to 2007—the end of *The Sopranos.*

It's Not TV, It's HBO: The Second Golden Age of Quality TV

Traditionally, the medium of television has never been the critics' darling. It has always lived in the shadow of "artier" media, such as theater, and especially, cinema. However, a remarkable change in this respect has taken place during the last two decades. The popular and academic perception of television—at least as far as fiction is concerned—has been radically altered. U.S. television has experienced a dramatic "rebirth" since the mid-nineties or so. A new aesthetic disposition toward U.S. quality drama has been awakened: the achievements of the small screen have given way to the notion that a TV series may be considered as a work of art, something unthinkable not so long ago (Anderson). This new frame of mind has led some critics to the conclusion that contemporary TV drama can be said to equal, and even surpass, cinema (Billen; Joyard and Prigent; Pearson; Martínez Roig; Casas). Joyard and Prigent's documentary film, *Hollywood: Le Règne des series*, concludes with these words: "In the realm of U.S. entertainment and culture, TV series have taken control of political discourse, social issues and aesthetic evolution, as cinema did in the 1970s" (my translation, 44:54– 45:13).

One of the reasons frequently pointed out for this phenomenon is the migration of talented personnel, especially scriptwriters, from cinema to TV. The small screen has become an attractive medium for the top writers to work in due to the freedom some cable channels like HBO offer their creators. Thus, the presence of names such as Aaron Sorkin, David Chase, Alan Ball, David Milch, David Shore, Michael Patrick King, or J. J. Abrams behind shows like *The West Wing, The Sopranos, Six Feet Under, Deadwood, House M.D., SATC,* and *Lost* provided these shows with an "exclusivity" stamp previously reserved only for cinema. This led many people to perceive them as auteur shows.

The newly acquired visibility of the TV series' creator has undoubtedly helped raise the genre's critical stakes, somehow proving Pierre Bourdieu's assertion that the "charismatic ideology" of authorship "is the ultimate basis of belief in the value of a work of art" (*The Field of Cultural Production* 76). However, recent technological developments have also contributed to blur the boundaries between cinema and television, at least in aesthetic terms. Thanks to digital technologies, production values in television have improved greatly: today's television enjoys higher resolution, more stable image and surround sound, a dynamic editing style, and a higher quality of visual imagery (R. Nelson). Contemporary "quality" dramas also distinguish themselves from their predecessors in their higher budgets, which in some cases come close to those of mainstream films. The result is a brand new televisual aesthetic that resembles the cinematic look of the big screen.

With its "revamped" look and its complex narratives, Quality TV is today amply celebrated, but it does not surprise us anymore. High production values and well-developed characters and story lines have almost become the norm rather than the exception on our screens, but where did this all come from? The answer is simple: it stemmed from the ferocious competition among channels during the post-network era. It was HBO that started the ball rolling. As one of its earliest slogans already announced ("Different and First"), this channel is generally believed to be the precursor of Quality TV as we understand it today. HBO is the brainchild of cable entrepreneur Charles Dolan, who got the franchise to bring cable to lower Manhattan in 1965. He managed to sell his idea of a new cable channel to Time Life, and HBO was born on November 8, 1972. During the 1980s the channel started to develop original programming, but it was the decade of the 1990s that witnessed its growth into a true media empire. With the number of subscribers increasing more than 50 percent between 1995 and 2007, HBO emerged in the late 1990s as "the most talked about, widely celebrated, and profitable network in all of television" (Edgerton and Jones, "HBO's Ongoing Legacy" 315). HBO as we perceive it today was born. [9]

During the last fifteen years or so, HBO has been a pioneer in the making of innovative quality programming, which has paid off not only in terms of revenue and awards, [10] but also in "intangible factors such as prestige, cultural influence and public awareness" (Carter), thus eclipsing all of its competitors. As a result, since the mid-1990s HBO has come to be perceived by critics and audiences alike as synonymous with quality in the television panorama.

How did this unqualified success come about? A sizeable portion of HBO's success lies in the economic model on which it is based (Kelso; Miller). Unlike commercial TV, HBO's business model does not measure success by audience ratings for individual programs, but by general audience satisfaction with the whole schedule, which is reflected on the viewers' monthly subscription renewal. This strategy allows for more "experimental" shows to survive, as they are able to accumulate an audience slowly, rather than having to deliver instant results. HBO does not address a mass audience, but a specific niche market composed of educated, affluent audiences. Relying on a base of subscribers means that the channel is free from government regulations and advertisers' constraints. Therefore, it is able to pursue innovation without having to worry about upsetting the sponsors. Moreover, it is not only that HBO is free to take risks: it is actually *obliged* to take risks in order to justify subscriptions. It needs to give viewers something they cannot see on regular television, and the only way to do this is by somehow distinguishing itself from the rest of the TV grid (Kelso).

Since the advent of the second era of TV, branding became a fundamental strategy for the survival of a channel in the busy TV schedule. HBO can be seen as the quintessential example of how to succeed in building a recognizable brand identity during the digital era. Throughout the years, HBO has managed to equate itself with "quality." Since the very beginning, it marketed itself as more than a TV channel, as a cultural phenomenon addressed to a "chosen" sociocultural elite. HBO has fostered its "quality" brand identity not only by devoting more money than any other network to production costs, but also to promotion. The channel has actively promoted its products as "works of art" and its creators as auteurs (Anderson). The ultimate goal of this strategy is not only to distinguish the brand from its competitors, but to gain subscribers by courting the perception that HBO's viewers are somehow "special," not so much regular TV viewers but consumers of "cultural capital." Subscription grants access to an exclusive club. It signals belonging to a social community that ranks above those who watch "regular TV." The channel's famous taglines ("It's Not TV, It's HBO"; "There's No Place Like HBO"; "Something Special's On"; "Get More"; "Simply the Best") are clearly meant to establish this distinction between what standard broadcast and cable stations have to offer and the "cultural capital" subscribers may obtain from HBO, which promises to grant them access to a higher, more exclusive, social status.

This is the context in which *SATC* is inserted. Its popularity, together with the success of *The Sopranos* (1999–2007) and *Six Feet Under* (2001–2005), helped HBO reach its highest point.[11] The channel's incapability to match its accomplishments with subsequent productions quickly sparked comments about its decline (Andersen; Pasha; Martin; Flint; Berman; Epstein et al.; Weinman, "Is It Time to Declare HBOver?"; Miller; Kelso; McCabe and Akass, "It's Not TV, It's HBO's Original Programming"). Competition from rival networks increased; HBO's success prompted the "popularization" of its modus operandi, and other broadcast and cable stations are now successfully deploying HBO's formula. However, maybe more importantly, HBO's main competition does not come from outside, but from within. That is, the channel is forever competing with itself, as its formidable past success makes it hard to live up to previously set standards. The decline of HBO should not be overstated, though. In a volatile industry characterized by constant flow, the fluctuation of audience ratings is only natural. Besides, HBO has never cared much for ratings, and subscriber figures are still impressive while the brand has not lost an inch of its cultural prestige. Nevertheless, in the long run, more important than figures is HBO's legacy in cultural and industrial terms: being responsible for changing the viewing expectations of television audiences in recent television history is no small feat. Not a bad accomplishment for a channel whose main motto is "It's Not TV."

A POSTFEMINIST NERVOUS ROMANCE? THE FILM CONTEXT

It is important to take into account the TV context in which *SATC* was born. The rise of the Quality TV phenomenon and the special idiosyncrasy of the channel that developed it played a crucial role in making *SATC* what it is— an original, high-quality product in between cinema and television. However, this book intends to approach the show from a film studies perspective, and more specifically, from a generic point of view. *SATC*'s commitment to Quality TV renders it closer to cinema than to traditional television in some aspects. This is especially evident in its production values and its efforts to establish a meaningful dialogue with its context. In this book, I argue that *SATC* tries to fill a "gap" in turn-of-the-century romantic comedy that the big screen has been unable to fill. For this reason, it is also necessary to contextualize the show within the history of Hollywood romantic comedy.

Romantic comedy is one of the most popular genres in film history. However, despite its popularity and endurance through time, it has been routinely sneered at by audiences and critics alike. The assumption of cultural lowliness that has traditionally accompanied the genre has turned it into a guilty pleasure for the public, and an "unworthy" object of analysis for academia, which has constantly belittled it either by omission—the amount of critical work published on this genre is significantly smaller than on other, more "serious" ones—or simply through plain derision, regarding it as simplistic, predictable, and hopelessly associated with a conservative view of love and marriage. Stacey Abbot and Deborah Jermyn, for instance, attribute this critical devaluation of romantic comedy to its address to a female audience and lightweight appearance; to its "cynical" manipulation of the spectator's feelings; and to the popular perception of the genre as "formulaic," "frivolous," and "anti-intellectual" (2). This negative view of romantic comedy as a genre is starting to be contested by academia (Jeffers McDonald, *Romantic Comedy*; Abbot and Jermyn; Grindon). In a similar vein, albeit in a much more modest manner, this book also aims to contribute to the difficult task of "rescuing" romantic comedy from the low cultural ground in which it is usually confined. Through the analysis of a text that fully participates in the conventions of romantic comedy, I expect to show that this genre may be much more complex and sophisticated than it is generally believed to be, if only for its innate capability to evolve with the times and establish a rich and complex dialogue with its social context.

Apart from its low cultural status, the scarcity of romantic comedy criticism in comparison to other genres can also be attributed to its elusive nature. Romantic comedy is a pervasive genre that is frequently intermingled with others. Its elusive nature makes it difficult to define it precisely. Definitions are abundant in the critical literature, though. Tamar Jeffers McDonald, for example, believes that a romantic comedy is "a film which has as its central narrative motor a quest for love, which portrays this quest in a lighthearted way and almost always to a successful conclusion" (*Romantic Comedy* 9). This definition is fairly accurate for what most of us understand by "romantic comedy." However, an important element is missing in it: its connection with its sociocultural context. Ewan Kirkland's definition may be more helpful in this respect. He envisions the genre as "a process of negotiation between broad generic conventions, specific textual requirements, and contemporary constructions of sexuality, gender and social relations" (n.p.) This conception comes closer to my theoretical approach, as it connects the formal aspects of the genre with its sociocultural dimension. Actually, both are virtually impossible to separate: text and context are inextricably linked, as romantic comedy is constantly evolving in order to address culturally specific discourses and anxieties. This ability to adapt to social and cultural transformations is not exclusive to romantic comedy, but a fundamental characteristic of film genre in general. However, romantic comedy is ideally equipped to deal with evolving discourses on masculinity, femininity, and the relationships between the sexes. This adaptability has been patent throughout the history of the genre, and continues to be reflected in recent developments, as the next section will show.

Romantic Comedy: From the "Nervous Romance" to the Present

As will be later discussed, *SATC*'s cinematic "precursors" are to be found in the "radical romantic comedies" (Jeffers McDonald, *Romantic Comedy* 59–84) or "nervous romances" (Krutnik, "The Faint Aroma of Performing Seals" 62–63; Neale and Krutnik 171–72) of the late 1960s and 1970s, which reflected the social turmoil brought about by the sexual revolution and second-wave feminism. Up to the mid-1960s, the romantic comedy panorama had been dominated by "sex comedies." This cycle's main premise was based on the woman's resistance to the man's sexual advances out of wedlock. However, the appearance of the contraceptive pill rendered this scenario obsolete. The availability of birth control made films based on the withholding of sex outdated and no longer in tune with the cultural moment. From the late 1960s onward, sex started to be conceived not only as a legitimate source of individual pleasure disconnected from reproduction, but also as the path toward self-realization and self-expression. This brought about an uncoupling of sex from love that prompted the acceptance of nonmonogamous and nonheterosexual lifestyles (Seidman, *Romantic Longings*). The weakening of the link between sex, love, commitment, and marriage caused a deep crisis for the traditional heterosexual couple. However, at bottom, this crisis was actually brought about by women's emancipation from their traditional roles as devoted wives and housekeepers. Apart from taking control of their reproductive lives, women made considerable advances in the public sphere thanks to the passing of laws that outlawed sex discrimination in employment (1972), did not allow sexually segregated classified ads (1973), or gave married women the right to get credit in their own names (1974) (Rosen). More importantly, after the legalization of abortion in 1973 marriage figures started to decrease, and the new no-fault divorce laws contributed to the rocketing of divorce rates, which increased 100 percent between 1963 and 1975 (Davis 287). In sum, female emancipation painted a whole new social picture for both sexes, one in which old certainties were crumbling down and heterosexual coupling was more complex than ever.

This social upheaval led film critic Brian Henderson to famously diag-
nose the death of romantic comedy in 1978. For him, love had become so
overanalyzed that its representation on the big screen was no longer viable.
On top of this, the social changes brought about by the sexual revolution and
the increasing importance bestowed on sex as a source of self-definition
made romantic love no longer feasible: "when the new self pulls itself together, it is away from the ground of sexual dialectic. To argue this is to
argue the death of romantic comedy" (Henderson 19). It has almost become a
cliché in romantic comedy criticism to point out how this prediction was
immediately followed by the genre's revival thanks to Woody Allen, who
inaugurated a new type of romantic comedy commonly known as "nervous
romance" (Krutnik, "The Faint Aroma of Performing Seals" 62–63; Neale
and Krutnik 171–72).

The intense turmoil that intimate culture was going through at the time
was documented by cinema in films like *The Graduate, On a Clear Day You
Can See Forever, The Heartbreak Kid, What's Up Doc?, Semi-Tough, The
Good-bye Girl, An Unmarried Woman,* and *Starting Over.* However, it was
Allen's "nervous romances" of the late 1970s, *Annie Hall* and *Manhattan,*
that really struck a chord with the audience. These films reflected the crisis
within a couple, in the tension between the lovers' wish to find love and their
cynical awareness of how difficult it is to maintain a meaningful relationship
in a social panorama shaken by female liberation. The advent of feminism is
not the only reason for the "nervousness" of this kind of romantic comedy,
though. Black and gay rights movements also started to gain visibility during
the 1970s, causing a considerable social stir. Paradoxically, this mood of
social upheaval weakened the political fervor and social participation that
had marked the decade of the 1960s. Instead, the 1970s were characterized
by a feeling of introspection and self-absorption. Not in vain is this period
known as the "Me Decade" (Wolfe 162).

Thus, much of the neurosis embedded in the genre stems from this preoccupation with the self; this translates into a remarkable self-consciousness in
the cinematic treatment of love. The "whole romantic thing" (Krutnik, "The
Faint Aroma of Performing Seals" 69) could no longer be embraced naively,
and the exhaustion of romantic clichés threatened the integrity of romance.
The genre is pervaded by a new self-reflexivity, which derives from an
increased awareness of the self and extends to three areas of the text. Firstly,
the "nervous romance" is self-conscious about the romantic relationship: it
faces the fact that romantic fulfillment and personal well-being might not go
hand in hand. Secondly, this self-reflexivity applies to the text itself, which
becomes self-referential, with characters who seem aware of themselves by
frequently addressing the camera directly or by quoting other texts. Lastly,
the "nervous romance" is aware of itself as a modern, more realistic type of
romantic comedy. This is done through a mixture of realism and romanti-

cism. In its attempts to prove that it is "beyond" the naivete of traditional romantic comedy, this genre also features open or unhappy endings, and more realistic elements than its audience was accustomed to, such as the inclusion of loss and death in the story lines, an emphasis on the importance of sexual satisfaction for women, or the deployment of more realistic language, which included swearing and honest discussions of sexual matters (Jeffers McDonald, *Romantic Comedy*).

The 1980s were marked by a "backlash" reaction against feminist gains during the previous decade and the rise of the New Right, which proposed a return to traditional values regarding the family and heterosexual coupling (Faludi). This neoconservative climate was also motivated by the AIDS crisis, which led to the stigmatization of casual sex. This provoked a revival of the conception of sex in connection with love, something intimately linked to courtship, romance, and monogamy. Even though the conception of sex as a source of individual pleasure and self-identity was not erased, the emphasis was rather on its social and spiritual aspects (Seidman, *Romantic Longings*). In cinema, this was reflected by what Steve Neale terms the "new romances" ("The Big Romance or Something Wild?" 287), a new kind of romantic comedy interpreted as a reaction to the "nervous romance" by means of a reassertion of the values of traditional heterosexual romance. Films like *Splash!*, *Romancing the Stone*, *Murphy's Romance*, *Something Wild*, *Peggy Sue Got Married*, *Blind Date*, *Moonstruck*, *Broadcast News*, *Overboard*, *Roxanne*, *Working Girl*, *Big*, *My Stepmother Is an Alien*, *When Harry Met Sally*, or *Pretty Woman* tried to counteract any threat of female independence by reaffirming the primacy of the heterosexual union. With this purpose in sight, the "new romances" make use of the signifiers of old-fashioned romance, embracing it fully, but not innocently: these films are haunted by the "already said," so they must find new ways of asserting the romantic myth while showing their awareness of the long tradition that precedes them in the representation of love on-screen. The result is a high degree of self-consciousness in the revisitation of past conventions. As Krutnik puts it, these films replace the agonized self-questioning of the "nervous romance" with an "ardent yet ironic embrace of romantic possibility" ("Conforming Passions?" 139). This ironic turn in romantic comedy leads him to talk about what he calls the "deception narratives" of the 1990s. These are films that "overtly frame romance as the construction of a representation, consolidating the couple through a blatant manipulation of signs and identities" (Krutnik, "Love Lies" 31–32). Examples include films like *Green Card*, *Housesitter*, *While You Were Sleeping*, or *The Truth about Cats & Dogs*. Writing in 1998, Krutnik does not refer to the 2000s, but I would argue that the "deception narrative" blueprint stretches up to the present day, with films like *How to Lose a Guy in Ten Days*, *Failure to Launch*, *The Proposal*, *17 Again*, *What Happens in Vegas*, *Did You Hear about the Morgans?*, *Just Go with It*, or

The Big Wedding. These movies are aware of the fundamental "lie" on which their love stories are based, but they are willing to sustain this lie anyway, thus acknowledging the impossibility of the romantic myth in the present while at the same time enacting it.

This is the context in which *SATC* is inserted: influenced by a conservative sociopolitical climate, the romantic comedy of the late 1980s and 1990s longed to return to the values of old-fashioned romance in the face of disquieting social changes, but could not help but recognize the difficulty of this task through an ironic rendering of the "whole romantic thing." This tendency does not seem to have changed much in the last decade. Writing in 2007, Jeffers McDonald refers to contemporary romantic comedy as "neo-traditional." She subscribes to Neale's and Krutnik's ideas about the genre's self-referentialism and nostalgia for the past, and adds some new interesting concepts. For instance, she points out a conspicuous peculiarity of contemporary romantic comedy: unlike previous cycles, the neo-traditional romantic comedy does not seem very interested in reflecting its context. This lack of relevance to contemporary life is the cause of a great deal of anxiety in the genre. This is reflected, for example, in the films' compulsive need to provide closed, happy endings for all of their story lines, no matter how contrived or unlikely they may seem (*Romantic Comedy*).

Another remarkable change in the "neo-traditional" romantic comedy with respect to previous cycles is its blatant disinterest in sex. In these films, sex is regarded as a somewhat immature preoccupation and replaced by a "vague intensity" between the couple. Unlike the "nervous romance," which presented sex as a fun and fulfilling activity—even as the path toward self-realization—the "neo-traditional" romantic comedy perceives sexual intercourse as unworthy or simply irresponsible, unless it is with the "right one" (Jeffers McDonald, *Romantic Comedy*; Jeffers McDonald, "Homme-Com"). Again, this tendency may be seen as a consequence of the political ascendancy of the Republican right with its "family values" ethos. Catherine L. Preston also considers the AIDS epidemic as a possible cause, or simply "the desire for a PG rating in a market environment increasingly hostile to sex outside marriage" (233). Whatever the reasons, this de-emphasis on sex is clearly felt in contemporary romantic comedy and it stretches from the early 1990s up to the present day, with films like *Sleepless in Seattle, You've Got Mail, How to Lose a Guy in Ten Days, Someone Like You, Just Like Heaven, Music and Lyrics,* and *Valentine's Day*, to name just a few.

These are some of the main developments in the most "conventional" type of romantic comedy. However, this overview of the present state of the genre would be incomplete without making reference to the diversification in form, content, and target audience that romantic comedy went through during the 1990s. As in *SATC*'s case, the genre has attempted to expand its appeal by targeting niche audiences. During this period, romantic comedy started to pay attention to ethnic diversity through the inclusion of African Americans (*She's Gotta Have It, Coming to America, Boomerang, The Preacher's Wife, Booty Call, The Best Man, Love & Basketball, Two Can Play That Game, Bringing Down the House, Hitch, About Last Night*) and Hispanic characters (*I Like It Like That, The Perez Family, Fools Rush In, The Wedding Planner, Two Much, Maid in Manhattan, Shall We Dance?*). Sexual preference is also explored in films like *Go Fish, Jeffrey, Chasing Amy, Billy's Hollywood Screen Kiss, Broken Hearts Club—A Romantic Comedy, Kissing Jessica Stein, All Over the Guy, A Family Affair, Better Than Chocolate, Imagine Me & You, Gray Matters,* or *I Love You Phillip Morris*. Contemporary romantic comedy also takes into account age difference, by producing films that address mature love (*Grumpy Old Men, First Wives' Club, The Mirror Has Two Faces, As Good as It Gets, Something's Gotta Give, Mamma Mia!, It's Complicated, The Best Exotic Marigold Hotel, Darling Companion, Love Is All You Need, Hope Springs, Enough Said*); films that present coupling within a broader network of family relations (*Three Men and a Baby, Father of the Bride, Home for the Holidays, Meet the Parents, The Family Man, My Big Fat Greek Wedding, Meet the Fockers, In Good Company, Guess Who, Monster-in-Law, The Family Stone, Dan in Real Life, The Big Wedding*); and youth-oriented romantic comedies (*Reality Bites, Clueless, 10 Things I Hate about You, She's All That, Never Been Kissed, American Pie, Get Over It, Juno, Nick and Norah's Infinite Playlist, Youth in Revolt, Adventureland, Scott Pilgrim vs the World, Warm Bodies*) (Krutnik, "Conforming Passions?"). Another source of diversification in the genre comes from the independent sector, which has been producing a considerable number of "alternative" romantic comedies that veer away from the mainstream formula. These offbeat romantic comedies often sport a more unusual appearance that challenges some of the conventions of traditional romantic comedy. They tend to rely on smaller budgets and present more idiosyncratic views of love through riskier premises and less archetypical characters. Examples include *Punch-Drunk Love, Garden State, Eternal Sunshine of the Spotless Mind, The Break-Up, Lars and the Real Girl, (500) Days of Summer, Gigantic,* and *Ruby Sparks.*

Romantic comedy's efforts to include a wider array of characters and situations have remained constant throughout the 2000s, a decade characterized by a greater tolerance toward romantic scenarios previously disregarded by the genre and by a conscious effort to expand the scope of their target audience (Echart). The best instance of romantic comedy's desire to address previously neglected niche audiences can be felt in its efforts to attract male viewers through an increased attention to the male half of the couple. This cycle has been referred to as "hommecom" (Jeffers McDonald, "Homme-Com") and includes films such as *High Fidelity, The Tao of Steve, Shallow Hal, 40 Days and 40 Nights, The 40-Year Old Virgin, Hitch, Dan in Real*

Life, Along Came Polly, The Heartbreak Kid, Forgetting Sarah Marshall, Knocked Up, (500) Days of Summer, and *The 5-Year Engagement.* These films introduce a male point of view in a traditionally "feminine genre," often making use of elements of scatological humor and slapstick to attract a male audience. The success of this cycle has been further exploited with the emergence of a group of movies that specifically focus not only on that male experience of love, but also of friendship, the "bromance," which deals with the relationship between its male characters. Examples include *Wedding Crashers, I Love You Man, Funny People, Superbad, Get Him to the Greek, Pineapple Express, Hall Pass, The Hangover, Role Models, Due Date, The Dilemma, Humpday, I Now Pronounce You Chuck and Larry, The Green Hornet, Chuck & Buck,* and *The Internship.* [12]

This brief account shows how the genre started to make a conscious effort to "diversify" itself from the 1990s onward, the context in which *SATC* was born. Even those romantic comedies that are not targeted at specific niche groups are incorporating discourses that seem to deviate from previous generic schemata, thus infusing new life into the genre. For instance, contemporary romantic comedy introduces variations with respect to previous cycles in its emphasis on friendship as a viable alternative to heterosexual love; in its focus on the difficulty of sustaining a satisfying relationship nowadays— which accounts for the precariousness of the happy ending; in its attention to the problems of adaptation both sexes experience as a consequence of the postfeminist ethos; and in the representation of interracial, interethnic, and transnational romance (Deleyto). *SATC* is not only chronologically inserted in this panorama of variety and diversification, but an active participant in the reshaping of generic boundaries. This book will hopefully show how this series helped rewrite the scripts of romantic comedy for the twenty-first century in a significant way.

When Woody Met Carrie

As a turn-of-the-century text, the general sensibility underlying *SATC* is closer to the contemporary postfeminist ethos than to the militant second-wave feminism of the 1970s. However, it could be argued that, from a generic point of view, the show is more connected to the so-called "radical romantic comedy" or "nervous romance" of the earlier period than with the cinematic context in which it is inscribed. *SATC* can be seen as a "postfeminist nervous romance," that is, the series is generically influenced by the cycle of romantic comedy popularized by Woody Allen in the 1970s, but at the same time, it is shaped by a postfeminist sensibility characteristic of its historical context.

Evidently, the social framework at the turn of the millennium is different from that of the 1970s. However, in some respects, things have not changed

so much since the sexual revolution shook the pillars of intimate relationships. Many of its consequences are still felt nowadays. Far from waning,
SATC shows how confusion about heterosexual dating protocols seems to
have grown; and more importantly, this instability appears to be particularly
affecting women in the postfeminist era.

In the frantic search for coupledom depicted in *SATC*, the series "resuscitates" the tension in the "nervous romance," tension between romantic wish-
fulfillment and the cynical awareness of its impossibility in the present era.
The characters in this genre are nostalgic about the past, when faith in the
couple was possible and heterosexual romance was a source of security and
stability, but at the same time, they are reluctant to seriously commit themselves to a partner in an age in which the certainties of marriage and the
couple are crumbling.

SATC's resuscitation of Allen's "nervous romance" includes both formal
and thematic aspects. Formally, *SATC* features typical Allen trademarks such
as a perpetual romanticization of New York. It also uses cinematic tech-
niques popularized by him in the 1970s, such as the voice-over flashback and
the consistent use of tracking shots. However, one of the clearest signs of the
influence of the "nervous romance" on the show lies in its self-conscious
style. In pure Alvy Singer fashion, much of the series' formal structure is
based on Carrie's direct address to the camera and constant voice-over.
SATC's beginnings are also characterized by an "ethnographic" spirit similar
to *Annie Hall*'s, as we get testimonials about relationships from random
people on New York's streets. However, it must be acknowledged that this
self-conscious visual style was considerably watered down with the progression of the series, which gradually settled into a more conventional look.

SATC's formal self-consciousness matches perfectly its self-reflexive nature in thematic terms. The show continues the tradition of the "comedy of
analysis" inaugurated by Allen in the 1970s (Babington and Evans 153). In
the series, just as in the "nervous romance," talking about sex is as important—if not more important—as sex in itself. The characters dissect every
aspect of their relationships obsessively, trying to find an insight into their
own self-identities. The "Me Decade" may be over, but the fixation with the
self does not seem to have decreased, at least in *SATC*'s world. The centrality
of sex in the series is actually one of its paramount features, and it includes
not only explicit representations of the sexual act, but more importantly,
extremely frank conversation about sex. The "nervous romance" pioneered
the inclusion of honest sex talk in the 1970s. At the turn of the millennium,
SATC raised the level of realism of such talk a notch or two, which created
considerable controversy during its heyday.

This contrasts strongly with the treatment of sex in the "neo-traditional"
romantic comedy. In these films, sex is frequently downplayed, deemed immature, irresponsible, or unimportant. Sometimes it is simply absent. When it

happens, it is always with the "right one"—if not, it is considered a mistake—and it is visually implied or prudishly shown (Preston; Jeffers McDonald, *Romantic Comedy*; Kirkland). This contrasts with *SATC*'s ethos. Even though the series is not *so much* about sex as its title announces, sex does play a paramount role in the narrative. Moreover, intimate matters are not only extensively talked about, but also explicitly represented, something very uncommon in the "neo-traditional" romantic comedy. Unlike in many examples of this genre, the sex in the series is actively integrated in the story lines and employed as a source of humor and narrative potential. This way of representing sex is clearly reminiscent of the "radical romantic comedies" or "nervous romances" of the 1970s, when sexual intercourse was not embarrassedly hidden from view, but used to define their characters and to move the action forward. This was the case in films like *Starting Over, An Unmarried Woman, Annie Hall,* and *Manhattan*, for example, in which sex was a favorite topic of discussion. Moreover, it was used to characterize their protagonists: in *Annie Hall*, for instance, we learn more about Alvy's (Woody Allen) narcissism and Annie's (Diane Keaton) repression thanks to our access to their sexual behavior. In this sense, *SATC* has much more to do with these films than with the cinematic panorama in which it is inserted. Admittedly, the treatment of sex in these 1970s films was more "serious," while in the show it is much more lighthearted. However, the fact that sex fulfills mainly a comic function in the series does not diminish its importance as a means of character construction and a fundamental pillar in the storytelling process.

Apart from the representation of sex, one of the greatest similarities between *SATC* and the "nervous romances" lies in their constant yearning for romance in the face of continual disappointment. Like the characters of this 1970s cycle, the girls in *SATC* navigate New York's dating scene with a mixture of hope and cynicism, as they long to find their twin soul, while acknowledging the difficulty of this task. The formal structure of *SATC* accentuates this idea. Thanks to its serial form, this TV program is better equipped than film to represent the perennial tension between people's romantic longings and the virtual impossibility of fulfillment, an inherent feature of the "nervous romance." The series offers us a kaleidoscopic view of single life in New York. This view is powerfully determined by a "cyclical" structure that combines hope and pessimism in equal doses as the girls usually dismiss potential suitors by the end of each episode, only to start all over again with renewed hopes in the next one. Thus, as the "nervous romance" did in its heyday, the series often features bittersweet or open endings. The 1970s films set out to represent the upheaval pervading heterosexual relationships at the time. Therefore unhappy or open endings seemed a plausible resolution to the conflicts presented. The "neo-traditional" romantic comedy of the 1990s and 2000s, on the other hand, betrays a deep anxiety in its unwillingness to acknowledge the improbability of the happy, unproblematic heterosexual union. For this reason, it is often at great pains to provide happy endings against all odds, which sometimes feel forced and unnatural. *SATC* clearly deviates from this trend. Thanks to its serial form, endings are manifold and—happy or not—they are never closed. In this way, TV reveals itself as a much better-equipped medium to reflect the instability and uncertainty of contemporary romantic relationships. Rather than trying to clumsily conceal the anxiety in which intimate culture is immersed, *SATC*, just as the "nervous romances" did, fully embraces this uncertainty, taking it as its leitmotif.

Another important connection between *SATC* and the "nervous romance" lies in the construction of its neurotic protagonist, which has many points in common with the Allen persona that became popular during the late 1960s and 1970s. The advances brought about by second-wave (and third-wave) feminism have not always been happy and smooth the turn-of-the-century woman, who has frequently found herself immersed in a kind of confusion and psychological unrest similar to that undergone by her male counterpart after the sexual revolution of the late 1960s and early 1970s. Carrie is a successful, independent, working woman. She is in her thirties and enjoys the pleasures of single life in New York freely, showing an evident sense of entitlement to equality. This indicates a full assimilation of the rights gained by second-wave feminism. However, Carrie's enjoyment of the perks of female liberation frequently conflicts with her desire to settle down in a stable relationship with a man. This dilemma is not only Carrie's, as it captures the sensibility of a whole generation of women who struggle to reconcile independence and romance. In this respect, Carrie's evolution throughout the series is remarkable, and by the end, she becomes ambivalent about marriage, as it requires sacrificing many of the pleasures of the single life she enjoys.

Evidently, this is a very different scenario from the late 1960s and early 1970s, when the "nervous romance" and the Allen persona made their appearance. However, despite the differences in context and gender, both characters show remarkable similarities. Their frantic quest for the right match in the educated, upper-class New York milieu constitutes their clearest resemblance. Both characters find themselves perpetually engaged in the search for the perfect partner. In the process, they overanalyze their relationships and feel permanently dissatisfied with them, no matter how fabulous their partners are. In this sense, many critics have pointed out that the Allen persona suffers from a chronic case of anhedonia, that is, the inability to experience happiness. Carrie's case is not so extreme, as she seems to be able to find fulfillment in different aspects of her life, like her relationships with her girlfriends, but the truth is that she just cannot feel fully satisfied with any of her romantic relationships, systematically dismissing potentially suitable boyfriends in her quest for a quasi-mythical partner. Vittorio Hösle points out that the "Allen persona searches for a woman who is both sexually and intellectually challenging, but if both criteria were satisfied, he would be bored" (30). This is basically what happens to Carrie: her relationship with Big (Chris Noth) is a constant source of dissatisfaction because of his inability to commit. However, when she finally finds everything she could wish for in a man with Aidan (John Corbett), inexplicably she breaks up with him. Carrie's systematic dismissal of potential suitors, and more importantly, of Aidan, points to the fact that the problem may not be in them, but in her dysfunctional experience of relationships. Nevertheless, despite constant failure, she keeps trying, never losing faith in eventually meeting her twin soul.

Carrie's enduring faith is actually one of the main features of the *schlemiel* character epitomized by Allen. According to Annette Wernblad, the *schlemiel* "is capable of keeping his faith in the most dire of circumstances. He is seen as the only morally sane man exactly because he remains young at heart no matter how cruelly the world treats him" (60). This is also applicable to Carrie, since she is constantly seen picking herself up and dusting herself off after every failed relationship, never losing hope. The connection between both characters is also pointed out by Tom Grochowski, who claims that "Carrie manifests the most impressive gender inversion of the Allen *schlemiel*" (153). Like the Allen persona, Carrie frequently embarrasses herself by making the wrong comment at the most inappropriate moment or by simply falling down when everybody is looking, as in the episode in which she trips on a fashion catwalk ("The Real Me," 4:2). The link between the two characters is also reinforced by Sarah Jessica Parker's star persona, which was frequently associated with the figure of the outsider trying to fit in the roles she played before *SATC*, like *Miami Rhapsody* and *If Lucy Fell*. Last but not least, both characters are also linked by their neuroses. Both are nervous, occasionally insecure, and constantly need to revise their relationships with others and with their own selves. If Allen was the hero for the age of anxiety in the 1970s, Carrie has become an icon of postfeminist neurosis.

At bottom, Carrie's extraordinary resonance with a female audience lies in the character's ability to reflect the complex web of meanings modern women find themselves immersed in. This character reveals the deep contradictions embedded in public discourses about female liberation and women's role in contemporary society. Post-second-wave generations like the girls in *SATC* have been raised with the belief that they can "have it all": a career, a satisfying family life, and, in the case of some women like *SATC*'s protagonists, a wardrobe full of designer clothes. This has created a series of expectations in women about what their lives should be like, which, in most cases, are difficult to meet. The problem is exacerbated by popular culture's discourses addressed to women, telling them that they must be independent, but they also need to find Mr. Right. This belief shapes the agenda of most texts addressed to women nowadays: from glossy magazines to cinema's romantic comedies, having a career without a partner is repeatedly portrayed as a highly undesirable option for women. This is confirmed by the popularity of a figure born in the mid-1990s: the singleton. The singleton is an independent, single woman in her thirties who realizes that "her success in other fields has been at the expense of the one thing that 'really' matters—finding a man" (Whelehan 136). She wants to have a career, but her biological clock is ticking, and she is quite desperate to meet Mr. Right. She identifies herself with feminist stances on independence but cannot help indulging in traditional heterosexual fantasies of being rescued from it all by Prince Charming. The best example of this postfeminist archetype is the protagonist of Helen Fielding's *Bridget Jones's Diary*, a 1996 book that is credited with almost single-handedly establishing chick literature as a genre (Gill). The success and rapid spread of this figure attests to the importance of the dilemmas it puts forward for the contemporary woman.

These dilemmas constitute, in fact, the basic premise around which *SATC* revolves. The negotiation between the girls' wish for independence and their desire for traditional heterosexual coupling is a recurrent issue throughout the series, but this dichotomy reaches its climax for Carrie when she considers marrying Aidan: while trying on a wedding dress she gets a rash, an obvious sign of her unconscious rejection of marriage. She breaks up with him and eventually retakes the relationship, but she is never able to commit herself fully. In this way, Carrie sabotages her own happiness once and again, unwilling to sacrifice her freedom for anything less than "perfection." That is what she is looking for in a man, and she will not settle for anything less. Interestingly, some critics argue that the dilemmas faced by the characters are not presented by the series as feminism's fault. Lotz, for instance, maintains that, rather, "their struggles result from the scale of their expectations" (108). However, weren't these expectations created by feminist gains? As some authors have pointed out (Lewis-Smith; Shalit), feminist advances have led to increasingly higher expectations about men (and about life in general) on the part of women, which results in greater disappointment when they fail to materialize. Leaving aside discussions about the show's feminist or anti-feminist ideology, it does depict a generation of women who have become much more picky and demanding in all aspects of life, from romantic entanglements to handbags. They live in a world in which women are granted the opportunity of choice. This is something previous generations could not enjoy, and is taken for granted by Carrie and her girlfriends. The whole series revolves around this rhetoric of choice: choosing a man, a career, or a place to live . . . even choosing a pair of shoes is presented as an issue of paramount importance. All these choices represent not just consumerist options, but women's newly acquired status in society as autonomous beings.

Women's newly found "freedom" is problematic, though, as it implies a series of contradictions that are appropriately encapsulated by the term "postfeminist nervous romance." The vast array of choices that extends before women's eyes in the postfeminist era is not desirable as it may seem at first sight.[13] As the series repeatedly shows, this abundance of choice may create confusion and indecision. Faced with so many options to choose from, the contemporary woman has lost the traditional points of reference in her quest for happiness. It cannot be forgotten that notions like "happiness" and "personal realization" are cultural constructs. Society tells the individual what being happy in the Western, industrialized world means and the steps she must take to achieve this state. Not so long ago, women's path toward the achievement of self-identity was well defined: it basically amounted to finding a husband and raising a family. If possible, the husband should meet a series of desirable features. Among these, being able to keep the family and to grant them a more or less comfortable lifestyle took precedence. Of course, having all these things did not guarantee automatic happiness, but that was what public discourse promulgated.

Today things are not so simple. The arrival of feminism in the 1960s came to "free" women from their oppression. Feminism's proposals were more or less straightforward, but postfeminist tenets are not so clear. Postfeminism mixes elements of traditional feminism with others that some critics regard as defiantly prefeminist. It defends women's independence, but proposes a "recuperation" of a kind of traditional femininity presumably lost during the second wave that allows for traditional feminine pleasures previously "forbidden" by militant feminism. As a result of this ideological entrapment, the idea of self-realization has varied considerably since prefeminist days. Being a woman in the new millennium is a more complex issue, as it frequently entails a difficult juggling of private and public responsibilities. In fact, the wide range of choices available for the contemporary woman sometimes means her own stigmatization, regardless of her choice: if she decides to put aside her career in order to devote herself to her family, she will be criticized and pinned down as antifeminist—as happens to Charlotte when she quits her job in "Time and Punishment" (4:7). If she chooses to pursue a career at the expense of having a family, she will be equally put down by popular discourses that affirm the need to have a man by her side if she wants to achieve happiness—this is the case in the episode entitled "My Motherboard, Myself" (4:8), in which Miranda's mother dies but the real tragedy seems to be having to attend the funeral without a man by her side. On the contrary, trying to "have it all" proves to be a strenuous task, which easily leads to neurosis, work overload, and self-mortification for not being able to attain the ideal role models presented by the media (as happens to Miranda when she becomes a mother). In the process, nobody assures women that happiness lies in having a successful career or a traditional family, or even in having both. In a postmodern world where complete certainties seem to have been lost forever, the rhetoric of choice sometimes leaves women with more questions than answers. As a result, attaining self-realization as a woman looks like an almost impossible task in today's society.

Another problem contemporary women have to face is the difficulty of defining Mr. Right after feminism. Postfeminist discourses instruct women in the need to find that mythical being, but there are no clear guidelines on what he should be like. This is clearly seen in *SATC*: Carrie dates innumerable men in the course of the six seasons. Most of them are attractive, intelligent, well off, and sexually proficient. However, she finds none of them completely satisfying. Apart from this, she has two important relationships: Big and Aidan. According to Joanna di Mattia, these two men represent two models of archetypal masculinity: "Mr Big, a classically phallic 'seducer' in the filmic tradition of Rhett Butler, and Aidan Shaw, a strong, sensitive 'rescuer' like the heroes of modern Mills & Boon romances" (19). Both men are appealing, but also limited as complete fantasies of Mr. Right. The unrestricted passion that Big represents is absent in Carrie's relationship with Aidan, who nevertheless is capable of providing a level of commitment and stability alien to Big. The fact that neither of them is able to fully satisfy Carrie's needs attests to the difficulty of defining Mr. Right in a postfeminist context that has done away with clear-cut ideas about traditional archetypes of masculinity (di Mattia). In this sense, Carrie's "problem" is much more complex than that faced by the Allen persona in the "nervous romances" of the 1970s: he was equally incapable of finding the right match, but he had a clear idea of what she should be like. His main impediment lay in the scarcity of that kind of traditional woman as a consequence of the sexual revolution. Carrie's circumstances are different: she has no shortage of suitors, but she is confused about Prince Charming's actual features.

As has been seen, public discourses about female liberation and women's role in contemporary society are highly contradictory. In the late 1960s and early 1970s, second-wave feminism championed women's total emancipation from their role as second-class citizens. After that, the 1980s witnessed a backlash reaction, as well as the birth of the postfeminist ideas that spread during the 1990s, shaping popular texts like *SATC*. The contradictory nature of postfeminism, with its mixture of feminist tenets and traditional ideas about femininity, has resulted in a sea of contradictions for the contemporary woman. This sense of confusion is faithfully portrayed by a show like *SATC*, which revolves around its protagonists' dilemmas about the "right" attitude toward issues like sex, independence, motherhood, work, and especially, finding the perfect partner. Carrie's high expectations in this respect make her romantic quest extremely complex. In a way, it could be said that Carrie's neurosis and frustration stem precisely from the same feminist ideas that have supposedly "liberated" her.

The "nervous romance" struck a chord with the audience because it was able to capture the mood of the times, faithfully reflecting the unrest experienced in the sentimental field during the late 1960s and 1970s. In this context, the Allen persona became the epitome of male angst in the face of social transformation. His unmanly characterization succeeded because it helped soothe the anxiety of a masculinity crisis caused by the advance of feminism. If the Allen persona of the "nervous romance" was mainly addressed to a male conscience in the 1970s, *SATC* can be seen as an updated version of the genre—what I have termed "postfeminist nervous romance"—as it has succeeded in powerfully engaging female sensibilities in the late 1990s and early 2000s, a moment of upheaval for women motivated precisely by an excess of options lying at their feet. Just as the "nervous romance" was a product of the sexual revolution, the "postfeminist nervous romance" can also be read as trying to show the consequences of female liberation and the advances of feminism at the turn of the millennium. However, there is an important difference between both "genres," as men and women seem to have traded places this time. Faced with so many options to choose from, modern women find themselves caught up in a web of contradictory meanings about their femininity, in a situation of crisis not unlike that suffered by men in the 1970s. In this way, the series shows that the feminist "earthquake" and its consequences are as relevant today as in its heyday. For all these reasons, it can be said that *SATC* is generically shaped by many of the conventions of the "nervous romance," but it keeps in touch with its contemporary context thanks to its updated postfeminist agenda. Shaped by a discourse full of contradictory meanings, the series participates in the postfeminist ethos that underlies most examples of 2000s romantic comedy, as it usually supports feminist attitudes and ideas but just as frequently indulges in traditional—some would say prefeminist—fantasies of heterosexual romance, in which Mr. Right does exist and a woman's only choice is to live happily ever after with him.

NOTES

1. Both series are also the work of *SATC*'s creators. Based on a similar formula to *SATC*, these shows were not very successful with the public (*Cashmere Mafia* was canceled after its first season and *Lipstick Jungle* lasted only two seasons).

2. *SATC*'s influence was felt on the big screen as well: *He's Just Not That Into You* (2009) is based on the eponymous best-selling book by *SATC*'s screenwriting collaborators (Behrendt and Tuccillo) and clearly inspired by *SATC* season 6, episode 4, "Pick-a-Little, Talk-a-Little" (specific episodes are identified by number throughout this book: 6:4).

3. See, for instance, Parks; Davidson; Lewis-Smith; Parker; Raven; Shalit; Barrick; Wolcott; Holston; Leonard; Ellwood; Orenstein; Henry; King; Brasfield; Gennaro; Piore; Limbaugh.

4. See Avins; Chang and Chambers; Flett; Sayeau, "Carrying On"; Wolf; Jermyn, "In Love with Sarah Jessica Parker"; Clark; Setoodeh.

5. See Chang and Chambers; A. Nelson, "Miss Bradshaw Goes to Washington"; Arthurs, "*Sex and the City* and Consumer Culture"; Gerhard; Skov Anderson et al.; Jermyn, *Sex and the City*.

6. See Hanks; Roberts; Ream; Greven; Merck; Gill; Baird; Macey.

7. Even though there are no formal studies on the real influence *SATC* has had on women's actual dating behavior, psychiatrists, relationship experts, and fans seem to acknowledge that the show changed "the way women view hooking up, if not their hooking up habits." According to Pepper Schwartz, a University of Washington sociology professor and relationship expert for Perfectmatch.com, "It did have some impact given that it was a sea change in how women talked about sexuality and what was shown on a network" (Marikar).

8. Deborah Jermyn points at *SATC*'s self-conscious indebtedness to these shows by comparing the resemblance between their opening sequences (*Sex and the City* 43). Also, *SATC* features Valerie Harper, *Rhoda*'s protagonist, in the episode entitled "Shortcomings" (2:15) as a clear homage to this series.

9. For more information on HBO's history see Rogers et al.; Edgerton and Jones; and Leverette et al., *It's Not TV*.

10. HBO reached twenty-nine million subscriptions in 2007—almost twice the number of its nearest rival, Showtime. Also, in 2004 the channel made history by winning thirty-two Emmy Awards out of its 124 nominations (Edgerton and Jones, "HBO's Ongoing Legacy" 317).

11. *The Sopranos* finale was followed by 11.9 million viewers. *SATC*'s final episode garnered an audience of 10.6 million and *Six Feet Under*, 4 million. These are impressive figures, taking into account that HBO only reached one-third of U.S. households—around 32 million compared to 100 million for broadcast television (Rogers et al.).

12. The creation of this cycle or subgenre in contemporary comedy is generally attributed to Judd Apatow, producer (and sometimes writer and director) of many of these films. The success of this kind of films has been such that some critics have even declared the "bromance" as the "new romantic comedy" (Setoodeh).

13. Of course, I am always referring to the kind of women represented in *SATC*, that is, white, middle/upper-class, heterosexual, and educated. This rhetoric of choice does not apply so unproblematically to other demographic groups. Working-class women or those belonging to racial minorities are not considered in the series and have much more difficult access to the array of choices *SATC* depicts as a given.

Chapter Two

Have We Become Romance Intolerant?

Romancing Consumption

The word *romance* brings to mind two different concepts: on the one hand, it is a specific and culturally mediated way of experiencing intimate relationships. As will be later explained, romantic love is worshipped today as some kind of mystical force, not only able to sweep us off our feet, but also to make good virtually every single lack in our life. In our post-Christian modern society, romance is perceived as today's secular religion (Illouz; Lindholm; Langford; Evans; Beck and Beck-Gernsheim, *The Normal Chaos of Love*). However, it cannot be forgotten that romance is also a well-established literary genre of unquestionable popularity. The figures say that romance fiction has the largest share of the consumer market; at 16.7 percent, it generated $1.35 billion in sales in 2013, becoming the top-performing category on the best-seller lists.[1] However, this genre—both in its cinematic and written forms—has been traditionally "looked down upon," when not simply despised, by both the popular press and academia (Regis). Romance novels in particular have been the subject of intense feminist criticism, especially during the 1970s (Greer; Firestone; Millett; Douglas). From the 1980s onward, some feminist writers attempted to vindicate these texts, defending them and making visible the double standard operating in the assessment of male and female genres. Thus, authors like Tania Modleski and Janice Radway highlighted the emancipatory potential of the pleasures these texts offer to female readers. Today, romance still does not receive the same amount of attention and respect as other genres do, but critical discourse on this genre has evolved considerably, expanding its scope beyond the consideration of gender to issues such as race or nonnormative sexuality.

The increased critical attention to romance may be partly justified by its resilience, both in the written and the visual media. Its unquestionable endurance confirms its relevance as cultural discourse. As Rosalind Gill argues, romance is "one of the most compelling discourses by which Western subjects are inscribed. Its tenacity in the face of social, cultural and demographic changes that include high rates of divorce, the growth of new family norms and broader transformations of intimacy shows that there is no necessary correspondence between changing patterns of sexual relations and romantic desire" (227). Thus, sociosexual protocols and living arrangements may change, but our craving for romance stays the same. The "staying power" that characterizes romance as a genre may lie in its outstanding capability to evolve and to adapt to changing social circumstances. In this sense, *SATC*, with its constant interrogation of its protagonists' romantic lives, constitutes a good illustration of romance's capacity to incorporate new—and sometimes conflicting—discourses into its credo. Gill underlines the way in which the show plays with the codes and conventions of romance, adapting them to the complex reality of its context. She states that *SATC* "constitutes a reinvention of the codes of romance for postfeminist consumer culture" (247). This chapter aims at exploring this assertion in greater depth, analyzing the relationship between contemporary beliefs about romance and the consumerist ethos of late capitalism in which they are inscribed.

Whether explicitly or tangentially, *SATC* exhibits a relentless obsession with romance. In the course of its six seasons, myriad questions are posed: Is romance still possible after the sexual revolution? Is it just a fabrication to keep women happily trapped in a submissive role? Is it a harmful ideal for a healthy sentimental life? Or is it a positive model that everyone should aspire to? Is romance limited by age, gender, or nationality? What are romance's connections with the consumerist ethos of our times? In *SATC*, romance is the elusive goal that keeps its romantic heroines permanently enmeshed in a never-ending quest. Since *SATC*'s characters meet a significantly large number of men through ninety-four episodes—many of whom are perfectly suitable candidates to the position of "permanent boyfriend"—it can be argued that the show pivots not so much around the search for a flawless partner, but around the search for flawless romance. As a result, the interrogation of contemporary notions of romance occupies a paramount position among the thematic preoccupations of the series.

The ideas that shape our modern beliefs about romance are complex and often contradictory. The idea of "romance" is not a natural given, of course, but a cultural construction firmly based on the cultural practices of its context. Eva Illouz explains the way in which romantic love became enmeshed with economic practices as the intersection of two processes: the romanticization of commodities and the commodification of romance. The first process started in the early twentieth century with the evolution of the mass market. The nascent movie industry and the emergence of a national advertising system helped establish new standards of romantic behavior influenced by the ethic of consumerism. At the same time, the theme of romance started to be used to sell products in the United States, thus giving rise to the "romanticization of commodities." In this process, the allure of romance works at two levels: not only does it impregnate the product itself—what Illouz terms "candid consumption," but also the leisure activity associated with the product, giving way to "oblique consumption" (26–39). The link between romance and commodities is so pervasive because it interlocks two powerful motives of American capitalist culture: "a euphoric vision of harmonious human relationships and the American dream that consumption affirms both democratic access to affluence and the originality of the individual self" (Illouz 82–83). Because of this, the association between romance and the consumerist ethos, which was established at the beginning of the twentieth century, has become increasingly complex and sophisticated, developing into an inseparable unit by the turn of the millennium.

Critics have been preoccupied with the implications of this connection and have assessed it differently. Illouz, for instance, does not consider it as something negative: for her, the quality of the romantic bond is not necessarily undermined by "consumerist love," since this kind of love "invokes values and principles that have had an emancipatory potential throughout Western history: individualism, self-realization, affirmation of the individual's personal qualities, and equality between the sexes in the mutual experience of pleasure" (152). On the other hand, critics like Mary Evans lament the way in which capitalist society has impacted modern relationships: for her, the influence of consumerist patterns in our love lives has turned fleeting romance into the preferred option of sentimental entanglement, which has come to replace stable relationships these days. Zygmunt Bauman shares Evans's views about the increasing elusiveness in the meanings attached to contemporary relationships. According to him, the consumerist ethos of today's society has degraded desire, reducing it to the category of mere "wish." Unlike desire, which needs time to germinate, wishes are momentary, born and dead on the spot and entailing no delay of satisfaction. For Bauman, today's relationships are based on the same model of consumerist "wish": disposable and easy to replace if "faulty" (11–13). Since the issue of consumption plays a paramount role in *SATC*, encompassing manufactured commodities as much as romantic relationships, the following sections will look at the way in which it is tackled in "The Ick Factor" (6:14), an episode in which the show's association between romance and the values of consumerist society is particularly evident.

Romance is a prominent theme in *SATC*, and before undertaking the textual analysis of the episode, I would like to foreground its importance by describing the general way in which it is dealt with in the show. The relevance of the topic is announced in the very first episode of the series. In it, Carrie's voice-over declares: "I totally believe that love conquers all. Sometimes you just have to give it a little space . . . and that's exactly what's missing in Manhattan: the space for romance" (pilot, 1:1). The series thus establishes the boundaries of the territory in which its quasi-ethnographic study of urban relationships is going to take place, somehow blaming New York for their precariousness. However, the messages put forward by the text are not as clear cut as its beginning may suggest. The show's initial presentation of New York as a place where romance is impossible will be repeatedly contradicted by the text, as this city's potential for romantic transformation is constantly foregrounded by the series. Similarly, *SATC*'s position on romance is often ambivalent. The episode entitled "The Chicken Dance" (2:7), for instance, deals with Miranda's friend's marriage to a woman he met only one month ago. This makes Carrie wonder: "In a city as cynical as New York, is it still possible to believe in love at first sight?" The episode thus contrasts the innocence of fairy-tale, old-fashioned romance with the generalized cynicism of Manhattan dwellers. The whole issue of Miranda's friend's hurried wedding is treated with detached irony by the girls. However, the episode's closing lines complicate its suspicious attitude toward romance: Carrie's relationships with men may be cynical, but she concedes the possibility that this may not be so for everybody.

The episode from the third season called "Are We Sluts?" (3:6) also explores the state of romance in the modern-day dating scene. Carrie is worried because she has been going out with Aidan for one week and a half and they have not slept together yet. When Aidan points out that one week and a half is not *that* long ("Don't people date anymore?") and he would like to keep the romantic suspense a little longer, she is ashamed to admit that the thought had not even occurred to her. Once again, she blames it on the city: "Is that what thirteen years of dating in Manhattan does to a woman?" This episode raises an interesting point: the girls have a theory that if one waits too long to have sex with a man, he becomes your friend, which, apparently, rules out sex and romance. Thus, in *SATC*'s world, love and friendship appear to be incompatible, which seems to contradict current sociological theories that propose friendship as the basis for durable relationships. Carrie's relationship with Aidan is largely based on friendship but it eventually fails, while her undying obsession with Big, with whom she cannot be friends, points to the fact that friendship does not feature in *SATC*'s formula for a successful relationship. This reinforces the idea that for women, friendship can only exist with other women, not with heterosexual members of the opposite sex.

The episode entitled "The Man, the Myth, the Viagra" (2:8) also deals with this issue. Moreover, it is directly related to the concerns expressed by second-wave feminists regarding the "dangerous" ideas that romantic texts instill in women's minds. The girls discuss whether fairy-tale endings actually exist in reality, and they conclude that they are just a myth with negative side effects on women's sentimental lives: "Urban relationship myth. Unbelievable fairy tales concocted by women to make their love lives seem less hopeless. Except it makes you feel even more hopeless because this fabulous, magical relationship is never happening to you." Thus, romance is cynically dismissed as a harmful construction that only distracts women temporarily from their sad love lives, making things worse, rather than better. However, this episode turns out to be uncharacteristically optimistic in its conclusion: Miranda, who has just met her husband-to-be, Steve (David Eigenberg), is positive that his willingness to see her again after what she believes to be a one-night stand is not sincere. Similarly, Carrie also distrusts Big's commitment to her when he fails to meet her friends. However, the final two minutes of the episode dismantle the girls' lack of faith in the myth of "happily ever after." The episode wraps up with a fairy-tale happy ending with no hint of irony: a slow-motion montage shows us Big's last-minute appearance, which encourages Miranda to give Steve a chance. She runs after him in the rain in a self-conscious climactic scene that relies on the audience's familiarity with the conventions of romantic comedy: "Maybe I can believe it," she declares. The romantic union is thus sealed with a kiss, and the magic power of this genre, with its blind faith in the possibility of romance, is fully enforced.

However, the optimism displayed in this episode is, arguably, a one-off. *SATC* certainly wants to believe in romance, but its doubts about its likelihood are never efficiently dispelled. This ambivalence is perfectly encapsulated in the episode entitled "Unoriginal Sin" (5:2), which also reflects the girls' weariness of this struggle. Even Charlotte, the eternal optimist, is losing her faith in romance after divorcing the man she had believed to be "the One." In this episode, Carrie is asked to compile her columns in a book, but first she has to decide on the tone of the volume. She searches herself for the answer and decides that her book will have an optimistic tone, but she admits that her decision might be influenced by her cynical side, which "suspected optimism would sell more books." Once more, the show wonders about the harmful potential of the romantic myth, comparing it with an addictive substance: "How do you bounce back when reality batters your belief system and love does not, as promised, conquer all. Is hope a drug we need to go off of, or is it keeping us alive? What's the harm in believing?" This episode also introduces a new idea: not only is it impossible for romance to coexist with friendship, but it is apparently also incompatible with growing old: "Maybe it's not advisable to be an optimist after the age of thirty," Carrie ponders. "Believing" is thus equated with the innocence, or maybe naivete, of youth. In this way, despite the episode's upbeat ending, Carrie's doubts are not safely contained by the text's resolution, which encapsulates once more *SATC*'s ambivalent attitude toward the issue.

As we shall see, "The Ick Factor" also offers valuable insights into the meanings attached to romance nowadays, even though it is also ambivalent in its treatment of this topic. The episode is also interesting because it explores the connection with another of *SATC*'s main preoccupations: contemporary capitalist society's consumerist ethos. The episode opens with Miranda's unceremonious marriage proposal to Steve—the man she once believed to be lying to her—while having a beer at an outdoor café. This is followed by a scene that shows us Carrie at her new love interest's impressive apartment. She is dating Aleksandr Petrovsky (Mikhail Baryshnikov), a famous Russian artist. The chic mise-en-scène and Petrovsky's piano playing create a quiet atmosphere meant to underline his "old-fashioned" style of courtship in contrast with the urban, frantic setting of Miranda's marriage proposal. It turns out that the song he is playing is dedicated to Carrie, which makes her feel uncomfortable. After that, we see the girls having lunch together, and we know these issues are going to be dissected in depth.

When an embarrassed Carrie tells her friends about Petrovsky's ways, Samantha and Miranda cringe at the thought. Charlotte, on the other hand, is delighted. For her, this kind of gesture is the epitome of romance, while for the rest, it is a phony and contrived act. Thus, as usual, Charlotte's optimistic view of relationships is contrasted with the others' cynicism. Her belief that romance does not have a place in women's lives anymore would be shared by Christina Nehring: the girls' discussion reflects this author's view that true romance has been cast off in contemporary society, which suffers from a chronic fear of authentic passion. Indeed, for Carrie, Samantha, and Miranda, romance represents an embarrassment or, at best, a harmless pastime. Romance is routinely ironized and made fun of in the show, among other things, because it is seen as a traditional form of patriarchal submission. For this reason, Miranda refuses to "surrender" to a kind of mystification she considers disempowering, instead taking the active role in proposing to Steve at a time and place far removed from the codes of traditional romance.

When Miranda announces she is getting married, her friends are stunned. However, despite their previous debasement of romance, Carrie and Samantha's emotional response to the news suggests that maybe they are not as convinced of their "antiromanticism" as it may seem. Miranda, nevertheless, is enraged at their reaction. The scene thus sets the tone for the episode, which is going to provide ambivalent perspectives on the topic of romance and its connection with the consumerist ethos of late capitalism through the three main couples' handling of their respective "romantic issues."

CONSUMERIST ROMANCE: CARRIE AND ALEKSANDR

After the piano-playing embarrassment, a similar situation takes place again at Petrovsky's apartment, where he reads Carrie a Russian poem. Once more, she feels uncomfortable. She reciprocates ironically by reading him some of her "favorite poetry": a fragment from *Vogue* magazine. She then proceeds to explain to Petrovsky the reasons for her uneasiness: "I write a column based on the assumption that romance is either dead or just phony. . . . Frankly, I'm just not used to these grand gestures." So, this scene tries to establish the opposition not only between Carrie's cynicism and Petrovsky's heartfelt romanticism, but also between a series of features that are symbolically enacted by each character. Carrie is associated with popular culture, Americanness, and youth. That is, she is a child of the pragmatic New World, in which women accept jokes and e-mails instead of poetry and love songs, as she herself admits. Given her cultural background and age, she is familiar with the mass-media culture of today, which grants her an acquaintance with the codes of romance and the postmodern uses to which it has been applied. Thus, her awareness of the "already said" prevents her from taking Petrovsky at face value. Aleksandr, on the other hand, stands for high culture and European sophistication. Not only does he come from the Old World, he is also older in age. This implies that his non-ironic take on romance was a reality not so long ago. However, this reality is clearly limited by geographical space, as the kind of romance he represents seems to be conflated with the refinement of Europe and with the world of high culture associated with it in the American imagination. In this sense, it is worth noting that the part of Petrovsky is played by Mikhail Baryshnikov, one of the greatest ballet dancers of the twentieth century. He brings about a series of meanings attached to his persona that contribute to the spectator's perception of his character as the epitome of European sophistication and high culture. The intertextuality raised by his presence in the series is heightened by Baryshnikov's personal acquaintance (and friendship) with Joseph Brodsky, the author of the poem he reads to Carrie (Wentworth). In this way, everything works in this scene in order to highlight the opposing grounds on which each character stands in relation to their fundamental beliefs about romance.

Carrie's response to Petrovsky's poetry with a quotation from a fashion magazine implies that, for her, romance is inextricably linked with the world of manufactured consumption represented by *Vogue*. Carrie's reply is meant to be tongue in cheek, but her reaction to Petrovsky's gift in the next scene reveals that the connection in Carrie's mind between romance and expensive commodities is a strong one. He wants to take her to the opera, and gives her the Oscar de la Renta dress she saw in the magazine. Carrie might feel embarrassed by poetry and music, but she does not seem to feel the least bit of unease at Petrovsky's new romantic gesture. On the contrary, she is ecstatic. Carrie's reaction reveals a striking double standard in the judgment of the "truthfulness" of his romantic gestures, which, at the same time, is very telling about society's connection between romance and consumption.

The disinterested values usually associated with romantic love are apparently set in direct opposition to those of capitalism. However, today's capitalist culture plays a paramount role in the way romance is constructed. Eva Illouz examines the connection between the experience of romance and capitalism's economic practices. She traces the beginning of this connection back to the golden age of capitalism—roughly between 1870 and 1930. The turn of the century witnessed the end of Victorian morality and its spiritual conception of love, which was replaced by a more secular vision. When religion started to decline as the focus of daily life, it was replaced by romance. What was new was not romantic love in itself, but the visibility of romantic behavior. At the time, the shifting patterns of consumption brought about by mass culture transformed the old romantic ideal into a "visual utopia." This was done mainly through the nascent movie industry's fixation with romance, which became increasingly linked with the emerging ethic of consumerism. This association was strengthened by the creation of the star system: movie stars, commodified in themselves, helped foster the interconnection of concepts like romance, marriage, consumption, and beauty. This connection was also furthered by the emergence of a national advertising system, which added the elements of self-expression and hedonism to the equation (Illouz).

This association of ideas has not only been perpetuated until the present day; in today's mass consumption society, the link between romance and consumption has been dramatically intensified. Moreover, this connection has arguably gone a step further these days, as the individual's access to commodities is even equated with happiness in a larger sense, and not only with romantic fulfillment (Evans). The scene in which Petrovsky presents Carrie with the expensive *haute couture* dress perfectly encapsulates society's interiorization of this ethos. As mentioned before, Carrie despises all forms of "romance," but she is delighted at the sight of the dress: "If I had been on a romance-free diet, this seemed like a good time to binge," she gurgles. This emphasizes the overwhelming power of late capitalist values: poetry and music are under suspicion, but commodities are not to be doubted as tokens of "true" romance. The mise-en-scène reinforces this idea: Petrovsky, impeccably dressed in a tuxedo, welcomes Carrie. The apartment is dimly lit, which creates an intimate atmosphere, but also helps to emphasize the significance of Petrovsky's present. The gift box is on a table, brightly lit from above. Lighting thus foregrounds the "stylishness" of the present, which is displayed as if it were a piece of jewelry.

Carrie's reaction when she unwraps the present confirms the "value" of Petrovsky's gesture. Thus, the dress is not only a very expensive piece of clothing; it becomes a fetish, a part of the cultural scenario of romance.

Figure 2.1.   Carrie receives Petrovsky's present.

According to Illouz, luxury goods fulfill two functions: on the one hand, they are "seduction aids" for men, since they help emphasize their social status. On the other, "they make the romantic moment an intense ritual experience in which the couple's feelings are intertwined with the ostentatious act of spending" (134). Luxury foregrounds formality and embellishment, which reinforces the intense meaning of the ritual in opposition to the instrumental qualities of the everyday, discriminating between the ordinary and the extraordinary moments in a relationship. These meanings are fully activated in this scene, marking it as a special, "magical" moment. However, in the light of subsequent events in Carrie's relationship with Petrovsky, his generosity when it comes to gifts can be read in a less positive manner. Gifts have ambivalent connotations: they are altruistic expressions of affection, but at the same time, the rules of reciprocity governing their exchange make them socially binding (Mauss). Carrie, being unable to reciprocate Petrovsky's expensive gifts, is thus disempowered in the relationship, since her inability to reciprocate places him in a superior position (Bourdieu, *Outline of a Theory of Practice*). The unevenness of their relationship will become apparent later on, and it will be one of the reasons for their breakup.

On their way to the opera, Petrovsky has another romantic gesture: he wants to dance with Carrie to the sound of street violins. However, before

Figure 2.2.   The stylishness of the gift is enhanced by lighting.

they get the chance to do so, she faints in his arms as a nineteenth-century damsel would. When she recovers, she announces: "It's too much. I'm an American. You've got to take it down a notch." Once again, the implication is that romance is a European prerogative that Americans cannot handle, even to the point of fainting when faced with it in its "purest" form. Thus, the next scene shows Petrovsky and Carrie in the most American possible scenario at hand: a McDonald's restaurant. Carrie feels much more comfortable here, and, despite the general disconnect between the place and Petrovsky's persona, he is able to "come down" to her level gracefully. Their talk feels intimate and romantic, because Carrie is at ease in a place that stands for American culture. The intimacy of this scene makes a strong contrast with the couple's previously failed attempts at romance. Their final "success" indicates that romance, to be believed today, needs to be coded in new, nonscripted ways. The old-fashioned icons no longer work in a postmodern context, and less hackneyed signs are needed in order to bestow a halo of authenticity on the romantic enterprise. Thus, instead of dancing under the moonlight, Carrie and Petrovsky dance under the fluorescent light of McDonald's arches. The replacement of the traditional romantic script of dinner and dance in a posh restaurant with the middle-class culture McDonald's represents suggests that in a postmodern era in which everything has been said and done, romance needs to be visually coded in a different way, that is, more in accordance with today's media-savvy audiences. Contemporary viewers are well aware of the conventions of romantic comedy and its iconography. For this reason, opera, poetry, and classical music no longer suffice to re-create true romance, having become mere clichés, empty signifiers. The audience's familiarity with these clichés makes it necessary for texts to rework their signs: visual representations of romance need to go off the beaten track to engage the audience's imagination these days. They still need to keep the same essence, but they must be wrapped up in different packaging. In the case of *SATC*, this new packaging consists of the romanticization of the middlebrow lifestyle, which is very much in accordance with the democratic character of the American ethos.

Thus, *SATC* proposes a fantasy in which money is not needed in order to enjoy romance. Petrovsky's kind of romance is associated with high culture and a well-off status. Carrie's ideal of romance, on the other hand, is much more "democratic": anyone can enjoy it. However, the replacement of highbrow romantic signs with more ordinary ones does not imply the rejection of consumerist values. The couple is still dressed in high-fashion clothes, and they are in McDonald's, one of the greatest symbols of American capitalist culture. In this way, the scene manages to artfully reinforce the legitimacy of

Figure 2.3. **McDonald's: a reworked scenario for "democratic" romance.**

Figure 2.4.   Dancing under the fluorescent light.

consumption while endorsing a new kind of "democratic romance." According to Charles McGovern, "the democracy of consumption also meant a universalizing of luxuries previously reserved for the rich. In this light consumption was a leveling force in the social structure and the heir to traditional republican hostility to privilege" (quoted in Illouz 72). The scene under analysis thus contributes to the illusion of America's classless society by foregrounding the possibility of romance through consumption, regardless of the individual's economic status. The fact that everybody can afford to dine at McDonald's highlights the idea that consumption assures democratic access to romance. In this sense, the unpretentiousness of McDonald's strengthens rather than diminishes the authenticity of the romantic experience, since "the power of the romantic utopia resides in its Janus-like ability to affirm the values of late capitalism and at the same time to invert them into symbols of primitive simplicity and pure emotionality" (Illouz 100). Thus, despite its status as a one of the greatest multinational enterprises of capitalism, McDonald's apparent "simplicity" produces the illusion that romance is a class-free experience, not only available to everybody, but more desirable than the European sophistication represented by Petrovsky. Carrie says she feels like a phony when she is with him but, paradoxically, the unfortunate denouement of their relationship suggests that the "democratic romance" professed by cynical Americans is ultimately perceived as much more genuine than the kind of romance evoked by traditional ideas of European refinement, which, in the light of the series' finale, is constructed as the actual "fake." The sight of Carrie and Petrovsky slow-dancing, framed by McDonald's fluorescent arches, nicely encapsulates all these meanings in an inventive way. It reaffirms the viewer in his or her allegiance to the capitalistic consumer ethos in its promise of democratized access to romance, while providing a necessary renewal of romantic comedy's iconography. In the end, all of these elements work to reassure the viewer of the possibility of romance in the contemporary panorama. However, it is only in this new, "reworked" context represented by the "fluorescent moonlight" that we can today laugh with romance, and not at it.

DOMESTIC ROMANCE: CHARLOTTE AND HARRY

After the girls' discussion of romance, we see Charlotte and her husband Harry (Evan Handler) coming out of Tasti-D-Lite, a low-calorie ice cream parlor. When she tells him about Petrovksy's ways, he promises to take her out on a romantic night on the town because he knows "how to do romance right. It's not just for foo-foo foreigners." This implies, once again, that romance is associated with European sophistication and not with the American frame of mind. It also implies that romance is something you "do": it is associated with a series of specific practices, such as "wining and dining." In this way, we see Charlotte and Harry having dinner at a posh French restaurant. They undergo the whole ritual self-consciously, but without irony. Charlotte is delighted, and despite their awareness of the romantic script they are following, they fully participate in the romantic experience they have fabricated for themselves. Since marriage and romance have traditionally been opposing concepts, they are willing to bridge the gap between the two through the enactment of practices more typical of the dating phase. From the beginning of the twentieth century, advertising and cinema have tried to solve the contradiction between romance and marriage through participation in consumer culture. The message transmitted by these cultural mechanisms is that the dullness of marriage can be avoided through consumption of the appropriate commodities and access to certain leisure activities, thus making passion and stability compatible notions. Therefore the middle and upper classes, like *SATC*'s characters, would be better equipped to overcome the contradictions of marriage than working classes.

One of the leisure activities that facilitate the ritualization of romance is dining out. The scene between Charlotte and Harry features all necessary elements to enact the fantasy: champagne, fancy food, candlelight, evening clothes, intimate atmosphere, soft music, and French language. Meals at restaurants are perceived as more romantic than those at home. This is because restaurants are conceived as self-contained spaces that allow people to step out of everyday experience "into a setting saturated with ritual meaning" (Illouz 128). Meals at restaurants have a much slower pace (Charlotte and Harry's dinner has seven courses), which places the relationship, rather than the satisfaction of hunger, at the center of the experience; and they take place in an alternative space to the home or workplace, which facilitates simultaneous isolation from the rest of the world and participation in the public sphere. The food is also more special or exotic than usual, and it is presented in a menu, a "formal cultural device that defuses the taken-for-grantedness of daily consumption of foods and ritualizes the act of eating, turning it into a symbolic event" (130). The symbolic meaning of the dishes ordered by Harry is foregrounded by the text: ordered in broken French, their suggestive names function as a kind of aphrodisiac for the couple, as they become fully immersed in the romantic fantasy evoked by the exotic menu. However, as the next scene is going to show, this fantasy is quickly subverted.

The couple is lying on their bed, presumably about to make love as a culmination of their romantic evening, when they are forced to rush to the toilet. They realize that their seven-course dinner has given them food poisoning and they spend the rest of the night dashing in and out of the bathroom. Thus, their perfectly planned romantic evening turns into a very unromantic nightmare. The lack of romance in Charlotte and Harry's perfectly scripted night contrasts with the romantic intensity experienced by Carrie in her spontaneous dinner at McDonald's. This reinforces the series' mockery of "fabricated" romance. It also emphasizes the idea that, in the postmodern era, individuals must look for their own blueprints for romance. Traditional romantic icons, scenarios, and gestures do not seem to work anymore, and feel worn out in a postmodern age characterized by cynicism and self-consciousness about the representation of romance in popular culture.

Another reason why Charlotte and Harry's romantic aspirations do not work out is also suggested by the voice-over: "Surviving a night of food poisoning together wasn't the stuff of great romance but it was the stuff of lasting love." The episode thus hints at the possibility that romance and "real" love cannot coexist. No matter how much they try, Charlotte and Harry's relationship cannot be romantic because it is too "real." This idea is recurrent throughout the series, which suffers from a chronic fear of the end of romance once a couple becomes consolidated. An example of this is Miranda's qualms when washing Steve's dirty underwear ("Drama Queens," 3:7) or Carrie's accidental farting while being with Big ("The Drought," 1:11). These quotidian "events" are not the stuff romance is made of, but they surely form part of the life of a couple. However, the girls are appalled when they happen because it seems that when a certain level of intimacy is reached, finding one's way back to romance is a difficult task. The basic incompatibility between romance and true love is further supported by larger story arcs in the series; for instance, Charlotte's relationship and her subsequent wedding with Trey (Kyle MacLachan) is full of romance in the traditional sense, but that does not lead to a good marriage. On the contrary, her relationship with Harry is anything but romantic, but he proves to be her most suitable partner so far. Similarly, Carrie's relationship with Petrovsky feels like a fairy tale, full of old-fashioned romance. Its highest point comes when she moves to Paris with him. However, shortly after, the relationship becomes more "everyday" and it is clear that romance alone is not enough to sustain it; as we will see later in this book, their arrangement does not work out because romance does not translate into a "real" relationship.

TRUE ROMANCE? MIRANDA AND STEVE

As previously stated, the episode opens with Miranda's marriage proposal to Steve. They are sitting at a table in the street, drinking beer. The decision to get married feels genuinely spontaneous, as it naturally springs from conversation. The announcement of Miranda's engagement to the girls is just as informal—she drops the bomb casually while having lunch and talking about Carrie's issues with romance: "I can't stand all that artificial hoo-hah. That's why I proposed to Steve over three-dollar beers," she declares. The girls are drop jawed at Miranda's unexpected revelation. They get emotional about the news and Miranda is upset: "Okay. Everybody stop. It's not a big deal. I'm not engaged. I'm not doing the big circus wedding. There will be no white dress or bridesmaids or posed pictures. I hate all that shit." Thus, for Miranda traditional weddings are "circuses," not the expression of genuine love between partners, and white dresses are symbols of patriarchal submissiveness or women's hypocrisy. When she goes to buy her wedding dress, she is angry at the shop assistant's suggestions because she refuses to wear virginal white. Besides, she goes shopping on her lunch break, not with her friends. Given the fact that shopping is presented in the series as the girls' main leisure activity, it would be reasonable to think that shopping for Miranda's wedding dress would be a joyous activity for the group. However, Miranda's decision to go alone and on her lunch hour means that this is not a pleasurable task. While planning the event with Steve, she reasserts her uneasiness with all the fanfare surrounding conventional weddings: "I don't want to make a big entrance. I don't want everyone staring at me." Steve suggests getting married on a boat going around the island, but she hates the idea. The problem with this is that they have never been on a boat together, they are not "boat people." She wants the wedding "to feel like them." That is, she does not want a copycat wedding from a brochure; she wants something original and different from "those millions cookie cutter weddings I had to suffer through." She wants to assert her individuality in the face of pre-made notions of romance surrounding weddings today. When she finally finds a small community garden in the center of Manhattan that she "doesn't hate," she decides to get married there.

The reason why consumerist romantic moments are culturally more prevalent than nonconsumerist ones is because they facilitate the ritualization of romance (Illouz). According to Evans, "the industry of romance has a definition of love which depends upon the fulfillment of the consciously created expectations of the market place. The couple (particularly the heterosexual couple) of late capitalism is a couple who can live, dress, consume and travel in ways which accord with the fantasies of consumption" (136). According to this notion, Miranda's marriage proposal is not "romantic" in the traditional sense because it ignores the consumerist practices that sanction the moment as such: there is no ring and the engagement is sealed over three-dollar beers rather than at a fancy restaurant. The "unconventionality" of the scene is also foregrounded by the reversal of roles in the proposal, since she is the one who takes the initiative. We are able to recognize this flouting of orthodoxy thanks to our familiarity with the conventions of such a moment in countless romantic comedy films. If "consumerist romantic moments serve as the standard against which nonconsumerist moments are constructed" (Illouz 125), Miranda's proposal is unmistakably marked as a "nonconsumerist," and therefore unusual, take on romance. This is extended to her choice of the place for the ceremony: the "ordinariness" of a community garden contrasts with the boat option, which is dismissed as artificial and contrived. Illouz's ethnographic study on the influence of social class on people's ideas about romance found that those belonging to the middle and upper-middle class rely on a broader range of romantic practices and are more likely to reject the concept of romance and praise the "mundane." Those in the upper-middle class are especially likely to despise the consumerist ethos, while the working classes tend to buy more uncritically into the ideas associated with manufactured romantic commodities. In this way, those belonging to the upper end of the social scale try to reassert their autonomy from romantic practices. This tendency among the upper-middle class may account for Miranda's vehement rejection of all the wedding paraphernalia: her emotional detachment from manufactured romantic practices is meant to reaffirm her critical "superiority." Her insistence on going off the beaten track in the organization of her wedding so that it feels "like her"—in this case cynical and skeptical about romance—matches Illouz's findings about the well-off classes valuing creative self-expression, and her impulsive marriage proposal dovetails with this social group's high regard for spontaneity.

However, despite being conditioned by her sociocultural background, and even though she always remains the most cynical of the group, the text makes clear that, at bottom, Miranda does not really despise romance, but rather the contemporary cultural and economic practices associated with it. In her conversations with her friends she appeals to a simpler, "purer" raison d'être for her wedding: "I don't even care about the wedding. I just wanna be with Steve." However, she does not simply want to have a quick ceremony at the city hall because she actually wants to "say those vows out loud to Steve in front of the people I care about." In this way, Miranda's alternative take on romance is presented to the spectator as the most authentic one.

The scene depicting Miranda's wedding is short but compelling. We see the couple in a cozy garden in the center of Manhattan surrounded by a very small group of people. The warmth of the scene is underlined by the reddish autumn colors of the garden, which match Miranda's clothes and hair. Together with the mise-en-scène, the editing also works to emphasize the "truthfulness" of the couple's bond: close-ups of Miranda and Steve, intermingled with shots of the wedding attendees, convey a deep sense of contained emotion in the scene. After the ceremony, the small wedding party is seen having a relaxed, informal lunch at a restaurant.

Due to contemporary society's fascination with "white weddings," Miranda's is conspicuously marked as opposed to tradition. Chrys Ingraham explains how today's obsession with weddings virtually impregnates every aspect of American culture, including film, television, the Internet, and the popular press. The wedding business has grown at such a rate that, these days, it can more accurately be referred to as the "wedding-industrial complex" (37): an average U.S. wedding cost $27,852 (a year's earning for many Americans) in the mid-2000s. In the case of the New York metro area, the average amount increased to $38,852, easily reaching $100,000 in many cases (44). Measured against these figures, Miranda's wedding is clearly characterized as "ordinary," or even "nonconsumerist." The high cost of "white weddings" clearly denies the lower classes access to the traditional romantic fantasy they promise. However, as happened with the McDonald's scene, *SATC* 's romanticization of Miranda's "nonconsumerist" wedding tries to democratize romance and offer a utopian view of America's "classless" society.

This is the text's intended reading for Miranda's wedding, and it is clearly a positive one. However, as happens very often in this show, the series' systematic silencing of class and race issues always lurks beneath the surface. At bottom, Miranda's attitude may be interpreted as yet another manifestation of the show's blindness toward social inequalities. The fact that getting married in a community garden is more romantic for her than doing so on a boat says a lot about the taken-for-grantedness of Miranda's socioeconomic status. Being able to access such "luxury" whenever she wants, she has the possibility to opt for the "mundane," which is thus infused with a new halo of romanticism detached from consumerist practices and perceived as more authentic and true to the individual self. Carrie's case is similar: being used to attending exclusive cultural events and wearing expensive outfits, she can afford to prefer McDonald's restaurants to the opera. *SATC*'s protagonists find the ordinary romantic because they live in a world far removed from economic necessity and they are able to access those (expensive) cultural practices any time they like. They know that they can buy their way into romance if they want to. This grants them the privilege to choose not to do so, thus reaffirming their individuality and cultural capital, as displayed in their self-consciousness about these practices. If we take into consideration this idea, it becomes clear that social class issues play an important part in *SATC*'s ideas about romance, but this is never made explicit by the text.

In any case, despite the series' subtexts, taken at face value Miranda's wedding scene is unambiguously constructed as a positive model for contemporary romantic practices, which, in general, tend to follow pre-established patterns of uncritical consumption. Chrys Ingraham laments how consumer culture in general, and the pervasiveness of the wedding-industrial complex in particular, has done away with our ability to develop a critical consciousness (222). Miranda's "nonconsumerist" wedding tells the viewer that she knows better, placing her on a level superior to those who uncritically buy into the lavish wedding paraphernalia. The value of her critical sense is reinforced by the fact that the scene feels truly romantic, which legitimates "simplicity" as romance's best chance of survival today. Once again, this also points toward romantic comedy's need to renew its conventions to convince savvy, postmodern viewers of the "truthfulness" of the love depicted on-screen.

However, *SATC*'s generic agenda to push the boundaries of romantic comedy goes further than that. Before the wedding, Samantha picks up Carrie in a taxi and tells her she has breast cancer. Carrie is deeply distressed, but she does not show it, since she does not want to upset Samantha or ruin Miranda's day. During the ceremony, the two friends' response to the couple's vows is clearly split between conflicting emotions. Despite the centrality of the heterosexual couple in the wedding scene, editing works to emphasize the importance of Samantha and Carrie's bond. When Miranda pronounces her vow to stay by her partner "in sickness and in health," we see Carrie reaching out for Samantha's hand. This is followed by a shot that visually encapsulates the two "engagements" taking place at the same time: the heterosexual couple is "framed" by the couple of friends, who stand in the foreground.

Here formal devices do not only emphasize the importance of friendship in the series, as they often do. It can be argued that *SATC* goes one step further, suggesting that the concept of romance nowadays can be extended to encompass friendship. As Chrys Ingraham points out in her exploration of the role of weddings in the naturalization of heterosexuality, the imagery characteristic of these events makes clear that "romance" is limited to en-

Figure 2.5.   Samantha and Carrie hold hands.

compass only the heterosexual couple. The centrality of the heterosexual couple in wedding scenes is a deeply ingrained convention in the romantic comedy genre. Cinema's preoccupation with weddings is especially salient nowadays: a myriad of recent romantic comedies revolve around weddings, while only a few of them deal with issues other than the progression of the protagonist couple toward the altar.[2] For this reason, the central role played by female solidarity in this scene, which takes away the limelight from the happy couple, pushes the boundaries of the genre by expanding its meanings to incorporate friendship as a possible, and highly desirable, site for a new kind of "romance" at the turn of the century.

The subordination of the heterosexual couple to female friendship is corroborated by the episode's concluding scenes, which take place in a small restaurant where the wedding party is celebrating the union. Miranda's family is conspicuously absent from her wedding. The only family member present at the ceremony is Steve's mother, who is unequivocally presented as a nuisance for Miranda: she corners her in conversation, praising her honesty in refusing to dress in white, while Miranda looks desperately at her friends. A point-of-view shot from her perspective makes clear that she would like to be in the company of her family of choice rather than the one she is now legally bound to. When she finally manages to get to her friends' table and learns about Samantha's illness, she refuses to go to "her people" in order to

Figure 2.6.   "In sickness and in health."

celebrate her "special day": "You are my people and we'll talk about it now!" she insists. In this way, Miranda's "special day" becomes Samantha's, as the episode's focus shifts completely in order to concentrate on her. Thus, the text goes against the tide, so to speak, in its representation of a wedding, since eventually the emphasis is not laid on the heterosexual union, but on the friends' bond. The camera underlines this link in the closing scene, framing the girls from outside the restaurant, absorbed in their private world, as it frequently does. The repetition of this closing device points to the endurance of the girls' friendship in all circumstances, for better or worse, in sickness and in health, just like the vows Miranda has recently pronounced. In this way, *SATC* adds another layer to the meanings evoked by weddings, suggesting that contemporary ideas about romance can be "stretched" to encompass friendship, thus hinting at the possibility of a new kind of romance for the twenty-first century—one that is not based on traditional romantic clichés and consumption-based scripts.

SHOPPING AROUND FOR LOVE

Disentangling *SATC*'s position toward romance is no simple task. This is mainly because the show does not offer a straightforward view on the issue, but highly ambivalent and often contradictory readings. The influence of our consumerist society on love relationships and on larger aspects of our lives has been an issue of remarkable concern for twentieth-century critics. Marx, for instance, regards consumption as incompatible with personal emancipation (Elster). *SATC* displays a complex relationship with consumption, but it tends to oppose these negative views. On the one hand, commodities in the show are frequently presented as a site of cultural resistance and self-identity; for instance, Carrie's deployment of fashion can be seen as an act of resistance to traditional notions of femininity, becoming "a site of identity and the reclamation of power" (Buckley and Ott 223). Similarly, the rhetoric of freedom promulgated by today's consumerist society clearly dovetails with *SATC*'s insistence on women's right to choose in every aspect of their lives, be it shoes or men. Therefore, the association between consumption and romance in *SATC* is not necessarily negative. Quite the contrary, it is this association's emancipatory potential that is normally foregrounded.

The "shop-and-choose" view of relationships legitimized by consumerist practices is not morally judged by the show. Its ambivalent attitude toward most of the issues featured in the series provides a nonjudgmental reflection of the way in which contemporary relationships have been affected by late capitalism's mentality. According to Scitovsky, our drive toward consumption is based on the excitement of novelty. However, *SATC*'s protagonists would not buy a new pair of shoes without shopping around. That is, freedom of choice among a large array of options is also a paramount component of consumerist satisfaction. The extrapolation of these pleasures—the excitement of both novelty and choice—to the realm of intimacy has radically altered people's romantic narratives at the turn of the millennium. The result is that the concept of the "great love" in our lives has been replaced by a more postmodern experience: the affair. Affairs have become the dominant model of romantic liaison today because they resemble consumerist patterns in its basic structure: "shopping around" for a partner gives way to the initial "high" of novelty, which quickly leads to a loss of interest in the "object." Since consumerism does not actually consist of accumulating goods, but of "using them and disposing of them after use to make room for other goods and their uses" (Bauman 49), the repetition of the cycle is guaranteed, turning affairs into "self-contained narrative episodes disconnected from one another in the flow of experience, resulting in a fragmenting of the experience of love into separate emotional units" (Illouz 174). In this light, it becomes obvious how a serial text like *SATC* is better equipped than film to reflect the changes undergone by romantic relationships at the turn of the century. Conditioned by the two-hour format and by its narrative conventions, traditional romantic comedy is often at a loss when faced with the responsibility of reflecting today's panorama of intermittent romantic engagement and disconnection.[3] Rather, the genre is more prone to telling great love stories that dissolve into the promise of a happily ever after. Since the reality of contemporary relationships is, sadly, otherwise, it can be argued that *SATC*, with its serial structure, can better grasp the fragmentation and discontinuity of the contemporary intimate panorama than its cinematic counterparts can.

As illustrated in the episode analyzed above, this fragmentation is largely motivated by the intrinsic incompatibility between fleeting romance and real intimacy. The postmodern romantic self tries hard to reconcile the intensity of the affair with the stability of a long-lasting relationship. The individual's struggle translates into a crisis of representation of love, since the "postmodern condition" is characterized by the disjunction between the signifier of romance and the signified of love (Illouz). *SATC* reflects this struggle: its protagonists date one man after another, in constant pursuit of the "signifiers" of romance, but find themselves perplexed at their lack of correspondence with the actual experience of a "real" relationship. Arguably, it is this disagreement, coupled with today's consumerist mentality, that propels them back into the romantic quest time after time.

However, despite the challenges faced by the romantic self in contemporary society, *SATC* generally does not offer a negative view of consumption in connection with the romantic experience. This does not mean that the link between the two is unproblematically endorsed, either. The analysis of the episode shows how romance's alliance with consumption is somehow nuanced to make it more in tune with the American "democratic" ethos. The ordinary and the mundane are thus presented as the new scenarios in which "real" romance can flourish, in opposition to clichéd symbols of European sophistication or expensive manufactured celebrations. *SATC*'s penchant for "democratic" or "ordinary" romance is partly accounted for by the characters' socioeconomic position: their well-off status guarantees them access to consumerist romantic practices any time they like. Therefore, simplicity is excitedly embraced as "exotic." This is also explained by the genre's need to update its conventions: in a postmodern context in which everything has been said and done, knowledgeable audiences are familiar with romantic symbols and protocols, which have been thoroughly emptied of their significance. The genre's need to reinvent itself is palpable in *SATC*'s will to push its boundaries by expanding the limits of what romance is able to encompass, in order to include friendship.

To conclude, it can be said that, at bottom, *SATC*'s recurrent obsession with the topic of romance betrays its desire to believe, not only in its possibility, but also in its compatibility with an enduring relationship. This is, however, a nearly impossible task in today's dating panorama. This contradiction makes *SATC* a deeply ambivalent text in its position toward the state of heterosexual relationships in general and romance in particular. This "indecision," however, captures accurately the tentativeness and confusion surrounding the intimate climate of its time, and this is effectively conveyed through its episodic structure. Conventional romantic comedy tends to offer a more reductionist view of romance, constrained as it is by the need to tie up all the loose ends by its conclusion. *SATC*'s vision is, if not more realist, at least more complex and multifaceted, and also more connected with its context, since its ambiguity springs from the postfeminist spirit that shapes the show. Perpetually caught between feminist and antifeminist discourses, *SATC*'s characters, although admittedly to different degrees, would like to surrender, to be rescued from it all by Prince Charming. However, their feminist allegiance will not allow them to give in to this fantasy, which enmeshes them in the intricate web of contradictory meanings about romance, sex, and femininity that characterize turn-of-the-century intimacy. In this way, the myth of romance is simultaneously rejected as a harmful construction and willingly embraced as the most desirable of states. In the end, it is difficult to extract a straightforward message about the series' stand toward the issue. What is clear, however, is that, thanks in part to the show's serial form, romantic millennial anxieties have never had a more committed forum for expression.

NOTES

1. Romance Writers of America, "Romance Industry Statistics," http://www.rwa.org/p/cm/ld/fid=580 (accessed 11 January 2014).
2. In the last two decades, romantic comedy has been especially fascinated by weddings. Recent films following this trend include *Four Weddings and a Funeral* (1994), *Muriel's Wedding* (1994), *My Best Friend's Wedding* (1997), *The Wedding Singer* (1998), *Runaway Bride* (1999), *The Bachelor* (1999), *The Wedding Planner* (2001), *My Big Fat Greek Wedding* (2002), *The Wedding Date* (2005), *License to Wed* (2007), *Made of Honor* (2008), *27 Dresses* (2008), *The Five-Year Engagement* (2012), and *The Big Wedding* (2013). All of these films are mainly concerned with issues such as the heterosexual couple's (un)suitability for marriage, their attitude toward the institution, or simply the celebration of the ceremony in itself. In any case, it is always the couple that takes central stage and few other topics are usually tackled. A notable exception to this trend are those films that address a male audience, such as *American Wedding* (2003), *Sideways* (2005), *Wedding Crashers* (2005), *The Groomsmen* (2006), and *The Hangover* (2009). These films are much scarcer and tend to put the emphasis on male bonding in the face of marriage.
3. A notable exception in this respect are multi-protagonist films. María del Mar Azcona devotes a chapter of her book on this new genre to its intersection with romantic comedies, in which she argues that a narrative format that includes various story lines and protagonists reflects more accurately today's volatile intimate scenarios.

Chapter Three

What's the Harm in Believing?

Romantic versus Democratic Love

Romantic possibilities seem endless today. Individuals appear to enjoy a much wider array of options to choose from than their parents and grandparents ever did. Evidently, the freedom to customize romantic life to fit one's personal aspirations is the prerogative of a certain group of individuals who are able to do so because of their privileged socioeconomic position. Those members of industrialized Western societies who are not pressed by more urgent issues concerning their well-being devote a considerable amount of energy and time to the writing of their romantic narratives. This is so because, unlike previous generations, who had a more clearly sign-posted path to follow in the management of their intimate lives, "romantic options" nowadays multiply before our eyes while social stigmas and prejudices become more diluted. These options include homosexual coupling, single parenthood, marriage (traditional or open), friendship networks, serial dating, serial monogamy (short- or long-term), cohabitation (with a romantic or nonromantic partner), "hooking up," or abstinence (by choice or not). The turn of the century has thus witnessed a remarkable boost in the ways in which intimate life can be "officially" organized.[1]

These changes have undoubtedly opened new doors for individual self-realization, but they have not made our pursuance of that state necessarily easier. In the past, the path toward personal fulfillment was more clearly marked. Today, this straightforward road is increasingly becoming a winding and hesitant trail, since the unprecedented number of choices lying at our feet these days seems to have brought about more questions than answers. Actually, it is more than that; all this sentimental "sophistication" and self-awareness has sometimes resulted in a paradoxical outcome, namely, a renewed faith in the traditional idea of "true love." The remarkable number of books published on love's many dimensions attests to people's enduring preoccupation with matters of the heart at the turn of the millennium (Jamieson; Langford; Evans; Kipnis; Bauman; Swidler; Shumway; Ben-Ze'ev; Beck and Beck-Gernsheim, *The Normal Chaos of Love*; Weeks, *The World We Have Won*; Nehring). Some sociological theories have tried to shed some light on the subject, proposing a democratic, friendship-like model for our intimate attachments more in tune with the capitalistic, market-driven society of our times. However, it appears that the more rational sociological discourses become, the more inclined the individual is to hold on to uncanny, metaphysical explanations for his or her emotions. The "soul mate" ideal, whose origin can be traced back to Plato's myth, has never been more present in popular representations of love. Paradoxically enough, we seem more willing than ever to believe in love's mysterious "magic" as the link between lovers, rather than in a "rolling contract" more akin to an economic merger. The more sociologists talk about "rational investments" in the couple, the keener popular culture seems to be on the representation of unfettered passions able to sweep individuals off their feet.

This paradoxical clash regarding contemporary discourses on love and intimacy will be addressed in this chapter. In a moment in which there is an unprecedented number of options at our disposal for the organization of our intimate lives, why this vehement insistence on pursuing old blueprints for romance? At a time in which gender roles seem to be much looser in the Western, industrialized world, what is still so compelling about the most traditional model of heterosexual coupling? What is so fetching about romantic love in a society that systematically scorns clichéd romantic notions? How can our postmodern self-awareness and romantic cynicism be compatible with the desire for a fairy-tale "happily ever after"?

All these questions are routinely tackled by *SATC*. With its serial structure, the show dissects the vicissitudes of contemporary romantic relationships from a variety of viewpoints, posing questions like: Can women aspire to "have it all," or should they settle for what they can get before it is too late? How much of oneself is acceptable to sacrifice in a relationship? Is "the One" just a harmful myth? What are the deal breakers in contemporary relationships? Have men really accepted women's new roles? Do women deep down just want to be "rescued" by Prince Charming? When it comes to relationships, is it smarter to follow your head or your heart? In general terms, all these questions are encompassed in one of *SATC*'s most pervasive preoccupations: love's eternal double bind between its potential emancipatory power and the limitations that it paradoxically imposes on the self. It can be argued that this is the main dilemma that lies at the very heart of the series, as the show portrays contemporary women as torn between a longing for intimacy and an intense wish to preserve their autonomous subjectivity, often framing the latter in contractual, even consumerist terms. For this chapter I have selected four episodes from season 4 that I consider representative of the show's struggle between romantic "surrender" and female independence, coupledom and singleness. The episodes deal with Carrie and Aidan's engagement and eventual breakup: "Just Say Yes" (4:12), "The Good Fight" (4:13), "All That Glitters" (4:14), and "Change of a Dress" (4:15). The aim of this chapter is to explore the above-mentioned dilemma, and how these discourses are articulated through the conventions of romantic comedy.

Sociological theories trying to make sense of the state of intimacy today are manifold. There has been a burst of writings on this topic during the last few years. However, broadly speaking, two general trends can be identified in contemporary definitions of intimacy. On the one hand, there are those who propose the norms of friendship as the model to follow for contemporary intimacy (Pahl; Giddens; Evans; Kristjánsson). This trend argues in favor of the democratization—and in its most extreme stand—the rationalization of love. On the other hand, other authors support the idea that romantic love is better equipped to cater to the individual's needs today (Luhmann; Levinas; Beck and Beck-Gernsheim, *The Normal Chaos of Love*; Nehring), since it is more in tune with the individualistic ethos of our times and it encompasses an element of passion generally overlooked by the "friendship model." This chapter will look at the way in which the series comes to terms with these two tendencies, arguing that the show's apparently cynical view of love actually betrays a deep wish to believe in the possibility of old-fashioned, unrestrained romance. The tension between love as a matter of "closing the deal" and love as Cupid's return to the co-op, to paraphrase Carrie's opening monologue, might well have left the show, in Carrie's terms, a "mess." The "mess" is managed, however, through *SATC*'s deployment and revision of conventions from the romantic comedy genre.

ARE DIAMONDS A GIRL'S BEST FRIEND? *SEX AND THE CITY'S* ROMANTIC DREAMS

The central plot of "Just Say Yes" concerns Aidan's marriage proposal to Carrie. It starts with "ominous" words: "My building is going co-op!" Carrie announces to Aidan as she walks into her apartment. This means that she either has to move, or buy the place, which she cannot afford. Aidan offers to buy both her apartment and the one next door, so that they can tear down the wall and live together. This is Carrie and Aidan's second attempt at their relationship after her infidelity with Big. However, this time everything seems to be going smoothly, so Aidan's offer is tempting. She does not really say "yes," but this does not stop him from unofficially moving in, leaving his stuff all over the place and upsetting Carrie. In the next scene we see her

cleaning up while he is taking a shower. While tidying his bag she acciden-
tally finds a proposal ring. She looks at it in astonishment for some seconds,
after which she runs to the sink to throw up. This is followed by a quick cut
to Charlotte's reaction to the news: "You're getting engaged!" she gurgles
excitedly. Evidently, her interpretation of the event is very different from
Carrie's. As usual, the girls have gotten together for lunch and they are
discussing the issue.

The episode's premise hinges on the many possibilities regarding
coupling in contemporary America (and elsewhere). Statistical research carried out by sociologists confirms that people do not regard "living together"
as implying the same level of commitment as marriage. The idea of "forever"
is still firmly attached to wedlock, as opposed to cohabitation. Thus, there is
still a clear boundary in the collective mind distinguishing the life project of
those couples who decide to marry and those who remain legally unbound
(Bawin-Legros; Pollard and Harris). Carrie's strong reaction to the thought
of marriage attests to this assumption, since she seems more or less ready to
live under the same roof as Aidan, but not for the firm attachment marriage
implies.

In order to convey this idea, the text also brings into play the audience's
familiarity with romantic comedy's conventions. Fans of the genre know that
the marriage proposal is usually the climactic moment in the couple's narrative, and all the paraphernalia surrounding this moment is perceived as holding a quasi-magical value. Thus, Carrie's prosaic discovery of her engagement ring—in her boyfriend's sports bag, among his dirty clothes—and her
"atypical" reaction to the prop that has traditionally elicited the greatest
amount of tears in the genre is not accidental. Traditional approaches to
genre criticism would say that this can be read as a clear subversion of
romantic comedy's conventions. However, according to less taxonomical
views, genres are not fixed categories that can be simply subverted, but a
fluid set of conventions (Altman; Neale, *Genre and Hollywood*). Genres find
themselves in a constant state of flux, constantly in tune with the cultural
context in which they are inscribed. With its repeated "challenges" to romantic comedy's best-known conventions, for example, *SATC* might be simply
reflecting the changing romantic milieu that frames its characters' love lives.
Carrie's reaction to the discovery of the ring is a sign of the volatile intimate
panorama of turn-of-the-century New York, a context that fosters (in this
show, at least) a pathological fear of deep attachments in general, and of
marriage in particular.[2]

Alongside this contextual understanding, Carrie's vomiting at the sight of
the ring might also be read as an internal shift within the conventions of
romantic comedy. Carrie's exaggerated reaction is not only "troubling," after
all, but also comic. In romantic comedy, humor often plays a paramount role
in the path toward romantic transformation. In the case of *SATC*, it also plays

an important role in its protagonists' occasional *rejection* of this transformation. That is, *SATC* stretches the boundaries of the genre by using humor not
only as enabler of romance but, sometimes more importantly, as a tool to
surmount the disappointments love repeatedly brings our protagonists. Since
SATC's lead women find themselves in a constant turmoil of relationships,
the latter function of humor often proves to be more useful than the one it has
traditionally served, at once marking and normalizing the girls' unsuitability
for coupled life.

   In either case, it is no accident that this scene's humor—and its emotional
conflict—centers on an engagement ring. The ring is a significant prop within romantic comedy's iconography, and its importance here is foregrounded
by the lunchtime discussion after Carrie's reaction. What seems at first to be
a conversation about Carrie's decision whether to get married or not ends up
revolving entirely around the ring itself. It turns out it is a disappointment: "It
was a pear-shaped diamond with a gold band," which apparently is a bad
thing. Carrie justifies her dislike for the ring because "it is not her"—that is,
she takes Aidan's mistaken choice as a sign that he does not really know her
and they are not meant for each other: "How can I marry a guy who doesn't
know which ring is me?" she demands. The conversation thus reveals the
importance that Carrie bestows on material objects, which, once again, points
to her association of (luxury) consumer goods with happiness and romance.
It is the ring that makes her throw up—presumably because she does not like
it—making her think the marriage is doomed to failure because of its unsuitability. Tellingly, she will be happy to accept Aidan's proposal later on in the
episode, when she is presented with a "good" ring. Of course, this connection
between consumption and happiness does not only concern Carrie; it also
affects the other characters, who also endorse the show's consumerist spirit,
extending the equation of ring and person first made by Carrie to Aidan as
well. "Wrong ring, wrong guy," Samantha thus declares, underscoring the
series' strong link between consumer goods and relationships.

When It's Right, You Know

With all the ring talk, Carrie's conversation with her friends does not help her
solve her actual dilemma: whether or not to marry Aidan. Once alone at
home, she starts to think about something Charlotte said: "When it's right,
you know." This is a place that fans of romantic comedy are familiar with:
love takes over you when it comes, leaving no doubt about its truthfulness.
However, faithful to *SATC* 's mission to interrogate every single romantic
cliché, Carrie wonders:

> Do you really know when it's right? And how do you know? Are there signs?
> Fireworks? Is it right when it feels comfortable or is that a sign that there

aren't any fireworks? Is hesitation a sign that it's not right or a sign that you're
not ready? In matters of love, how do you know when it's right?

To know when it is "right" is another way of phrasing a concern that has
been repeatedly addressed in the show: the concept of "the One" or the soul
mate. The roots of this idea might be traced back as far as Aristophanes's
famous account of love in Plato's *Symposium*, but it has grown pervasive in
late-twentieth/early twenty-first-century American popular culture. For example, a national Gallup Poll carried out at the time of *SATC* broadcasting in
the United States (2001) showed that 94 percent of surveyed people (single
women and men between twenty and twenty-nine) were seeking a soul mate
to marry, and 87 percent were confident they would find it (Trimberger).
Their confidence is remarkable: after all, this idealizing account of love as a
quasi-demiurgic process implies that we will recognize "the One," that we
will be recognized in return, and that the relationship between "soul mates"
will be flawlessly harmonious, a completion of each self by the other. No
wonder, then, that the idea of "soul mates" depends on supernatural discourse, the discourse of miracles, rather than on the liberal discourse of
"closing the deal" or consumer choice. Thomas Moore says that a soul mate
is "someone to whom we feel profoundly connected, as though the communi-
cating that takes place between us were not the product of intentional efforts,
but rather a divine grace" (xvii). The problems with this "divine grace"
version of love are manifold. After all, what if we never meet our twin soul,
or meet him or her and are not recognized as "the One"? If total harmonious
fusion proves impossible—if "the One" leaves us, say, as a consequence of
some misunderstanding, or if we have to inject our "intentional efforts"
(Moore xvii) into the relationship to make it succeed—does that mean we
were mistaken? Will we never, now, be "complete"? The "soul mate" model
of love puts extraordinary pressure on the individual's actual romantic relationships, potentially spoiling them as they fall short of this ideal. At the
same time, this model implies that personal fulfillment can only be achieved
through coupled love, thus devaluing one's network of friends and other
nonromantic partnerships.

Given the popularity of this myth of love, and the ambivalence it might
provoke, it is no wonder that the writers of *SATC* were fond of the topic. In
"The Agony and the 'Ex'-tacy" (4:1)—an episode that ponders the question,
"Soul mates: reality or torture device?"—the protagonists discuss the different aspects of this myth. Charlotte believes in it blindly, while the rest are
skeptical:

Miranda: Soul mates only exist in the Hallmark aisle of Duane Reade
Drugs.

Charlotte: I disagree. I believe there's one perfect person out there to complete you.

Miranda: And, if you don't find him, what? You're incomplete? It's so dangerous!

Carrie: All right, first of all, the idea that there's only one out there? I mean, why don't I just shoot myself right now? I like to think people have more than one soul mate.

Samantha: I agree! I've had hundreds!

Carrie: Yeah, and if you miss one, along comes another, like cabs.

Charlotte: No, that is not how it works.

[. . .]

Samantha: The bad thing about the one perfect soul mate is that it's so unattainable. You're being set up to fail.

Miranda: Exactly, and you feel bad about yourself!

Samantha: Yeah, it makes the gap between the Holy Grail and the assholes even bigger.

This dialogue touches on three main doubts about the twin soul ideology: whether the twin soul actually exists, whether there might be more than one "the One," and whether the ideology itself might be a harmful construction. Notably, however, the exchange also contains hints of another, contrasting ideology of love: one based on consumer choice among multiple options. "If you miss one, another comes along, like cabs," Carrie quips, and her joke underscores the power that the consumer of love might have in an ideal romantic marketplace, one in which the possibilities of romantic transport are multiple and available to anyone with sufficient funds. Carrie's relentless self-questioning about Aidan's suitability—and basically about the suitability of every partner she has—shows her acting like a wary consumer, evaluating each "cab" as it comes into view, but her wariness would surely not be so intense if it were not for the high expectations this kind of myth has instilled in her. Indeed, we might say that on some level, conscious or unconscious, Carrie is turning twin soul ideology against itself, using it to justify the actual (consumerist) choice she has already made. That is to say, Carrie's fondness for the single life is the main reason behind her doubts about Aidan, and all this talk of "the One" essentially helps her rationalize her unwillingness to marry. She would hardly be alone in this self-justification: in fact, Trimberger connects the pervasiveness of the twin soul myth with many contemporary women's single status, while certain sectors of popular discourse warn women that they will have to forsake this myth and settle for "Mr. Good Enough" if they want to settle down (Gottlieb; Lipka).

However we interpret Carrie's motivations, *SATC*'s treatment of the topic makes clear that the twin soul ideal forms an important part of the contemporary "resuscitation" of romantic love. Such quasi-religious faith in love as the path toward personal fulfillment has largely replaced other reasons for long-term partnership and/or marriage (Trimberger). Beck and Beck-Gernsheim explain this phenomenon thus: they maintain that we are immersed in a new age characterized by a deep transformation of the relationship between the individual and society. This transformation is based on the disappearance of fixed traditions, institutions, and beliefs, which turns the individual into a fully autonomous being both blessed and cursed with the responsibility of decision making. Moreover, the present demands of the labor market (mobility, flexibility, competitiveness) are turning the preservation of personal relationships (marriage, parenthood, friendship) into an increasingly difficult endeavor (*The Normal Chaos of Love* 3–8). Thus, the incompatibility between the demands of the labor market and those of relationships, and the increased instability brought about by the loss of traditional certainties, make the establishment and consolidation of intimate relationships more difficult than ever. Paradoxically enough, this situation has propelled love to the top position in people's priorities. The individualization process that Beck and Beck-Gernsheim believe is taking place in contemporary societies may seem to pull the sexes apart, but it actually makes the need for close relationships stronger. The dilution of tradition causes people to turn to love as an antidote to their fear of loneliness (*The Normal Chaos of Love*). In this way, romantic love is put on a sort of pedestal, heralded as today's "secular religion," with the soul mate ideology as its main dogma. In our post-Christian modern society, love has become the center of our personal lives as we try to discover who we are. The parallels with religion are manifold: both "ethoi" hold out the promise of perfect happiness, both represent a source of escape from everyday reality, both give individuals the opportunity to "find themselves," both offer some sort of mystical "salvation," and both give meaning to our life in moments of crisis. This new faith in romantic love thus becomes a reaction against individualism: people place all their hopes in their love lives in an attempt to find safety in an increasingly fragmented world (Beck and Beck-Gernsheim, *The Normal Chaos of Love*). Thus, love becomes more important than ever for the modern individual. However, as will be later explained, it is also more difficult than ever to attain.

This is reflected in the episode under analysis, since Carrie's dilemma about marrying Aidan or not is entirely concerned with whether he is "right," that is, whether he is "the One" for her or not, and it glosses over other factors that have traditionally played a paramount role in the decision to get married: economics, friendship, sexual attraction, community and family approval, and so on. This tendency toward the idealization and romanticization of love, the preoccupation with that "special someone" able to cater to the individual's every need, is particularly in tune with romantic comedy's ethos, since the genre has always been based on the wish to believe in the possibility of the perfect romantic communion. But we cannot overlook the way that "perfect romantic communion" in this show puts a distinctive twist on this enduring wish. Love here entails a reconciliation or perfect accord between spiritual ideals and their material instantiation, the right guy with the right ring. As Carrie says in the opening episode of this fourth season, "The Agony and the 'Ex'-tacy" (4:1), the soul mate ideal consists in the "belief that someone, somewhere, is holding the key to your heart *and your dream house*. All you have to do is find them" (my emphasis). One key for both: otherwise, the search goes on.

WHY HASN'T HE ASKED ME YET?

Let us return, now, to "Just Say Yes." As I mentioned earlier, Carrie discovers Aidan's ring shortly after he offers to buy both her apartment and the one next door, so that they can tear down the wall and live together: a gesture that would suggest he sees himself as the "someone" who holds the key to her heart and her dream house (or at least her co-op). Carrie's initial reaction to the offer is lighthearted and flirtatious:

Carrie: Would that make you my landlord or my roommate?

Aidan: A little of both.

Carrie: What would the rent be like?

Aidan: Like . . . this? [kissing her]

Behind the flirtation, however, lies a serious problem. If the modern couple is supposed to be a democratic, freely chosen contract between equals (Giddens), where does this agreement leave Carrie? Will she live in the apartment in exchange for sexual and emotional gratification for Aidan? His gesture looks romantic and disinterested, but it actually gives him the upper hand in the relationship. As is always the case in the series, *SATC* refuses to acknowledge explicitly the important role played by class and economic issues in its romantic dynamics, even as it implicitly returns, again and again, to precisely those factors.

The truth is that Carrie never falls for "poor" men. Even though she has dated men who were not particularly well off, the three men she has had serious relationships with (Big, Aidan, and Petrovsky) were far above her in the economic and social ladder, and Carrie's conception of her partners' suitability seems deeply shaped by their "provider" status. She is not the only woman in the show to behave this way; in fact, the series follows remarkably traditional patterns when it comes to the definition of gender roles within the couple.[3] In theories of democratic love, relationships are presented as nego- tiated contracts entered by mutual agreement (Giddens). However, mutual agreement does not automatically imply equality. The democratic contract between the couple does not mean the end of domination; rather, it is "an effective means by which consent of the subordinate is at once secured and made hidden" (Langford 12). The fact that Carrie is attracted to well-off men and seems happy with this situation, that she *chooses* her wealthy partners, does not diminish the economic inequality that underlies her relationships; it simply conceals it. Carrie's agreement to be supported by Aidan, paying her rent in kisses, thus does not lessen her economic dependence on him, but it does suggest that kisses are the way that this inequality might be masked, at least for a while, by the discourse of romance. In particular, the soul mate version of love does not stoop to consider such "prosaic" questions as materi- al conditions, thus conveniently overlooking the practical aspects of the un- ion. Conversely, the more material conditions reassert themselves, the less wholeheartedly one can embrace or espouse this romanticized version of love.

Carrie herself seems conscious, on some level, of this tension between love as a contract between equal subjects and love as the "divine grace" that merges true soul mates. Immediately after the scene where Carrie and her friends discuss Aidan's ring, we see the couple having dinner together at a posh restaurant. She has not yet decided whether to marry him or not, a decision that would be made on the basis of romantic love or twin soul ideology, of "knowing that it's right." Instead, she accepts his proposal of living together, a more rational, contractual domestic arrangement in which it seems that economic and political factors can be acknowledged. "So . . . yes," she tells Aidan. "I say yes to living together. I think we're ready for that step. Yes, we still have to work out the money, 'cause I don't want a free ride. We're still individuals, but we'll be sharing a life and an apartment." The episode never clarifies what kind of financial arrangement their new life plan is going to follow, but even this brief nod to financial reality shows how an economic understanding of relationships ("we still have to work out the money") entails a sense that the two members of the couple remain distinct "individuals," a version of romance that stands in sharp contrast with the idea of "completion" found in twin soul ideology.

Even as Carrie accepts cohabitation, however, a second sharp contrast characterizes the scene. Carrie's rational, qualified "yes" to living together takes place in a mise-en-scène that invokes neither reason nor egalitarian contracts, but rather the emotional and erotic extravagance of romance. The restaurant in which they are having dinner is elegant, they are dressed in formal clothes: in sum, all the "signs of romance" are "activated" in this scene. In accordance with capitalist society's scripts of romance and romantic comedy's conventions, everything around them indicates—both to Carrie and to the viewer—that this is the moment in which Aidan is going to make his proposal. The scene's editing increases her and our suspense by having Aidan reach for his pocket in slow motion. However, our expectations are disrupted when it turns out it is his wallet that he was reaching for, not the ring. Romantic comedy's mise-en-scène has tricked both Carrie and the viewer, and paradoxically, she feels both relieved and puzzled. "Why hasn't he asked me yet? What if he realized I'm not 'the One'?" she wonders nervously in a phone call to Miranda the following day. It is as though Carrie were untroubled by her own willingness to think rationally and economically about the relationship, but the suggestion that Aidan is likewise thinking about it in any terms other than twin soul ideology—reaching for his wallet, not a ring—fills her with self-doubt.

Carrie's ambivalence and anxiety are typical of her character, but they are not reducible to individual psychology. Rather, they illustrate the difficulties faced by lovers in a particular institutional context, one that, once again, we can understand through the individualization theory of Beck and Beck-Gernsheim (*Individualization*). As the sociologists explain, in wealthy Western industrialized countries previously stable institutions of family, marriage, parenthood, sexuality, and love are no longer fixed or secure, and must therefore be negotiated by individuals on a case-by-case, couple-by-couple basis (*The Normal Chaos of Love*). The disappearance of traditional points of reference puts pressure on individuals to supply their own guidelines for living, and the dissolution of traditional blueprints of action forces us to make choices, not in a vacuum, but in a context that is cluttered with competing, often contradictory values systems and life narratives. This freedom of choice appears to open the door to the possibility of happiness, but the constant need to decide every aspect of life also creates anxiety, irritation, and never-ending questions, whose answers provide only "precarious freedoms" (Beck and Beck-Gernsheim, *Individualization* 6).

In preindustrial societies, the purpose of marriage was to contribute to the family's prosperity. Today, it is not stability that is sought after, but freedom, love, and self-realization, and there are no clear-cut, uncontested guidelines to follow in order to reach these. The disintegration of traditional certainties and institutions opens a sea of possibilities, condemning us to design our own biography in accordance with the dictates of an ostensibly "true" self that turns out to be as elusive as any soul mate. Indeed, there is a link between these two searches. In these times of uncertainty, the individual's romantic life gains unprecedented significance, as he or she turns to love in search for answers, idealizing it as a source of security and self-identity. Decisions about love, sex, romance, marriage, even erotic lifestyle are therefore elevated to more-than-practical importance, since only in these decisions can the true self be made securely visible and knowable. In the theorists' terms, these decisions are "deified," even as "[e]very day life is being post-religiously 'theologized'" in what is otherwise an increasingly secular world (Beck and Beck-Gernsheim, *Individualization* 7).

In this sense, *SATC* in general and this episode in particular constitute a faithful reflection of the contemporary individual's constant state of self-scrutiny, especially in the romantic realm. It could even be argued that a TV series like *SATC* is better equipped than cinematic narratives to reflect accurately the maze of introspection in which the individual is today immersed. Unlike film, which is usually forced to offer less nuanced readings of their characters' existential and romantic fates due to time constraints, television can better portray the uncertainty and volatility that characterizes the contemporary intimate panorama, as well as the psychological unrest produced by individualization processes. *SATC* captures this spirit of uncertainty and self-questioning, not just in any given episode, but in its formal structure *as a series*. Since the answers it provides by the end of each episode are merely provisional, the cycle of self-interrogation is bound to repeat again and again with a different romantic ideology—twin soul, consumerist, or something else—being embraced and contested by turns.

Not the Marrying Kind?

Aidan has not proposed to Carrie yet, but we know the moment is inexorably approaching. However, before that happens, there is a significant short scene between Carrie and Big. She is looking for a cab in the busy streets to get home, with no luck. Suddenly, Big appears and "rescues" her from the chaos of the New York traffic with his updated version of a white horse: a black limousine. She gets in the car and they talk about her relationship with Aidan. This scene is remarkable because it is totally gratuitous. Uncharacteristically for a twenty-five-minute sitcom, it does not make the action move forward. The scene's function is to remind the spectator that Big is still there, "lurking" in the back of Carrie's mind as a reminder of the single life she is about to leave behind.

The scene seems uncalled for in terms of plot advancement, but it makes sense in the context of romantic comedy. A recurrent trope within the genre is that of the "wrong partner." For the heroine to recognize her "right partner," he must be contrasted with his opposite, an ill-fitting suitor (Neale,

"The Big Romance" 288). Big seems to fulfill this role here, since Aidan certainly cannot be faulted in his behavior toward Carrie. The function of the wrong partner is also to problematize the romantic union, to pose obstacles to the final reunion of the lovers, something Big has certainly done in the past, since his affair with Carrie led to her first breakup with Aidan. However, the text's serial structure allows for greater complexity in the reworking of its conventions than the traditional romantic comedy usually does, since the roles of the right and wrong partner are not as clearly defined.

With the benefit of hindsight, the viewer knows that Carrie and Big will end up together, which problematizes Big's categorization as wrong partner. Once again, this helps emphasize the confusion and uncertainty surrounding people's positions in the romantic game nowadays. However, even without the knowledge of retrospection, there are certain textual clues in the scene that point in this direction. Carrie and Big's verbal exchanges are sharp and lively, thus underlining the chemistry between the two. Their witty banter in this scene is reminiscent of the 1930s screwball comedies. At that time, due to the restrictions of the Production Code, sexual tension between the couple had to be suggested through playful dialogue, thus implying more than was actually shown. *SATC* is not precisely curtailed by censorship, but it resuscitates this convention in order to convey the couple's compatibility. Carrie and Big's verbal sparring is also highlighted by editing. The scene, which is nearly two minutes long, is composed of no less than forty-eight shot-reverse shots to accompany the characters' quick remarks, which gives it a vivacious pace. The dynamism of their relationship is also emphasized by the setting of their conversation: they are literally "on the move" inside Big's limo, a fancy environment that—as do most luxury goods in the series—functions as enabler of romance. As we have seen, the appeal of upper-class privilege is the best aphrodisiac in *SATC*.

Carrie and Big's banter is also a subtle way of conveying Big's romantic interest in Carrie: "[r]ather than speaking seductively, the males in screwball comedies typically scold, lecture, admonish, or preach. In the codes of the screwball comedy, what this tells us is that the man cares, but it also mimics rational persuasion, something that corresponds to the presumption that the woman must choose her mate" (Shumway 389). In this case, Big's teasing remarks about Carrie's relationship with Aidan seem to go against his own interests, since their encounter gives her the final push in her resolution to marry: Big does not believe she is the "marrying kind." Is her decision conditioned by her will to prove him wrong? In spite of the episode's happy denouement, subsequent events suggest this might be the case.

Maybe You Just Have to Say What's in Your Heart

The ambivalence and multiplicity of discourses surrounding contemporary love is summed up quite memorably in the actual proposal scene of "Just Say Yes." It is late at night, and Aidan has tricked Carrie into walking his dog with him. At one given moment, he kneels down to pick the dog's excrement and surprises Carrie by putting a ring box in her hand while she is not looking. She is clearly struck, but her face lights up when she opens the box and sees the ring: it is not the one she had seen the previous day in his sports bag. Overcome by emotion, she accepts his proposal. How are we viewers meant to take this scene?

On the one hand, Aidan's proposal demonstrates the series' endorsement of a particular ideal of "democratized" romance, one in which simplicity and lack of artifice are the hallmarks of true love. Having pulled out the conventional stops of romantic luxury in the earlier dinner scene—the false or feinted proposal, which ended with Aidan reaching for his wallet—the episode now stages a self-conscious intervention in the conventions of romantic comedy by having a marriage proposal, traditionally the genre's climactic moment, play out in the middle of the street, in pajama-like clothes and while taking the dog out for a pee. The romanticism of the scene is heightened

Figure 3.1. Aidan's proposal.

Figure 3.2.   "I do."

precisely because of its quotidian staging, as well as its unexpectedness. It is as though, in order to create an atmosphere of believable romance in the postmodern era, conventions have to be inverted or reworked. The show thus seems to be in agreement with those who think that the sphere of consumption has "undermined the capacity of people to engage in an authentic experience of romance" (Illouz 112), since in order to reach an authentic moment, Carrie and Aidan have to leave the world of consumption behind. They are not the only couple to do so: as the analysis of "The Ick Factor" (6:14) in the previous chapter has shown, some of the most self-consciously "romantic" moments in *SATC* often take place in nonconsumerist situations. "Authentic" love would thus seem to demand a retreat from or rejection of consumerist romantic scenarios, as though freedom from the world of money and things were needed in order certify the truth of the feelings involved.

However, *SATC*'s apparent embrace of this "nonconsumerist" ethos is deceptive, and the romantic utopia proposed by the show remains just below the surface, powerfully determined by economic factors—or rather, to be more precise, consumption remains the arena in which the truth of love is proved. When Aidan kneels down, Carrie's face transmits her unease with what is to come. However, her expression changes completely when she sees the new ring. Nothing in the emotional or interpersonal situation has changed—Aidan is still proposing marriage, as she feared he would—but the material object that embodies and enacts his proposal *has* changed, so much so that the first thing Carrie says when she opens the box is "Oh, my God. It's not . . . It's such a beautiful ring!" Just as in the brunch scene, then, the real issue here is not the serious consideration of whether to spend her life with Aidan or not, but the virtues of the ring in itself, that is, the ritual of consumption enacted in the marriage proposal. Helped by the endorphin-fueled high of Aidan's consumerist gesture, Carrie lets herself get carried away and agrees to marry him, rationalizing her decision with these words: "Maybe there are no right moments, right guys, right answers. Maybe you just have to say what's in your heart." These words admit implicitly that she has not really worked out whether Aidan is her soul mate or not, but she lets herself be taken in by the magic of romance anyway—and, the skeptical viewer notes, by the rightness of the ring. Despite the series' habitual cynicism, in this scene everything works in order to create a climactic romantic moment. The full power of romantic comedy is summoned up with no hint of irony, resorting to one of its most reliable clichés: in matters of love, follow your heart, not your head. To use a term from Beck and Beck-Gernsheim, Aidan's choice of the right ring allows Carrie to "theologize" her decision to "just say yes" to marriage.

We are not finished, however, with unpacking the complexity of the scene. It may well be true that Carrie's momentary impulse to "say yes" to romantic love illustrates the temptation of deracinated, well-off urban lovers—even the most cynical among them—to idealize love as a source of "salvation" because it offers what Beck and Beck-Gernsheim describe as "person-related stability" (*The Normal Chaos of Love* 32–33). "The more other reference points have slipped away," they explain, "the more we direct our craving to give our lives meaning and security toward those we love" (*The Normal Chaos of Love* 50). In this context, marriage takes a new meaning. It does not just provide a social structure for the individual's life; it becomes a matter of identity, as we seek ourselves in the other. Aidan's choice of the "right ring" may not prove that he is the "right guy," the "someone, somewhere" who "is holding the key to your heart and your dream house," as Carrie mused at the start of season 4, but it does suggest that he knows and ratifies Carrie's identity in the way she (and perhaps the viewer) secretly craves.

Who, though, really chose that "right ring," enacting this intimate knowledge? Rather than having the happy couple kiss to seal their engagement while the closing credits unfold, this episode ends with a coda devoted, not to Aidan and Carrie, but to Carrie and Samantha. Carrie knows that Samantha dislikes the idea of her marriage and thinks she is not going to take it well. They meet in a bar and she tells her the news. Once again, they talk about the ring, not the engagement in itself, and it turns out Samantha helped Aidan pick the new, "right" ring, just as Miranda had previously helped him pick the "wrong" one. In effect, Carrie's circle of female friends are shown to be the ones who give her "person-related stability," functioning simultaneously as the modern version of a premodern social network that must give a suitor their approval and as modern (or postmodern) lovers and love objects in their own right. Despite her misgivings, Samantha gives Carrie her "blessing," much as a parent would, even as she demonstrates that it is she, not Aidan, who knows what ring "is" Carrie, and thus who recognizes Carrie's true self. Once Samantha gives Carrie "consent" to her marriage, they embrace, and one cannot help but feel that this constitutes the episode's true happy ending, reminding us that underneath the apparent obsession of the show with the search for Mr. Right, its heart lies with an apolitical version of female sisterhood. By having the girls close the episode rather than the heterosexual couple, the text seems to imply that their relationship is more important, and certainly, more lasting.

Beneath the glossy, comforting surface of its Hollywood-like happy ending, "Just Say Yes" is thus marked by significant tensions and paradoxes, an exemplary instance of the mix of romantic ideals and discourses in *SATC* as a whole. On the one hand, the episode illustrates *SATC*'s secret longing to believe in the possibility of true romance—or, as we might now put it, the episode demonstrates that Carrie, too, is subject to the contemporary tendency toward the romanticization of love brought about by individualization processes characteristic of modern liberal capitalism. In a world devoid of the old certainties that gave a sense of security to the individual, she—and some of her viewers—take refuge in romantic love as the one context in which market values are suspended, rational choice is set aside, and our elusive "true selves" can be known. At the same time, the episode undercuts or unmasks this "theologizing" longing, revealing how deeply it remains embedded in a neoconservative nostalgia for financial inequality between the sexes and by the consumer culture that twin soul ideologies of love purport to escape. In a final twist, the episode offers an alternative context in which affection, consumerism, and a "person-related stability" seem to coexist quite amicably: that is, the world of female friendships, in which the fraught search for "the One" who will perfectly complete a partial self is replaced by an ineluctably multiple, deliciously imperfect exchange of affirmation, critique, communication, misunderstanding, forgiveness, recognition, and more.

If the episode finally immerses the viewer in the utopian world of romantic comedy, appealing to one of its basic tenets—just do what your heart tells you—it offers two competing sites for that "happily ever after." The first is in Carrie and Aidan's romance, but as viewers know, this does not last; they break their engagement only three episodes later, keeping the series in motion. The second, of course, is in the circle of friends who know and appreciate one another as much as they know and appreciate luxury culture: the right shoes, the right dress, the right ring, the right spot for lunch. Focused on women and meant for a female audience, the show might well be said to romanticize, or even "theologize," female friendship, deploying it in the service of consumer culture and various forms of racial and class privilege— but that is the subject of another book. For now, suffice it to say that if diamonds are a girl's best friend in the postfeminist fantasy of *SATC*, that is because a girl's best friends are, like diamonds, in this fantasy forever.[4]

TO BE IN A COUPLE, DO YOU HAVE TO PUT YOUR SINGLE SELF ON A SHELF? THE DEMOCRATIZATION OF LOVE

"Just Say Yes" (4:12) ends with a happy ending worthy of any mainstream romantic comedy. However, due to its serial form, *SATC* cannot maintain the "suspension of disbelief" most cinematic "happily ever afters" require. On the contrary, it is forced to lift the curtain again, breaking the spell by revealing what happens the morning after. This section analyzes the next two episodes—"The Good Fight" (4:13) and "All That Glitters" (4:14)—showing how the romanticization of love is, to a large extent, a pervasive tendency regarding the *idea* of marriage, but this ideal is difficult to sustain in the everyday reality of the couple. Paradoxically, people today hold the concept of marriage to a higher standard than previous generations have done, but they are much more pragmatic about the actual experience of coupled life. Ethan Watters, acting as spokesperson for his generation, says, "We might have been idealistic about marriage, but we were hardened realists about relationships . . . we were idealistic in thought and intention while we were hardened and realistic from experience" (177). The following section will show how the next two episodes reflect the bizarre coexistence in popular discourses of a tendency to romanticize marriage—or at least the lasting union with one's "soul mate"—and the need to adopt a more rational approach toward the actual experience of relationships. These episodes show how romantic rapture is ultimately incompatible with the dynamics of the everyday, and a more rational model is needed—one that is not based on the "fusion of souls" and projective identification proposed by romantic love, but on a negotiated contract between the members of the couple more akin to contemporary sociological theories of "democratic love," in which the preservation and development of each individual's self-identity is a prerequisite for the successful union.

"The Good Fight" narrates the first time Carrie has ever shared her apartment with a man. The opening words of her voice-over link in with the "twin soul" ideology explored in the previous episode, and already announce its problematization in the present one: "Someone once said that two halves make a whole. And when two halves move in together, it makes a whole lot of stuff." Aidan has moved in, crowding the space. The first scene already conveys Carrie's anxiety about the situation: she can barely open the entrance door with all the boxes Aidan has piled up there. Her angst is increased by his inquisitive questioning about what she has been doing. To make things worse, Carrie discovers that Aidan has brought a plant with him, a great offense in her book, since she kills "everything she brings in." The cramped apartment constitutes thus an unsubtle metaphor for Carrie's suffocation in Aidan's presence. Nevertheless, she consoles herself by thinking that the situation will not last too long, since her elderly neighbor is supposed to move out soon and they will be able to occupy the apartment next door too.

Carrie tells her friends about it in the next scene, bitterly mourning the traumatic loss of her personal space and privacy. It turns out that what she misses most is her "SSB: Secret, Single Behavior," that is, "things you would never want your boyfriend to see you do."

The next day she meets her neighbor and she is dismayed to find out she will not be moving out for thirty days. Carrie is happy to learn that Aidan is equally distressed with the situation, but her glee does not last long, since he suggests making room for his things by cleaning out Carrie's closet. Aidan's fateful words are underlined by an extra-diegetic gong that accompanies a

Figure 3.3.   Carrie feels suffocated.

zoom-in on Carrie's panic-stricken face. Despite Carrie's horror at the idea of getting rid of her clothes, she starts to accept that she will need to make some concessions. At one point, she reflects: "I realized I was holding on to a Roberto Cavalli outfit and throwing away my relationship." However, when she sees Aidan's dog chewing on a Manolo Blahnik sandal, she loses control. They start a fight that keeps escalating till she walks out of the apartment. The fight is over Carrie's "excess" of clothes and shoes, but taking into account the important role played by fashion in the show and how it is used to express Carrie's personality, it becomes clear that what is really at stake in this scene is her identity. Aidan's inability to understand Carrie's love of fashion emphasizes the differences that separate them, while his taking over of her wardrobe represents not only the invasion of her private space, but an all-out threat on her independent single self. Carrie and Aidan's fight is one of the longest scenes in *SATC*'s six seasons. The conspicuousness of this scene shows that the "happily ever after" from last episode was just an illusion. It was one of the rare moments in which the series let itself be carried away by unfettered romanticism, and now Carrie has to pay the price for her unreflective actions. Unlike conventional romantic comedies, which draw the curtain at the peak of romantic fulfillment, this feeling cannot be sustained in the everyday experience of relationships. In this way, *SATC* contrasts the romantic vision of love displayed in the previous episode with a much more prosaic, "everyday" view in this one.

Carrie leaves the apartment and goes to a café with her laptop. She starts to reflect about the difficulty of managing conflict within relationships: "The hard thing about fighting in relationships as opposed to Madison Square Garden: no referee. There's no one to tell you which comments are below the belt or when to go to your separate corners. As a result, someone usually gets hurt." Indeed, the lack of rules at a subinstitutional level creates a good deal of confusion within the couple, which is entirely left to its own devices in the regulation of crises. In the absence of external standards, the lovers need to find internal ones, making their own rules. This implies a constant effort to negotiate and to find common ground upon which the couple can be established. This is a view of relationships that contrasts with the effortless discourse of romantic love. In democratic models of love, the members of the couple are entirely responsible for its workings. They make up their rules according to subjective criteria, and, as Carrie points out, there is no referee in this process: "In creating their own laws, lovers open the door to a form of lawlessness as soon as the magic of being in love has flown away and their own interests take center stage" (Beck and Beck-Gernsheim, *The Normal Chaos of Love* 195). In this way, as Carrie and Aidan's situation shows, once the magic of romance has been diluted, the couple's freedom to regulate itself shows its negative side when things go wrong.

Carrie and Aidan make up eventually. Initially, neither is willing to apologize first, but after three days without speaking to each other, Carrie finally gives in. Things seem to go back to normal: the next scene shows Carrie being inquisitively questioned by Aidan upon her arrival. She resents her loss of independence and, as a compromise solution, she asks him to be left alone for one hour every time she comes home, which he agrees to do. Then, she draws a curtain that is meant to delimit her private space from his, and she proceeds to relax. However, not one minute has gone by when she opens the curtain again and accommodates herself in Aidan's lap. Thus, despite the episode's misgivings about cohabitation, *SATC* seems to finally argue in favor of coupled life at the end of this episode. However, unlike the "blissful" happy ending of the previous episode, "The Good Fight" provides a more realistic conclusion. In general terms, the negotiation process Carrie and Aidan undergo in order to keep their relationship afloat is much more akin to contemporary discourses on democratic love than to the romantic resolution of the previous episode. Their relationship is here portrayed as being closer to Giddens's "rolling contract," that is, open to negotiation and constantly subject to reflexive examination (192). This "rolling contract" is a fundamental part of the "pure relationship," which Giddens defines as a social relation "entered into for its own sake, for what can be derived by each person from a sustained association with another; and which is continued only so far as it is thought by both parties to deliver enough satisfactions for each individual to stay within it" (58). This is the kind of relationship on which posttraditional societies are based: the democratic partnership between equals thus replaces the traditional idea of marriage for life. The pure relationship is not based on romantic love, but on what Giddens calls "confluent love." This kind of love consists in "disclosing intimacy," in opening oneself out to the other, rather than on the projective identification of romantic love. Confluent love facilitates the reflexive project of the self and replaces the "special person" ideal with the "special relationship." This means it is contingent, thus jarring "with the 'for-ever,' 'one-and-only' qualities of the romantic love complex" (61–62). In this sense, it is clear how the sobering approach to Carrie and Aidan's relationship adopted by this episode is much more in line with Giddens's rational view of love, as the twin soul fantasy of "Just Say Yes" gives way to a more realistic experience of relationships.

Giddens's model of democratic love has been equally praised and criticized. One of its problems is that an inherent feature of the pure relationship is equality of resources. Unlike romantic love, which has always been imbalanced in gender terms, confluent love presumes equality between the members of the couple (195). This, however, is not the reality of most couples. Wendy Langford criticizes Giddens's democratic ideal, arguing that the democratization of love he proclaims has not been achieved yet, and what is worse, this new discourse of equality based on a contractual kind of love obscures the power inequalities that still exist within the couple (10). She claims that "traditional" configurations of love are still present in contemporary relationships. What has changed is that the relationship between gender, power, and love is now obscured by the individuals' conscious attempts to contain the contradictions in their experience (20). Langford believes that Giddens's idea of democratic love is just an ideal, not a reality, which allows for "the reproduction of a social order characterized by gender polarization, alienation and hierarchies of power, while we at once articulate the discourse of egalitarian coupledom" (152).[5] This is the case for Carrie and Aidan: as has been previously discussed, their relationship is far from equal in economic terms. Carrie is very much dependent on Aidan in their new living arrangement, which gives him the upper hand in the relationship, but this reality is never explicitly acknowledged by the text, and Carrie's decision to make amends with Aidan is justified by her change of heart. The very important matter of Carrie's financial position is never really considered, thus hiding the inequality that exists in their relationship despite appearances of "democracy."

Another problem with the pure relationship is that its negotiated character makes it intrinsically fragile: according to Giddens, "[i]t is a feature of the pure relationship that it can be terminated, more or less at will, by either partner at any particular point" (137). The pure relationship basically seeks communion with the other as a means of realization of the self, so it is bound to be extremely contradictory and likely to fail (Rubin). Since the concepts of commitment and obligation have been replaced by personal satisfaction as the only raison d'être of relationships, these are inherently "fissiparous, unlikely to last longer than the convenience they bring" (Bauman 90).[6] This imbues contemporary relationships with a highly rational character, modeled after capitalist society's principles and characterized by a utilitarian attitude toward love based on the individualistic ethos. Just as business contracts include revocation clauses, contemporary partnerships also have a contingent character, "till death do us part" having been replaced by "till further notice." Carrie and Aidan's relationship exemplifies this frailty: as we will see later on, when Carrie refuses to marry, Aidan makes the unilateral decision of dissolving the couple. She has not fulfilled her part of the contract, therefore, he is entitled to terminate it without further explanation, since it no longer lives up to his expectations of personal satisfaction. Thus, despite *SATC*'s occasional "yielding" into the temptation of romantic love and its deep wish to believe in it, the text usually displays this kind of pragmatic approach to relationships: its self-reflexive character is very much in tune with Giddens's rational view of love. As this episode shows, when the series forgets its "self-analytical" spirit, trouble ensues.

However even though Carrie and Aidan eventually split up, in this episode the couple is still together, and apparently satisfied. Despite their quar-

Figure 3.4. **Carrie walks happily into the sunset, alone.**

rels, the episode seems to argue in favor of coupledom, glossing over Carrie's need for independence with these words: "That's the thing about needs: sometimes when you get them met, you don't need them anymore." Once again, the text appears to be deceiving itself in its attempt to provide a happy ending. Nothing in the episode, nor in the series as a whole, suggests that Carrie is really willing to give up her independence. Moreover, it can be argued that this final scene already points subtly to the bleak denouement of Carrie and Aidan's story, since the text's verbal message is visually subverted by the images it accompanies: once more, the closing scene is not devoted to the couple. We only see Carrie walking out of her apartment thirty days later. She stops to drop in a litter bin the plant Aidan had brought with him: as predicted, it did not survive. This is a sign that their relationship will not survive either. Moreover, her outfit reveals that she has not really given up her "Secret Single Behavior": she appears glamorously dressed in high heels and the Roberto Cavalli outfit she was supposed to throw away the day of their big fight as a sign of her compromise within the relationship. Thus, it becomes evident that she is not actually willing to leave her "single self" behind. The high-angle long shot of Carrie's confident strutting in the middle of the road underlines her singleness in a positive way and suggests that being single is Carrie's real "essence" and that she is not really willing to give up on it. Thus we see Carrie confidently walking "into the sunset" on her own, while the extra-diegetic music ("A Whiter Shade of Pale") used in the previous scene to enhance the romance between Samantha and her boyfriend still plays on. However, since Carrie is seen joyfully walking alone, instead of in Aidan's company, the evocative melody acquires a different meaning in this scene, conveying another kind of romance: the individual's romance with oneself, and the need to be faithful to nothing else but one's self-identity.

ALL THAT GLITTERS . . . IS NOT (ROMANTIC) LOVE

The next episode, "All That Glitters," further develops the topic of "The Good Fight." It continues exploring Carrie and Aidan's "adjustment" problems. More specifically, rather than issues of personal space, it addresses explicitly the incompatibility between single and coupled life. The episode starts with their disagreement on what constitutes an "amazing" Saturday night in New York. He wants to stay at home and watch the game while eating fried chicken. Carrie abhors the idea, so she calls up her friends and they go out. They go to a trendy gay club, and the show makes a point of emphasizing what a great time they have there. Carrie makes a new friend, a gay shoe distributor called Oliver (Murray Bartlett). When she gets home, she is disappointed to find Aidan asleep and unwilling to have sex, which confirms the disparity in their lifestyles. The next day Carrie meets her new gay acquaintance for brunch. They talk about their respective relationships. Oliver has a boyfriend, but they have an open relationship because he does not believe in monogamy. He asks Carrie about her relationship with Aidan, and she tells him about her engagement unenthusiastically. When she gets home, she reflects on her situation with Aidan and her conversation with Oliver:

> Once we've found what we want, why are some of us reluctant to let go of our single selves? . . . Why does becoming a couple imply settling down? Maybe we shouldn't expect to get everything from one man, but feel comfortable getting different things from different people. But when do separate interests become separate bedrooms? To be in a couple, do you have to put your single self on a shelf?

Therefore, this episode explores two intertwined issues: the apparent incompatibility between single and coupled life, and the possibility of a third option based on a more "evolved" set of rules modeled after the gay "blueprint."

In a postfeminist context in which women seek to reconcile their newly acquired independence with a satisfying romantic life, Carrie's struggle between her single and coupled selves strikes a chord with the audience, capturing faithfully an ongoing debate in the sociological field. Like Carrie, Beck and Beck-Gernsheim wonder how to combine contemporary "do-it-yourself biographies" with a shared life with a partner (*The Normal Chaos of Love* 53). At the beginning of modern times individualization was an exclusively male privilege. However, since the late nineteenth century, and especially since the 1960s, social changes have boosted women's autonomy. The disappearance of the old female role within the couple, together with women's increased expectations about marriage, have resulted in a great deal of confusion for both sexes, who find themselves trapped between old and new models (*The Normal Chaos of Love*). In this way, the difficult balance between freedom and commitment prompts the question: "Can love survive liberation? Or are love and freedom irreconcilable opposites?" (*The Normal Chaos of Love* 65). This is one of the main questions *SATC* tries to answer.

As this episode shows, in an era that bestows the highest level of priority on the development of one's "true self," holding on to a stable relationship is a particularly challenging endeavor. This is not to say that love is simply forgone today. Quite the contrary: the reflexive project of the self as championed by Giddens is to be attained precisely through romantic interaction with the opposite sex. Love is conceived of as the exploration of the self, the answer to a lack in self-identity. As Bellah and colleagues point out, "[t]he love that must hold us together is rooted in the vicissitudes of our subjectivity" (90). In other words, it is in the sharing of one's real self that the essence of love actually lies. However this is a difficult task, since there appears to be a very fine line between "sharing" and "losing" oneself in the other. Paradoxically, the passive adaptation to the other's wishes may have as a consequence becoming less desirable. That is, in a harmonious union, the lovers must reconcile sharing and mutuality with the assertion of their individual projects. The difficulty of this enterprise is accurately reflected in the episode under analysis: Carrie desires a life in common with Aidan, but she does not want to lose herself in the process. According to this theory, she cannot afford to do it, either, since this would eventually mean the relationship's demise. The opposition established between single and coupled life in this episode is at bottom another way of expressing this dilemma: the difficult balance that must be found between freedom and individuality for the couple to survive.

This constitutes one of *SATC*'s central quandaries. This preoccupation with the apparent incompatibility between independence and the security provided by a stable relationship is constantly interrogated in the series. This topic is regularly dealt with in the show in one way or another, and a number of tentative answers are provided. In its will to open a variety of possibilities for consideration, *SATC* hints at one possible solution to this dilemma by looking at a more "open" blueprint for relationships based on a model already explored by some members of the homosexual community. In her brunch with her new gay friend, Carrie and Oliver reflect on the limitations of the traditional heterosexual couple:

Carrie: Your boyfriend doesn't mind if you date other men?

Oliver: Not date. Have sex with.

Carrie: Right. Oh, right! The international gay rules.

Oliver: Absolutely. Blow jobs only. No last names. The gym is a free space. And never, ever show up at the same place wearing the same shirt. I just crossed over into a whole other set of rules.

Carrie: Well, you've certainly worked out more options than "till death do us part." That's all we've come up with, and frankly, I find it a little limiting.

Oliver: I know monogamous gay couples. But I'm a realist. I don't expect to get everything from one man.

The history of sexuality and intimacy seems to indicate that gay lifestyles are way ahead of heterosexual culture in the organization of intimate life. Homosexual couples were the pioneers of the pure relationship (Giddens 35). Their lack of access to traditional marriage gave them freedom to set up their own rules in all aspects of the relationship. Thus, it is argued that during the last decades of the twentieth century, heterosexuals gradually adapted to those trends set by the homosexual community, including a greater variety of sexual practices, the idealization of egalitarian relationships, and the acceptance of the notion that offspring are not necessary to consolidate the couple (McLaren 221). Thus it seems reasonable to surmise that Oliver's refusal to believe in the monogamous ideal might be considered as the next logical step in the development of heterosexual relationships. The show seems to reject the expectation of getting everything from a single person and hints at a daring option for the future of heterosexual relationships—a nonmonogamous model, free from deep emotional investments in one single person as be-all and end-all of one's life, which nevertheless does not exclude the possibility of a deep attachment to a partner.

Carrie toys with this idea, playfully "cheating" on Aidan with her gay friend—"gay boyfriends are the loophole of monogamy," she reasons. She starts to consider the possibility of trying to combine the perks of single life with one man—going out and having fun—and the advantages of being in a couple with another, that is, love and stability. However, since this is still untested terrain for heterosexual relationships, she is uncertain about its outcome: "It's the greatest relationship ever or we are headed for separate bedrooms," she reflects. The next day, she tries to put this theory into practice, leaving Aidan at home while going to a very exclusive club with Oliver. She hangs her engagement ring around her neck in a symbolic attempt to find a way for her single and coupled selves to coexist. Aidan does not seem very happy about the gesture, but he does not object. Once in the club, Carrie realizes that her plan is not going to work out. She feels neglected by her date, as Oliver keeps flirting with every man in the club. It becomes clear that the gay friend does not seem to be a real answer to Carrie's problem. Disappointed, she walks out, realizing that "her single self life had a shelf life that had just expired." With this reflection in mind, she goes home to Aidan, who welcomes her back lovingly.

The implication in Carrie's words is that singleness is associated with youth; when you are older, you need to become part of a couple. Despite its general support of single life, *SATC* sometimes betrays a fear of "expiry dates," that is, it is often afraid that women may become pathetic if they continue to live the single life after a certain age. This fear is explicitly stated in the last season, for instance ("Splat!" 6:18), and it may be seen as one of the reasons why Carrie decides to move to Paris with Petrovsky. So, despite social changes, there still remains a deeply entrenched fear of "spinsterhood" lurking in the back of women's minds, which arguably motivates Carrie to go back to Aidan. In this way, the episode provides a happy ending that, once again, seems to dismiss the needs Carrie has been expressing so far. The episode appears to conclude that coupled life is preferable to singleness, but as happened in the previous episode, the very last scene suggests otherwise. If the visuals of the last scene of "The Good Fight" subverted the apparent happy ending, now it is the voice-over that seems to contradict the images: in the last few seconds of the episode we see Carrie and Aidan comfortably cuddling in bed. Aidan is fast asleep, but Carrie is wide awake. The cozy image of the couple is contradicted by Carrie's words: "That's the thing about relationships: sometimes they look prettier from the outside. And what's inside can be different than it seems." As in the case of Charlotte and her first husband Trey, who are posing as a happy couple for the cover of *House and Garden* magazine while on the verge of divorce, the picture-perfect image of Carrie and Aidan we see does not necessarily correspond with what is going on between them. This message is further underlined by the episode's closing image: the line "what's inside can be different than it seems" coincides with a shot of the miniature reproduction of New York Carrie was holding when she reflected on how the city was a "flurry of fun and friends" that makes settling down difficult. Since New York is consistently associated in the show with single life and fun, this clearly implies that what is really "inside Carrie" is not a "married" self, but decidedly a single one. Since being "true to oneself" seems to be today's precondition for a successful relationship, it becomes clear that Carrie and Aidan's relationship is doomed.

In these three episodes the series explores the contemporary struggle between the desperate wish to believe in romance and the increasing rationalization of love. Due to its serial structure, *SATC* shows how the romantic impulse to marry one's soul mate in search of a fairy-tale "happily ever after" inexorably gives way to a progressive disbelief in the possibility of the survival of romance in contemporary society. It can therefore be argued that the starry-eyed, romantic view of love is easier to uphold in cinema, which is able to freeze its protagonists in the perfect bliss of the climactic happy ending, while television is more prone to offer a more pragmatic approach to love. This rationalization of the romantic discourse is one of *SATC*'s trademarks, and it arguably constitutes a remarkable contribution to recent developments in the romantic comedy genre. *SATC*'s approach is not new: it follows the "tradition" started by Woody Allen's "nervous romances" of the 1970s and continued by the "confessional comedies" of the 1990s (Levy, *Cinema of Outsiders* 273, 508; Deleyto 165–66).[7] However, these films were a minority trend within the genre as a whole, mainly because these were chiefly developed in the independent circuit. It can be argued that not only has *SATC* revitalized this "genre," it has taken it to a new dimension: thanks to its endurance through time and its remarkable cultural impact, the "romance of self-analysis" practiced by *SATC* has entered the mainstream, acquiring an unprecedented visibility after the show's success, both on the small and big screens.[8] Of course, *SATC* is not entirely responsible for this tendency. As argued in this section, *SATC*'s obsession with the self-conscious (over)analysis of intimate relationships managed to capture its audience's imagination because it faithfully reflected the rational, self-reflexive approach to relationships that pervaded turn-of-the-century sociosexual life. Since reality and representation feed off each other, it is no wonder people are especially receptive to this kind of narrative. After all, it is their own lives that they are watching on the screen.

DO WE REALLY WANT THESE THINGS, OR ARE WE JUST PROGRAMMED? THE TRIUMPH OF INDIVIDUALISM

The episodes previously analyzed articulate an opposition between an idealist and a more realist approach to relationships. The former can be equated with contemporary discourses on romantic love, while the latter is more akin to discourses on intimacy, which privilege closeness and companionship over passion. The episode entitled "Change of a Dress" (4:15) further explores these two models' suitability as blueprints for contemporary relationships, but it ultimately argues in favor of neither of them. The denouement of

Carrie and Aidan's story proposes instead that the road toward self-identity and personal satisfaction may not lie in romantic love nor in the pure relationship, but in one's honest relationship with oneself. This achievement and upholding of this state is no easy task, though, but a reflexive project that must be self-consciously pursued by the individual.

At the beginning of this episode, we see Carrie having dinner with Charlotte and Aidan. She meets an acquaintance who enquires about her new life, but she forgets to mention her engagement. Charlotte points it out, and her friend is excited about the news. She reaches out for Carrie's hand in order to admire the ring, but she is surprised to see Carrie is wearing it around her neck. Her rationale for this is that in that way it is closer to her heart. Carrie's friend thinks it is a very romantic gesture but, as the previous episode had suggested, it actually represents her reluctance to get married. Carrie's choice of accessories also points to this fact: she is wearing so many strings of pearls that the ring is hardly visible, suggesting she is not particularly willing to tell the world about her engagement, nor to fix a date for the wedding.

After that, Aidan starts to pressure Carrie to start with the wedding arrangements. He suggests a quick wedding in Hawaii or Aspen, but Carrie is reluctant to talk about it. The next day, she tells Miranda about her lack of enthusiasm with the whole issue. Just as Miranda is not really excited about her pregnancy, Carrie feels apathetic—to say the least—toward her engagement. The girls wonder if there is something wrong with them, which suggests that, despite social change, traditional gender roles are still deeply ingrained in people's minds. Uncharacteristically for her, Carrie is not even excited about picking a dress. To remedy this, Miranda comes up with the idea of going to a horrible bridal shop she knows to try on tacky wedding dresses. This is meant to be a kind of shock therapy aimed at "curing" Carrie of her aversion to weddings. Carrie hesitates, but Miranda's promise to try on some dresses as well persuades her to accept.

Once in the shop, they pretend to be traditional brides, glowing about their future weddings. They put on a show for the shop assistant, asking for dresses that make them look like "giant cupcakes." In the dressing room, everything is pink and white and they laugh hysterically at the over-the-top, puffy dresses they try on. *SATC*'s extreme sense of fashion style always seems to hint at the series' awareness of the constructed nature of gender, but this scene can be read as an explicit comment on the performance of femininity. As Judith Butler famously argued, "[t]here is no gender identity behind the expression of gender; that identity is performatively constituted by the very 'expressions' that are said to be its results" (*Gender Trouble* 25). The girls seem to be aware of this: their laughter at their "hyperfeminine" gowns reveals their self-consciousness about the "masquerade" they are enacting. This scene makes clear that *SATC*'s protagonists are very much aware of the constructed nature of their roles as future mothers and wives, which allows them to laugh them off. The mise-en-scène also reinforces the idea of femininity as performance: the dressing room actually looks like a theater stage, complete with curtain and all. However, the scene's "theatrical" mise-en-scène can be understood not only to be mocking conventional femininity; it also reveals a self-conscious awareness of romantic comedy's iconography. The wedding dress is one of the most relevant props within the genre. Carrie and Miranda's ridiculing of it thus points to the series' constant efforts to question the conventions of "traditional" romantic comedy, updating them for a more media-savvy, and possibly more cynical, audience.

The girls are having fun trying on the dresses, but when Carrie sees herself in the mirror the mood changes, as she starts to suffocate: she cannot breathe and she develops a rash. She says that the dress is too tight, but it is the idea of marriage that suffocates her. Despite her previous mockery of conventional feminine roles, this scene shows their enduring pervasiveness in contemporary society. Again, this is underlined by the mise-en-scène: we see Carrie recovering from her panic attack while being almost "engulfed" by wedding paraphernalia.

Carrie's strong reaction to the wedding dress makes her finally voice what she had been suspecting all along: she does not really want to marry.

Figure 3.5.   Performing femininity.

Figure 3.6.   Engulfed by wedding paraphernalia.

She discusses the issue with her friends, wondering why women should get married after all.

Carrie: I'm missing the bride gene. I should be put in a test tube and studied.

Samantha: It's not just you, I don't want to get married.

Charlotte: Ever?

Carrie: Why do we even have to get married? Why? Give me one good reason. Aside from the not wanting to die alone thing, which is something to think about, I admit.

Charlotte: Well, for me, when it was good, it gave me a sense of security.

Carrie: But I feel secure now. Things are great with us. And you know what they say: "If it ain't broke . . ."

Samantha: . . . Don't marry it!

[…]

Miranda: Carrie, I'm gonna ask you an unpleasant question now. Why did you ever say yes?

Carrie: Because I love him. A man you love kneels in the street and offers you a ring. You say yes, that's what you do.

Carrie's assumption that when a man kneels in front of her, a woman is somehow "obliged" to accept his proposal, suggests the deep influence exercised by popular romantic narratives on people's conceptions of love and romance. This conversation also exposes the manipulative power of romantic comedy: it makes evident that the "happily ever after" promised by the proposal scene in "Just Say Yes" is nothing but a cliché endlessly repeated in popular culture narratives. It shows that the influence of romantic comedy's climactic endings is so powerful that they may end up directing people's narratives of the self, unconsciously imposing a romantic script for them to follow. Wendy Langford expands on this connection between reality and fiction. According to her, there is a fit between emotion and recognizable cultural narratives: "We feel emotion when we sense a match between an actual or potential story and our ideal one . . . cognition of a match generates emotions, the contrary realization leads to negative emotions" (33). Because of this, romantic intensity is not only experienced by the individual, but self-consciously acted upon since it is necessary to "write oneself" into romance, which is done by means of "imitation" between one's story and culturally recognized fictional narratives. Illouz makes a similar point, pointing out how reality and fiction feed off each other; she observes in her ethnographic study how people's most memorable romantic stories mimic the intensely ritualized temporal structure of mass-media love stories. Carrie's acceptance of Aidan's proposal despite her qualms, because a woman is supposed to say "yes" when a man kneels down and proposes, shows how cultural representations of romantic love may have a direct influence on the shaping of people's romantic narratives. This phenomenon is better summarized by La Roche-foucauld's sharp remark about the constructed nature of the experience of romance: "there are people who would never have been in love if they had not heard talk of it." In the media-saturated world we inhabit, we may have heard too much about love, which accounts for our text-mediated experience of it.

This conversation does not only show the influence of a popular fictional genre on the individual. It also seems to implicitly support a feminist perspective on the insidious power of romantic discourses in the perpetuation of the patriarchal social order. When asked why she said yes to Aidan's proposal, Carrie answers: "Because I love him." In the traditional romantic ethos, falling in love is usually equated with freedom (Person). However, feminist critics argue that "the experience of romantic love is a delusion which, far from providing an escape from unsatisfactory life conditions, actually helps to bring them into being" (Langford 23). From this point of view, love is not the path toward women's freedom and self-realization, but the most subtle and effective way of exercising power, because the language of the heart masks the perpetuation of patriarchal social relations. In its depiction of Carrie's "suffocation" within her relationship, *SATC* seems to share this feminist take on love, since it explicitly contradicts its equation with freedom by presenting Carrie's love relationship as the "imprisonment" of her true self.

Once at home, Carrie starts to reflect on the conversation, and more specifically, on the concept of "happily ever after" and the individual's need to conform to certain social impositions:

> I tried to get my mind around the concept of happily ever after. As progressive as our society claims to be, there are still life targets we're all supposed to hit: marriage, babies, and a home to call your own. What if instead of breaking out in a smile, you break out in a rash? Is something wrong with the system or is it you? And do we really want these things? Or are we just programmed?

Individualization processes force us to make our own decisions, but it also induces sameness in these very choices: it puts a considerable pressure on the individual to conform and behave in a standardized way. This is because today's apparently private decisions are actually largely tied to outside influences, such as political developments, economic circumstances, state legislation, and public expectations (Beck and Beck-Gernsheim, *The Normal Chaos of Love*). This applies to everybody, but the pressure to "hit certain life targets" seems to be particularly acute in the case of women. The generation of women portrayed in *SATC* constitutes a vanguard generation that started to create a new blueprint for coupling by systematically postponing marriage. Being the first to undertake this task implies a considerable degree of anxiety, of course. Watters points out how this generation of women is undergoing a moment of transition in which their personal and professional accomplishments are still perceived to conflict with their hopes of finding happy marriages, thus implying that this will not be so in the future. According to Watters, in years to come the achievements of women's single years will be directly connected to their "value" as partners, as has always been the case of men, who tend to marry later than women after having accomplished a certain measure of material success and personal maturity. However, the righteousness of this "plan" has not taken hold yet in relation to society's perception of women's life trajectories. For Watters, turn-of-the-century women struggle with the apparent incompatibility between personal success and a happy marriage, forging what he calls the "marriage delay" (181). So, he does acknowledge women's difficulty in reconciling personal happiness with stable coupledom, but never really rules marriage out of the question as their ultimate aspiration. Arguably, *SATC* follows the direction pointed out by Watters in its depiction of women who seek fulfillment out of wedlock, but goes one step further, since it does not simply represent women who regard their accomplishments in their single years as assets for marriage eligibility. *SATC*'s characters are not just "forging the marriage delay," but sometimes bypassing marriage altogether. As I will try to show in the rest of this book, *SATC* puts forward the possibility that women's "happily ever after" may lie in something different from traditional marriage.[9]

The Missing Bride Gene

Overcome by pressure, Carrie runs to buy some cigarettes—she had quit because of Aidan—but she changes her mind in the last minute and decides to buy some wedding magazines instead. Once in her apartment, she tries to "reprogram" her attitude by browsing through them while he is working in the apartment next door. However, as she turns the pages and Aidan's knocking noises become louder and louder, she starts to get nervous. He is trying to break down the wall between the two apartments—a symbol of his attempts to join his life with Carrie's. However, her distress—emphasized by the disturbing intra-diegetic heavy-metal music—implies that the breaking down of her "wall" is a painful experience for her. Upset, Carrie finally confronts Aidan. Her secret unwillingness to marry has been haunting her ever since she accepted his proposal, which is visually conveyed by the shot that precedes Carrie's "confession": she is kneeling on the floor with her head down and we can see the engagement ring hanging down from her necklace. It looks like a very heavy load that prevents her from standing straight. However, this weight is lifted when she confesses that she is not ready for marriage yet. As always, he is very understanding, but seems to be taken a little aback by Carrie's revelation. Carrie, on the other hand, feels relieved.

Even though honesty is commonly believed to be the basis for healthy intimate relationships, it can also be viewed otherwise. Honesty is also a way of relieving one's conscience. That is, it is a form of self-care, not of building the relationship (Cramer). As we will see later on, Carrie's decision to share her doubts with Aidan is basically motivated by a type of self-interest very much in tune with the contemporary cult of self-identity linked to contemporary individualization processes. It is precisely this cult of the self that is nowadays discouraging women from the idea of marriage. Apart from this, it is evident that advances in women's demands for equality during the last few decades have also played a central role in today's changing marriage patterns.[10] This is a reality faithfully represented by *SATC*: Carrie's unwillingness to marry is directly connected with her independent status as a working woman. Even though the pure relationship is assumed to be only possible between equals, Mary Holmes supports the idea that, unlike in the past, women like Carrie have fewer benefits to be won out of heterosexual relationships: "for middle-class women with more access to the privileges of individualization connected with well-paying jobs, entering a relationship may threaten rather than enhance their status. Protection from marginalization and precariousness may necessitate making relationships less central in their lives" (253–54). In this sense, *SATC*'s questioning of the advantages of marriage in an age that has done away with one of its basic incentives for women—financial security—dovetails with third-wave feminism's conflicting views on this institution. Despite third-wavers' disagreement on the meanings of marriage today, one thing is clear: among the middle classes, romantic commitments are today generally sought after solely for the personal gratification they may entail, not to secure one's economic well-being.

The series in general, and Carrie's refusal to marry in particular, is very representative both of this postfeminist attitude and of general demographic trends. However, it could be argued that it paradoxically goes against the grain of contemporary film and TV representations of marriage. I have already pointed out romantic comedy's obsession with weddings during the last decade. TV's preoccupation with the topic is not far behind, with all kinds of wedding-related issues cropping up on our small screens in different genres and TV formats.[11] However, this cinematic and televisual interest in wedlock does not seem to match people's actual romantic behavior. Some authors see the media's current "wedding fascination" as part of a larger "marriage movement" meant to counteract "antimarriage tendencies." The conservative movement for family values that arose in the United States during the 1980s turned its attention to marriage during the mid-1990s.[12] Its defense of marriage was usually based on bitter attacks on singleness. This climate was reflected in the publication of numerous books, such as *The Case for Marriage: Why Married People Are Happier, Healthier, and Better Off Financially* (Waite and Gallagher), *The Unexpected Legacy of Divorce* (Wallerstein, Lewis, and Blakeslee), *For Better or for Worse: Divorce Reconsidered* (Hetherington and Kelly), *What Our Mothers Didn't Tell Us: Why Happiness Eludes the Modern Woman* (Crittenden); or the documentary *"Let's Get Married"* (Kotlowitz). Cultural attempts to influence social behavior were also accompanied by actual state-sponsored measures to boost marriage to the detriment of other kinds of lifestyles. The Bush administration viewed marriage as the solution for "every social ill from poverty and teen pregnancy to drug use and poor education" (A. Nelson, "Miss Bradshaw Goes to Washington" n.p.). As a result, $400 million in federal funds were allocated in 2002 to pro-marriage initiatives, most of which were meant to encourage women on welfare to get married (Kumbier). In 2004, the efforts of the Bush administration were strengthened with the introduction of the

"Healthy Marriage Initiative" (HMI), which allotted a total of $1.5 billion to the promotion of the institution (Lamanna and Riedmann).

The combination of these state-sponsored initiatives and the cultural exaltation of marriage in the media—which also includes the old "gambling with fertility" discourse [13] —is reminiscent of the scare tactics used against women during the 1980s "backlash" (Faludi). Because of this, *SATC* constitutes a remarkable exception to the marriage frenzy pervading the U.S. cultural climate at the turn of the century, not only for its firm resistance against the dominant pro-marriage tide, but also for its endorsement of a less simplistic and more nuanced view of marriage than the one provided both by the Bush administration and popular culture representations. Without rejecting it nor embracing it altogether, *SATC* treats marriage as a complex issue that deserves close consideration. Unlike the promises of politicians and the "happily ever afters" of Hollywood romantic comedy, *SATC* questions marriage's advantages for women in the new millennium, and shows how a wedding does not necessarily provide a happy ending, but "just an ending," as Samantha points out in "Don't Ask, Don't Tell" (3:12). In doing so, the series' impact is twofold: on the one hand, it plays an important role in helping destigmatize those women who refuse to follow traditional life paths. Parallel to, or maybe as a consequence of this, *SATC* pushes the boundaries of the genre a step further, giving visibility to a more reflective tendency within contemporary romantic comedy.

Is Something Wrong with the System, or Is It You?

Carrie and Aidan's last scene together reinforces the series' critical position toward marriage, bringing closure to the plot started three episodes earlier. The couple is returning from the "Black and White Ball," and they are elegantly dressed for the occasion. Aidan has a tuxedo on and Carrie is wearing a long white dress almost indistinguishable from a bridal gown. Aidan proposes to go to Las Vegas and get married on the spot. Carrie is upset, as he seems to have forgotten their previous conversation and she feels pushed:

Carrie: I'm not ready for marriage.

Aidan: Well, I am. I'm sorry if that scares you, but I am. People fall in love, they get married. That's what they do.

Carrie: Not necessarily!

In their discussion, Aidan appeals to the "life targets" Carrie has been questioning throughout the episode. In this scene, she reaffirms her position, defending another kind of "happily ever after" seldom represented by romantic comedy. In a way, this scene mirrors the proposal scene, as the couple once again elucidates the fate of their relationship late at night in the streets of New York. Their wedding-like clothes and the beautiful setting—Aidan's new "proposal" takes place against a fountain—seem to set the appropriate mood for romance. However, this time, the series does not allow the magic of romantic comedy to take hold. A bleaker reality imposes itself as Carrie, no longer infatuated by the mise-en-scène of romance, rejects the traditional lifestyle implied in the "happy ending" proposed by Aidan, which leads to their breakup.

Despite its similarity to the proposal scene, the sheltering space of romantic comedy does not seem to work anymore. New York, the romantic scenario par excellence, witnesses here the disintegration of romance. This reveals that *SATC*'s New York is not the one-dimensional space portrayed in many romantic comedies today,[14] but a multifaceted, complex, and contested space in which desires of personal communion and self-realization collide with each other. The four episodes analyzed here show the contradictory meanings attached to this urban space by the series: the streets of New York are as likely a setting for romantic fulfillment as for its breakdown. In any case, this does not diminish the city's potential for romantic transformation; it simply

Figure 3.7.   The mise-en-scène of romance does not work this time.

puts new energy into it, turning it into an intricate "romantic playground" in which you win some, you lose some. This dovetails with Deleyto's idea about the often fleeting nature of romantic transformation; the "metamorphosis" undergone by the characters of romantic comedy as a result of the benign influence of its magical space is not necessarily a permanent one. This is the case for *SATC* for two reasons: first, because the show does not support the "soul mate" ideology, but a much more contingent perspective on love. And second, because this view of relationships as something ephemeral and "cyclic" is largely determined by its form. The serial structure of the text prevents the magical space of romantic comedy to have permanent effects on the couple.

When Carrie tells Aidan that she is not ready for marriage and she is not going to marry him just to make him trust her, he decides to break up with her. In the very last scene we see Aidan sleeping on the floor of the apartment next door, which was meant to be their home. In the middle of the night, Carrie sneaks in and lies next to him. This image is accompanied by Carrie's voice-over, which closes the episode: "There are some walls you can push through and some you can't. That was the only night we would ever spend on the other side of the wall. The next day, Aidan moved out." With this succinct line, the text puts an end to Carrie's most important relationship to date. The way in which this is handled, and the strong contrast established with the romantic naivete displayed by the first episode analyzed here, says a lot about the culture of entitlement and personal fulfillment that characterizes present-day relationships. The individualization process has strengthened people's "walls," making them practically insurmountable. It has gradually done away with the idea of the couple as a shared contract to which individual needs should be subordinated. On the contrary, the new sentimental order rests upon an ethic of self-care exclusively based on one's duty to oneself. In this new context, "[s]acrifice is condemned because it arises from a sense of obligation instead of the self's authentic wishes" (Blum 346). In this new intimate culture, personal satisfaction is viewed as the prerequisite for happiness, and being true to oneself is seen as the "supreme ethical act" (346). Aidan's unilateral decision to end the relationship when faced with a circumstance that deviates from his preconceived life plan, instead of trying to adapt to the situation, attests to the pervasiveness of this ethos. So does Carrie's position toward the matter: she also privileges her individual project of self-realization over the couple's well-being. In the past, both characters' decisions would have probably been considered selfish. However, the new frame of mind created by the individualist philosophy never questions the individual's right to self-preservation. As a result, the righteousness of their attitudes is never doubted. This poses a virtually unsolvable conundrum: how to reconcile one's personal development with a shared life project?

SO, CAN LOVE SURVIVE LIBERATION?

This chapter started with an analysis of an episode that reflected a remarkable tendency to romanticize relationships at the turn of the millennium. In "Just Say Yes," the series leaves aside its cynicism momentarily to abandon itself to the utopian happy ending of romantic comedy. However, the spell does not last long. Unlike films, which draw the curtain at the peak of romantic intensity, the serial form of *SATC* unveils what happens the morning after, when desire has been fulfilled, revealing that contemporary relationships cannot be solely sustained on romantic dreams, but must rely on a more rational model of intimacy based on a democratic contract between the members of the couple. According to this ethos of negotiation, Aidan decides to break their "contract," but this decision is motivated by Carrie's refusal to let go of what she considers to be her "true self." Thus, it can be argued that the show goes a step further in the last episode in its proposal of a viable model for the personal attainment of individual happiness these days: the ending suggests that the key to personal well-being lies neither in the romanticization nor in the rationalization of love, but rather, in being true to one's self-identity. In the case of Carrie, her "true self" seems to be her "single self" and, as the text shows, if its preservation involves breaking up with the loved one, that is what must happen. The episode's conclusion implies that happiness does not reside in the pure relationship, but in an honest relationship with oneself and the honest development of the reflexive project of the self. In this way, *SATC* challenges conservative pro-marriage discourses by proposing singleness as a more desirable option than coupled life. The episode's resolution is thus consistent with the show's overall ethos. A broader perspective on the series reveals that Carrie's attachment to her "Secret Single Behavior" is generally stronger than her wish to have a stable partner. In general terms, *SATC* makes verbally explicit its protagonists' will to be coupled, but it tends to contradict this impression visually: the moments in which the girls enjoy the perks of singleness—such as going out, shopping, having brunch, or having affairs—are those that tend to linger in the mind of the spectator most powerfully, since these are the times in which the characters seem happier and the series shines at its brightest for its wit, sharpness, and fun.

Carrie and Aidan's final breakup endorses, therefore, an alternative view of relationships more akin to the "more evolved" philosophy put forward—according to the series—by some sectors of homosexual culture: the idea that the expectation to get everything from a single person is an unrealizable hope. However this idea is in permanent tension with the ethos of romantic comedy—finding "the One " and living happily ever after with him or her—which is also central to the show. Therefore, it can be argued that *SATC*'s trademark ambivalence in its position toward relationships stems from the very basis on which it is laid: the need to find the Great Love that will make you complete clashes with the text's engagement with its zeitgeist in its need to reflect new social trends that acknowledge the impossibility of this ideal. This is translated at a textual level in a more traditional deployment of romantic comedy's conventions in the first episode, only to be debunked in the following ones, thus reflecting a new intimate reality that cannot be ignored by the text. The instability of the meanings attached to the "wrong partner" in the series, Carrie's and Miranda's mockery of wedding paraphernalia, Carrie's physical sickness at the thought of marriage, the deployment of humor and romantic music to convey the predilection for singleness over coupledom, the preference for "simplicity" rather than luxurious or elaborate settings for the enactment of "true romance" . . . All these "twists" on the viewer's generic expectations convey the impossibility of innocently perpetuating the conventions of traditional romantic comedy in the face of ongoing social changes like contemporary individualization processes.

In this way, it could be said that *SATC* deploys the language of romantic comedy in order to articulate discourses that sometimes differ significantly from the very basis on which the genre has been traditionally built. Genres are ideology-free categories by themselves, that is, they are not attached to any particular ideology (Deleyto). However, they do tend to be governed by a specific structure underlying the text in a more or less fixed way, which Rick Altman calls the genre's "syntax." According to him, genre formation depends on the successful combination of a certain "semantics" with a specific syntactic structure. By "semantics" Altman understands a text's "building blocks": a list of common traits among films belonging to the same genre, such as shared topics, plots, key scenes, character types, props, recognizable shots, or locations. By "syntax," he refers to the text's underlying structure, that is, the way in which those building blocks are organized. For him, genre is located at the intersection between semantic and syntactic elements (87–90, 219–25). According to this approach, it could be argued that *SATC* deploys romantic comedy's semantics but uses a different syntax. That is, it features the same "building blocks" as the average romantic comedy—conventions like the "meet-cute," the "wrong partner," the city as space of romantic transformation, a romantic soundtrack, humor, "typical" romantic settings and rituals like dining out or going to the opera, obstacles to be overcome by the couple, and the happy ending—but these are organized differently than they are in the average feature film. Due to its serial structure, *SATC* cannot delimit clearly the roles of the "right" and the "wrong" partner, for instance. On the contrary, a character like Big is depicted in much fuzzier terms, constantly stepping in and out of both roles. Similarly, the sinuosity in the characters' romantic lives imposed by the serial structure renders the city of New York a much more ambiguous and contested space for romantic transformation than film has traditionally allowed it to be;

SATC's New York may work both as enabler of enduring love and impediment to it. The text's length also allows for a much more culturally specific and idiosyncratic depiction of the city. Lastly, *SATC* frequently makes use of the "happy ending" convention, but in a much more tentative way, since its cyclical structure makes it impossible for unreserved romantic fulfillment to be achieved, as this chapter has shown.

Of course, it could be argued that the series' attitude toward these conventions is not entirely based on free choice, since the developments of its story lines are powerfully determined by its serial structure. Unlike films, TV series require incompleteness and discontinuity. Drawing from the sitcom, *SATC* revolves around a fixed set of characters that remain constant despite its plots' twists and the comings and goings of peripheral characters—the girls' suitors, in this case. This means that, unlike cinematic romantic comedies, whose main aim is to bring the lovers together so that they can be "whole," *SATC*'s protagonists have to remain forever incomplete, fragmented by textual imperative. However, the same formal structure that limits some of *SATC*'s textual choices also frees it from some of romantic comedy's conventions, allowing for a greater flexibility. As this chapter has tried to show, contemporary intimate discourses happen to be more in tune with the fragmentation, instability, and uncertainty depicted in the "seriality" of Carrie and company's relationships than with the "absolute" happily ever afters generally promised by feature films. It is thanks to its serial structure that *SATC* is able to provide a quasi-ethnographic view of the intimate culture it depicts, which is arguably more representative of the fragmentation and fleetingness of present-day relationships. By incorporating conventions from the sitcom genre, *SATC* inventively tweaks romantic comedy's syntax, pushing the boundaries of the genre in a direction that is much more in keeping with its context. By having bittersweet rather than happy endings, ambiguous suitors rather than right or wrong partners, and by chronicling a never-ending string of romantic affairs rather than a unique narrative of the Great Love or the soul mate, as cinema usually does, *SATC* may be particularly well equipped to capture the contradictory and episodic nature of the turn-of-the-century intimate panorama. This confusion is faithfully rendered in the show's tentative tone: *SATC* never provides a definite answer to the conundrum between love and freedom, but the chronic failure with which the girls' romantic hopes are perpetually confronted suggests that the new millennium might be a particularly ill-fated stage for relationships between men and women in the course of gender history, one that makes us wonder indeed whether love can survive liberation.

NOTES

1. I am aware that alternative romantic lifestyles have been at work for decades, but this has taken place mainly in the private sphere. It can even be argued that previous periods enabled more freedoms because of a lack of public discourses about certain practices. There has been interesting work on how gay subcultures worked (see for instance, *Gay New York: Gender, Urban Culture, and the Making of the Gay Male World, 1890–1940* [Chauncey], or *Twilight Girls and Odd Loves: A History of Lesbian Life in Twentieth-Century America* [Faderman]). *Intimate Matters: A History of Sexuality in America* (D'Emilio and Freedman) also explores similar territory and shows the radical changes in public assumptions about and discourses over intimate relations through time.

2. *SATC*'s conflicted approach to marriage is mainly reflected in its protagonists' different attitudes toward it: Charlotte and Samantha represent diametrically opposed views, while Miranda, and especially Carrie, stand in an ambiguous middle ground. Despite her willingness to marry Big in the *SATC* film, Carrie seems to reject the idea of marriage throughout the series, as it becomes obvious when she gets a rash from trying on a wedding dress ("Change of a Dress," 4:15).

3. The series offers numerous examples of how a well-off economic position is always implicitly presented as men's prerequisite to be considered for the "title" of Mr. Right. The girls sleep around with all kinds of men, but their serious suitors are always wealthy: that is Charlotte's case with her two husbands, and Samantha's with her boss Richard Wright (James Remar). When the men are not richer or do not occupy a higher social position than the girls, relationships tend to go astray. In the last season, for instance, Carrie dates Jack Berger (Ron Livingston), a writer who seems to meet all of her expectations. However, the relationship fails because he is not at the same professional level as she is. Samantha's relationship with the young waiter Smith (Jason Lewis) is not taken seriously until he becomes a famous model/actor. A similar thing happens with Miranda's husband-to-be, Steve. Their relationship is problematic because he feels inferior to her, which largely motivates their breakup. However, when they come together for the second time, he has been magically "upgraded" by the series from bartender to bar owner, which seems to green-light the relationship. Nevertheless, the clearest sign of *SATC*'s soft spot for Darcy-like male characters is Big: very much like Austen's hero, he is the wealthiest character in the show, and he is consistently presented as Carrie's knight in shining armor.

4. A previous version of this section has been published in the *Journal of Popular Romance Studies*. Thanks are due to the *JPRS* reviewers and, especially, to Eric Selinger for his careful editing of this piece.

5. Lynn Jamieson coincides with Langford in her disbelief in Giddens's optimistic view of democratic relationships. Her book, *Intimacy: Personal Relationships in Modern Society* (1998), sets out to assess the supposed shift toward "disclosing intimacy" and the "pure relationship" in real life. She concludes that this model is only present in public stories about intimacy, but the "pure relationship" as described by Giddens is not a widespread reality. Firstly, this is because coupledom cannot be based on the rules of friendship only, since it implies a sexual relationship. And secondly, this is because Giddens underplays inequalities between men and women, bracketing off material, economic, and social aspects of the relationship—Giddens's ideal of "disclosing intimacy" is based on "knowing and understanding." Jamieson argues that this conception presumes a world in which everyday needs are easily taken care of. Few relationships are sustained exclusively on disclosing intimacy in disconnection from more practical issues, such as caring and sharing.

6. Zygmunt Bauman relates the fragility of the "pure relationship" with a chronic fear of commitment characteristic of today's society, which constitutes fertile ground for the blossoming of superficial, fissiparous relationships. He laments that "[l]oose and eminently revocable partnerships have replaced the model of a 'til death do us part' personal union" (90). Bauman is not alone in this view, as Roger Scruton similarly regrets the replacement of old notions of loyalty within the couple with a negotiated contract characterized by self-interest, that is leading us into a world of "thin attachments and purely contractual ties" ("Sex in the Commodity Culture" 62).

7. Examples include *sex, lies and videotape* (1989), *Rambling Rose* (1991), *Singles* (1992), *The Wedding Banquet* (1993), *Ruby in Paradise* (1993), *Clerks* (1994), *Smoke* (1995), *The Brothers McMullen* (1995), *Before Sunrise* (1995), *Swingers* (1996), *Beautiful Girls* (1996), *Walking and Talking* (1997), and *Box of Moonlight* (1996).

8. Cinematic examples of this tendency include *High Fidelity* (2000), *Sidewalks of New York* (2001), *Bridget Jones's Diary* (2001), *Before Sunset* (2004), *Sideways* (2004), *Trust the Man* (2005), *Must Love Dogs* (2005), *The Groomsmen* (2006), *The Break-Up* (2006), *Friends with Money* (2006), *2 Days in Paris* (2007), *Definitely, Maybe* (2008), and *He's Just Not That Into You* (2009). On television, there are shows that also revolve around the self-conscious "dissection" of relationships, like *Dawson's Creek, Cashmere Mafia, Lipstick Jungle, Mistresses, Grey's Anatomy, How I Met Your Mother, Queer as Folk, The L Word,* and *Girls*.

9. I am aware that the centrality of marriage in the two cinematic sequels of *SATC* seems to contradict this assertion. The films seem to give conventional marriage the last word by finally pairing up Carrie and Big. Although the second film hints that there is the possibility for romance within marriage, through the flirtation of Carrie and Aidan, the rest of the film rather hysterically condemns this. However, as previously said, I consider the films as completely different texts in terms of form and ideology, since they sometimes contradict many of the series' main tenets.

10. At the time the episode under analysis was first broadcast, the average marriage age for women was twenty-five (as opposed to twenty during the 1960s). The 50 percent divorce rate also means that cohabitation is becoming an increasingly attractive option. This implies that at the time of the episode's airing, only 25 percent of people were living in the traditional nuclear family lifestyle (Kantrowitz and Wingert).

11. Chrys Ingraham identifies an unprecedented prevalence of weddings in turn-of-the-millennium TV fiction. Examples of the centrality of marriage and wedding ceremonies in contemporary TV series include *Frasier, Dharma and Greg, Friends, The Nanny, Jag, Spin City, Baywatch, Suddenly Susan, Dr. Quinn, Everybody Loves Raymond, NYPD Blue, For Your Love, To Have & To Hold, Will & Grace, CSI, 7th Heaven, Gilmore Girls, One Tree Hill, How I Met Your Mother, The New Adventures of Old Christine, ER, Bones, Desperate Housewives, Grey's Anatomy,* and *Boston Legal,* not to mention reality shows like *Amazing Wedding Cakes, Keasha's Perfect Dress, Say Yes to the Dress, Brides of Beverly Hills, Bridezillas, My Fair Wedding with David Tutera, For Better or for Worse, Platinum Weddings, The Bachelor, The Bachelorette, Whose Wedding Is It Anyway?, Who Wants to Marry My Dad?,* and *Four Weddings*.

12. At the center of the marriage movement is the Institute for American Values, together with the National Marriage Project at Rutgers University; the Religion, Culture and Family Project at the University of Chicago; and the Coalition for Marriage, Family and Couples Education in Washington, D.C. (Trimberger).

13. Despite the lack of reliable data on the claim that modern women must decide between career or family, the turn of the century has witnessed the proliferation of books that try to scare women into early motherhood, like Sylvia Hewlett's *Creating a Life: Professional Women and the Quest for Children.* The hype surrounding this publication motivated considerable press coverage on influential media such as *New York Magazine,* which unapologetically declared "Baby Panic" to have broken loose (Grigoriadis May 20, 2002), or *Time* magazine, which produced a cover entitled "Babies vs. Career" (April 15, 2002).

14. Tamar Jeffers McDonald argues that the city of New York has been dispossessed of its cultural specificity in contemporary romantic comedy, being nowadays reduced to a kind of shorthand for the evocation of romance (*Romantic Comedy*).

Chapter Four

What's Love Got to Do with It?

The Representation of Female Sexuality

On May 2, 1991, Fox broadcast an episode of *Beverly Hills 90210* in which Brenda (Shannen Doherty), one of its protagonists, lost her virginity. She celebrated the "event" with her friends, but her glee did not last long. Darren Star, creator of the show, tells in an interview how the network bosses were appalled by the show's treatment of the issue. In the next season Star was obliged to punish Brenda for her lighthearted approach to sex, showing the terrible consequences of her actions in the guise of a pregnancy scare and the eventual breakup with her boyfriend (Weinman, "The Macleans.ca Interview"). Thanks to the freedom granted by cable TV, seven years later, Star was able to paint a very different picture of female sexuality in *SATC*—one in which women's sexual dalliances not only went unpunished, but were joyously celebrated and cheerfully dwelt upon.

Not even a decade separates Brenda's ill-fated sexual fling and Carrie's promiscuous romps, which prompts the question: What changed in the meantime? There is no easy answer to this question. It has been pointed out that the turn of the millennium has witnessed a particularly quick pace in the "sexualization" of mainstream culture (McNair), a phenomenon that, paradoxically, coexisted with an increased "moralism" regarding sex and its representation in contemporary U.S. society (Bart). However, the changes undergone by public sexual morality at the fin de siècle are relatively small in comparison with the evolution experienced by female sexuality—and its representation—since the 1950s and early 1960s, prior to which women's sexual desire was not generally publicly acknowledged. Today, society's attitude toward women's entitlement to sex is very different.

This change regarding public views on female sexuality is, of course, framed by a wider modification of attitudes toward sex in general during the twentieth century. This change includes a more complex view of the meanings attached to sex: freed from its reproductive function and increasingly associated with physical and emotional pleasure, "[s]ex has become sexuality; or rather sexualit*ies*" (McNair 2). This greater openness has prompted an unprecedented optimism about sex, which is now regarded as a "beneficial, joyous phenomenon connected to personal health, happiness, self-fulfillment and social progress" (Seidman, *Embattled Eros* 5), a recreational activity (D'Emilio and Freedman), and a democratic endeavor (Giddens). To this positive view of sex should be added an increased proliferation of sexual identities, which have gained greater acceptance with the advance of the century.

All these discourses were born with the turn of the century, roughly speaking. They have reshaped sex and sexuality for the new millennium, thus showing their constructed nature. This has been reflected upon by numerous authors, but Michel Foucault was one of the first ones to explore the fabricated nature of sexuality. In *The History of Sexuality, Volume 1: An Introduction*, he connects sexuality with the circulation of power and discourse, arguing that the power relations that shape the changing discourses on sexuality play a fundamental role in determining the way we think about it. Sexuality is not something fixed, inherent to the self, that can be simply repressed by power, but a fabrication that emanates from certain discourses and that channels a variety of different power relations (103–14). Similarly, sex in itself is not something "universal" either. On the contrary, for Foucault sex is even more of a construct than sexuality is. When sex is talked about or represented in popular culture, it is not the actual physical act that is being referred to, but rather, the meanings that contemporary society has bestowed on it. Thus, sex is not an "anchorage point that supports the manifestations of sexuality," but "a complex idea that was formed inside the deployment of sexuality" (152). That is, it is a concept made up by—and not pre-existent to—the deployment of sexuality and shaped by public discourse.

In the media-saturated world we live in, film and TV play a key role in the creation and circulation of public discourses. Our views of what is permissible and/or desirable in sexual terms is largely influenced by the general beliefs and assumptions disseminated by the media, which have traditionally functioned as a public forum of debate for different social issues, including sex and sexuality. Thanks to its "democratic spirit," its easy accessibility, and its private character—unlike cinema, TV can be enjoyed in the privacy of the home—television has proved to be a particularly useful arena for the discussion of issues such as sexual morality in the public and private spheres, the proliferation of alternative sexual identities and lifestyles, or the normalization of an increased variety of sexual practices, thus progressively widening the limits of sexual representation.

This pushing of boundaries on TV has been slow and steady, lacking especially memorable "historical" landmarks, which may as well account for the very effectiveness of the process. One such TV touchstone was *The Mary Tyler Moore Show*, which featured a single female protagonist who was unapologetically single and dating men and on the pill during the 1970s. In the more conservative 1980s and early 1990s, *Murphy Brown* was the focus of a far-reaching national media controversy when Dan Quayle, George Bush's vice president, accused the show of immorality in its legitimation of single motherhood (Crotty). During the late 1990s, the greatest sexual TV "shock" would not come from fiction, but from the news bulletins: the Lewinsky scandal seemed to break the last taboo regarding sexual representation on TV at the end of the century. *SATC* was first broadcast in the year of the Clinton-Lewinsky scandal, 1998. In this new climate of sexual "openness," *SATC* presented itself as a show willing to go the extra mile in terms of what was still permissible or acceptable on the small screen. Taking advantage of the controversy that sex inevitably brings about, *SATC*'s very title already announced its intention to "shock" its audience—although never with "exploitation" purposes—and to take TV representations of female sexuality one step further.

As the previous chapters have shown, *SATC* is concerned with representing the permanent state of flux that relationships find themselves in at the turn of the century. This changing panorama in sexual mores is faithfully documented by the show, especially during its first seasons. If the previous chapters have shown how the presumably "natural" emotion of love is articulated in *SATC* through mediated discourses like romance or the pure relationship, this chapter will be concerned with the show's construction of sex and sexuality—a construction that is historically specific. With this purpose in mind, I will address three main issues that I consider relevant: the cultural messages delivered by the series regarding contemporary women's attitude toward sex; its acknowledgment of Giddens's notion of "plastic sexuality" and the role it plays in the construction of the individual's identity; and *SATC*'s contribution to the creation of new meanings about sex and sexual identity at the turn of the millennium. These issues will be taken into consideration against the generic background of the text, since questions of sexual identity and sexual attraction have always been at the core of romantic comedy's thematic preoccupations. This chapter will analyze how these issues are filtered through the comic perspective of this genre.

Before undertaking the exploration of *SATC*'s representation of sex, I would like to briefly place the show in the TV context in which it was first broadcast. The proliferation of sexual discourses on television has increased notably through the years, both in terms of quantity and "quality," that is, the variety of positions from which different sexual options are explored. This is due not only to people's change of attitude toward the issue, but also to the shifting legal status of the depiction of sex on-screen. The relatively "permissive" legislation of the late 1960s and 1970s gave way to a "family values" backlash during the 1980s and early 1990s that relaxed gradually as that decade came to a close. The regulation of sexual representation on U.S. television can be understood as "an ongoing struggle between traditional religious moral discourses and liberalism" (Arthurs, *Television and Sexuality* 21). Even though government interference in TV contents is very small nowadays, Christian fundamentalism is still a major influence on what is deemed appropriate for broadcast. Since the U.S. television industry is basically a market-based private enterprise, the pressures of certain groups make it much more restrictive than a system of state control would. Thus, the internal self-regulation of U.S. television basically pivots around its relationship with its audience. Because of this, and despite the disagreement of certain puritan sectors, the general increase of tolerance regarding sexual matters on the part of audiences has given way to the normalization of a wider range of sexual identities and practices and a growing informality or "boldness" in language (Arthurs, *Television and Sexuality*). Moreover, apart from this increased permissiveness in broadcast television, the variety of cable channels brought about by the digital era has resulted in the identification of very specific audience "niches" to which sexual messages are addressed. The TV grid now caters for a highly individualized range of viewers, which includes women as potential consumers of sexually charged texts.

Although *SATC*'s generic ascription is difficult to pin down—that is actually one of the text's assets—its treatment of sex may be most usefully compared to the sitcom's approach to the issue. Partly because 1980s and 1990s sitcoms were mainly focused on families, sex was not only generally understood in the context of familial intimacy, but also ostensibly "hidden" from view: it was assumed to take place offscreen, but never actually shown or explicitly talked about. It was often referred to, though: chaos or comic disruption frequently stemmed from the mild transgression of sociosexual rules. Thus, sex was generally treated as a sort of mild taboo that was addressed by means of innuendo, ironic humor, and sexual jokes that were not too provocative. Because of this, sitcoms did not tend to participate in the construction of what is "sexy." They assumed this definition and used it as background against which disruptions were made fun of (Smith). Such was the case of sitcoms like *Family Ties, Cheers, The Cosby Show , Who's the Boss, Night Court, Growing Pains , The Golden Girls, Alf, Full House, Family Matters, The Fresh Prince of Bel-Air, Blossom, Step by Step, Home Improvement,* and *Everybody Loves Raymond.* As the decade moved on, some sitcoms started to offer more "daring" views of sex, like *Roseanne , Seinfeld, Frasier, Cybill, The Single Guy, The Naked Truth, Caroline in the*

City, Suddenly Susan, Friends, Will & Grace, Union Square, and *Just Shoot Me.*

More dramatic genres have traditionally put greater emphasis on sex than the sitcom. Shows in the 1990s like *Beverly Hills 90210, Melrose Place, Models Inc., Central Park West,* and *Dawson's Creek* made abundant use of sex in their plots, but this was frequently explained by the dynamics of the soap opera, which revolves around its characters' sentimental entanglements with each other. Other series were far more explicit in their depiction of sex, like the erotic drama *Red Shoe Diaries,* but this is a show better classified in the sexploitation tradition, as its plot was a thinly veiled excuse for the display of soft-core sex. Female-centered comedies and dramas like *Dr. Quinn: Medicine Woman , Xena: Warrior Princess , Ally McBeal, Buffy the Vampire Slayer, La Femme Nikita, Felicity, Charmed,* and *Gilmore Girls* offered, if not more explicit representations of sex, at least more interesting portrayals of female sexuality.

However, as previously explained, the strong dependence of broadcast TV on the audience's perception of the "appropriateness" of its messages puts a clear limit on the degree of sexual explicitness of its contents. As already discussed, *SATC* was possible thanks to a premium cable channel's interest in the project. Once again, the series must be understood as an HBO product, and this should be taken into consideration when making comparisons with concurrent shows in network television. Not being tied to audience ratings nor sponsors, HBO has regularly made use of those elements that could not be shown on broadcast TV, such as sex, violence, and profanity, in order to establish its distinct brand identity (McCabe and Akass, "Sex, Swearing and Respectability"; Leverette, "Cocksucker, Motherfucker, Tits"). As far as sex is concerned, HBO included sexual content in its TV grid from the beginning, but this was done mainly through the docudrama format, as in *Real Sex, Taxicab Confessions,* and *G-String Divas.* These programs could be described as pseudoreality shows and were presented under the guise of "informational TV," never as pornography—even though their audiences' real motivations to watch them are open to interpretation (Leverette, "Cocksucker, Motherfucker, Tits"). Thus, the open display of sexuality on the small screen seemed to be acceptable as docudrama, on account of its pseudoscientific will to "illustrate," but it was unusual in the realm of fiction. Some HBO shows like *Dream On* started to break new ground in the inches of naked flesh that were appropriate to show on TV, but *SATC* was the very first fictional HBO series to revolve entirely around sex. *SATC*'s real "breakthrough" was not in its representation of nudity though, but in its uninhibited—and explicit—approach to female sexuality.

SATC was not only the first show with a premise entirely based on sex on HBO, but on U.S. television in general. Unlike the sitcoms that preceded it, nothing was taboo in *SATC,* something already announced in its title. The show presented itself as innovative due to its lack of inhibition. By 1998, its contemporaries did feature sex in some of its plots, but *SATC* made sex its core motivation, engaging in self-conscious exploration of sex and all of its possible ramifications. *SATC*'s will to "shock" the viewer did not lie in the display of titillating sex scenes, but in the use of frank, even raunchy language in the analysis of sexual liaisons. In this way, thanks to its "sex talk"— rather than its "sex action"—*SATC*, unlike most previous sitcoms, did make a remarkable contribution to the shaping of new meanings about sex and sexuality at the turn of the millennium. The following section will explore how this was done.

SEX AND THE SINGLE GIRL

SATC was a groundbreaking show not merely for its open depiction of sex but, more precisely, for its specific focus on female sexuality. Throughout its six seasons, *SATC* offers a variety of messages concerning the new role of women in the sexual realm. From issues of personal pleasure and self-care to questions of self-definition through sex, *SATC* displays its affinity with third-wave feminism's ideas in its stress on women's sexual freedom above everything else. As Maglin and Perry point out, for third wavers, "[s]exuality, in all its guises, has become a kind of lightning rod for this generation's hopes and discontents (and democratic vision) in the same way that civil rights and Vietnam galvanized (a previous) generation in the 1960s" (xvi). In keeping with the spirit of the third wave, one of *SATC*'s main concerns is the assertion of women's sexual autonomy, and the debunking of the traditional view of female sexuality as subordinated to men's. This issue constitutes the implicit foundation of the show and it is also explicitly dealt with numerous times throughout the series. An example of this is the pilot episode, which wonders whether modern women are able to have sex like men, that is, without any kind of sentimental attachment. The fact that this topic is addressed in the very first episode points to its importance throughout the series.

The pilot episode introduces the characters, and the very first time we see the girls together they are having a conversation that will be representative of the general tone of the show and its main preoccupations. Samantha puts it this way:

> If you're a successful single woman in this city, you have two choices: you can bang your head against the wall and try and find a relationship . . . or you can say "screw it," and just go out and have sex like a man. . . . This is the first time in the history of Manhattan that women have had as much money and power as men plus the equal luxury of treating men like sex objects.

The four friends discuss the issue and Carrie starts to consider the pros and cons of this idea. The upside is that if women are able to attain men's supposed ability to satisfy their physical urges without the need for an emotional connection, they will have the upper hand in relationships. In *SATC*, sex equals power, and being in total control of the former would imply a radical turning of the tables in the gender struggle. Carrie decides to test this hypothesis. By chance, she meets Kurt (Bill Sage), an old flame who took advantage of her repeatedly in the past. She does not have any feelings left for him, so she wants to see if she can "take revenge" by "having sex like a man." She goes to him decidedly and, in a short, straightforward verbal exchange, sets up a "sex date" with him for the same day. Carrie's attitude in this scene plays self-consciously with the sexual scripts associated with traditional gender roles. The typical sexual script for men includes the active pursuit of sexual partners, while women are more likely to wait to be chosen (Frith and Kitzinger). *SATC*'s reversal of roles continues in the next scene, where we see the couple having sex in his apartment: Carrie leaves Kurt after her climax, without reciprocating. For *SATC*, this selfish attitude in bed amounts to "having sex like a man." Even though this may be seen as a somewhat simplistic approach to male sexuality, sociological studies do tend to back *SATC*'s idea that men are more capable of undertaking sex only for the sake of pleasure while women's sexual scripts are more likely to include affection and the desire to please men (Alksnis et al.; Frith and Kitzinger).

Thus, Carrie leaves feeling "powerful, potent and incredibly alive." She feels as if she "owned this city. Nothing and no one could get in my way." However, precisely as she utters these words she bumps into a stranger and the contents of her handbag are spilled onto the pavement, suddenly undermining her feelings of control. She kneels down to pick them up, and this is when she meets Big for the first time, as he gallantly helps her pick up her stuff. The choice of this very moment for the "meet-cute" (Neale, "The Big Romance or Something Wild?" 287; Mernit 111) with the man who will be Carrie's main love interest during the series, coupled with the juxtaposition of Carrie's initial feeling of empowerment with her clumsy and nervous antics afterward, points to the fact that, in the future, it will be difficult for her to maintain this empowered position toward sex in her relationship with Big.

Despite this, the episode is successful in turning on its head the age-old notion of female sexual victimhood. Up to the second half of the twentieth century what Cas Wouters calls the "lust balance" between men and women remained firmly in place. The Victorian assumption that "the more spiritual love of a woman will refine and temper the more sensual love of a man" (van Calcar 47) was maintained well into the twentieth century, and it was not until the sexual revolution that women's carnal desires started to be taken seriously. These changes in sexual morality ran parallel to the emancipation of women during the 1960s, when sex became a legitimate "recreational" activity separated from love for both sexes. This gave way to a backlash during the late 1970s and mid-1980s, which was surmounted in the late 1980s, bringing about a "lust revival" and a further emancipation of women's sexual impulses. Finally, the 1990s witnessed a "lust and love revival": female desire was further emphasized, but sex outside of relationships, without being stigmatized, became less popular than before (Wouters).

Despite its firm support of female sexual autonomy, *SATC* reflects this contemporary tendency toward the integration of sexual and relational desires. When Carrie meets Kurt again she realizes that her new approach to sex is not really working out. This encounter takes place in a disco called Chaos, a place "just like that bar in *Cheers* where everybody knows your name . . . except here they were likely to forget it five minutes later." This reference to the more conventional sitcom *Cheers* underlines the difference between *SATC*'s representation of sexual morality and more traditional examples of this TV genre. Unlike the warm coziness and familiarity of the bar in *Cheers*, *SATC* depicts a complex universe of social relations far more detached and disconnected. Kurt's interpretation of Carrie's selfish behavior in bed confirms this point: far from being upset, he tells her he is happy because she has finally understood the kind of relationship he is looking for, after which he proceeds to kiss a gorgeous Asian girl. Carrie's reaction to this information is not what she had expected: "Did all men secretly want their women promiscuous and emotionally detached? And if I was really having sex like a man, why didn't I feel more in control?" Her confusion is further enhanced by her conversation with Big as he takes her home in his limousine for the first time. They discuss whether it is possible to have sex without feelings. That is not his case, he asserts. For Big, the answer to her confusion is clear: she has never been in love, something that, based on the look on her face, appears to be true.

In this way the episode seems to argue that sex is not really satisfactory for women outside of a context of intimacy. Despite its emancipatory initial premise, the series displays a conspicuous hesitation when it comes to conferring women the status of fully autonomous sexual subjects. This "fear of freedom," as Wouters calls it (203), may be attributed to the deeply ingrained resilience of the traditional lust balance, whose influence cannot be easily bypassed, something that is acknowledged by the show through Carrie's confused look at the camera in the frozen frame that closes the episode. In spite of this, the pilot episode sets the tone of the series in its refusal to provide a closed reading of its final message. Despite the failure of Carrie's "project," the resolution of Miranda's and Samantha's story lines throw into question again the advisability of detached sex: Miranda "uses" Skipper (Ben Weber) for sex, even though it is obvious she has no feelings for him, and Samantha ends up having casual sex with Charlotte's date. Both cases are presented without a hint of negative judgment or indication that the women feel uneasy about their choices. This ambivalence is symptomatic of the difficult integration of the two extremes that make up the lust balance. In connection with the contemporary ideal of integration between sexual and emotional fulfillment, Wouters predicts a "further sexualization of love and an erotization of sex" in a quest for a more satisfactory lust balance (208). The price to pay for this will be a sizeable intensification of ambivalent emotions between the two yearnings. The postmodern individual will pivot from one longing to the other in an effort to integrate the two, and this is a process that, as *SATC* shows, is not necessarily meant to elevate the individual to a higher level of happiness or enlightenment.

This feeling of confusion or ambivalence regarding women's stand toward "unattached" sex will be a constant throughout the whole series. *SATC*'s tentative discourse seems a reasonable initial premise, but the end of its final season confirms that the passing of time has not clarified the text's ideas in this respect. *SATC*'s first season revolved heavily around sex. It had a more "anthropological" feel, dealing with a different sexual issue practically in each episode. However, as the series progressed, it opened its scope, privileging psychological introspection rather than the uncritical pursuit of sexual liaisons, and the more general topic of intimate relationships, including romantic love and long-lasting partnerships, took center stage. A major cultural theme in this respect is the antithesis between sex and intimacy. Corless Smith argues that "TV genres are positioned at various points along the axis of physicality and emotionality, and it is these locations that further assign them to one genre or another. There are also programs that take this dichotomy as their subject, exploring or illustrating it rather than assuming a generic posture towards it" (122). This is *SATC*'s case: the series has repeatedly interrogated the complex—and often antithetical—relationship between physical gratification and emotional sharing, wondering whether it is possible to have sex outside of a relationship and whether a relationship may be maintained without sex.

There are episodes that put forward the question of whether a truly intimate relationship may survive without sexual satisfaction. In "Oh Come All Ye Faithful" (1:12), for instance, Samantha falls in love for the first time in the series, but the man's penis is too small. This generates a deep frustration in her and, despite her efforts to improve her sex life with her boyfriend, the relationship finally breaks. Like most of *SATC*'s episodes, this one shows how female sexual satisfaction is a prerequisite for a successful relationship. This message is not only endorsed in the case of sex-obsessed Samantha, but also in Charlotte's, the most traditional and less sex-driven in the group. At the beginning of the series she is dating an apparently perfect man ("The Drought," 1:11). She is already choosing the china for the trousseau, when she realizes that his "respect" for her actually means that he is on a medication that suppresses sexual desire. Charlotte decides sex is more important to her than a house in the Hamptons and she ends the relationship. Similarly, her marriage with her seemingly perfect husband Trey later in the series ends up on the rocks due to his initial impotence.

The show also explores the opposite possibility: being in a relationship just for the sex. In the episode entitled "The Freak Show" (2:3), Charlotte dates "Mr. Pussy," an incredible oral sex performer. She tries to build a relationship with him, but this turns out to be impossible. As Miranda points out, "Charlotte's not having a relationship, she's having multiple orgasms." The incompatibility between both things is also evident in "The Fuck Buddy" (2:14). This episode reveals the existence of a new kind of liaison at the turn of the century: a friend one uses only for sex. Carrie tries to establish a relationship with her fuck buddy, but there is no emotional connection. A similar thing happens to her in "What's Sex Got to Do with It?" (4:4). This episode wonders explicitly whether great sex and a good relationship can be found together. Carrie has mind-blowing sex with a jazz musician with a very short attention span. The man's inability to focus on something for longer than one minute makes it very difficult to talk to him. For her part, Charlotte is seeing Trey again after their separation. They manage to have sex in the bedroom for the very first time, but they are not living together as husband and wife, which upsets her. On the opposite end is Samantha, who is dating a woman. The proof that she is serious about the relationship is that she is not rushing into sex, as she usually does, but delaying the moment. This situation makes Carrie wonder:

> She wasn't having sex because she wanted to have a relationship and I was having mind-blowing sex hoping to turn it into a relationship. So there you have it: we've got a relationship without sex, and sex without a relationship. Which had a better shot at survival?

The answer given by *SATC* to the question is that neither is likely to be successful: both things are needed. Both Charlotte and Samantha seem to get the sex and the relationship by the end of the episode, thus providing a happy ending of sorts for them—although these relationships will eventually fail. Carrie's case is different: she breaks up with her jazz musician because she realizes she wants to have both a sexual and an emotional connection. As previously mentioned, as the series goes by, it becomes less sex centered and more relationship focused. Maybe because the characters grow older, they are more likely to pursue fully fledged relationships rather than casual sex. "Let There Be Light" (6:13), one of the very last episodes in the series, tackles the same topic dealt with in the pilot: the possibility of having a casual relationship with a man only for the sex. Carrie has just met Petrovsky and thinks she can take him simply as an occasional lover. His high-flying status as international artist and the long list of love conquests under his belt makes her think that he cannot be more than that. However, after sleeping with him she realizes she cannot simply have unattached sex with him. This episode belongs to the second half of the last season, but it seems to reach the same conclusion as the very first episode of the series: sex outside a relationship is not as satisfactory for women as it may be for men. This seems to throw into doubt Samantha's optimistic claims in the first episode: this may be the first time in history that women may have the luxury of treating men as sex objects. . . . What remains to be seen is whether choosing to do so is a good move in women's quest for happiness.

SATC's argument in favor of the integration of sex and affection does not mean that women's craving for sex for the sake of it is condemned. As Wouters argues, the loss of the popularity of sex outside relationships does not mean casual sex has become a new sin. Far from being stigmatized, recreational sex is routinely encouraged in *SATC*, thus illustrating the radical change undergone by women's attitudes toward sex and sexuality in the last decades. The episode entitled "The Big Journey" (5:7) provides a case in point, since it once again deals with the possibility of women's enjoyment of no-strings-attached sex, but in a more lighthearted way. Carrie has to go to San Francisco for the promotion of her book. Her journey has a second purpose, though: she is planning to meet Big there. She has not had sex for a long time and she is hoping to "use" him as her "male prostitute." The girls joke about the idea of opening "a brothel with cute men and 500-count Egyptian cotton sheets." The business could even develop into a franchise called "Starfucks" and Samantha would be the madam. The girls' conversation reveals a tongue-in-cheek, yet empowering position toward sex, which is nevertheless highly dependent on the characters' belonging to a privileged social group. This episode is a good example of how comic banter between the girls is normally used in the show to underline its unreserved acknowledgement of women's physical needs. Indeed, laughter plays a very important part in the legitimation of female desire in the series. *SATC* features nudity and abundant sex scenes, but never with titillating or exploitative purposes. Sex is extensively shown and talked about, but always with a comic function. The girls' outrageous conversations, their sexual adventures, and the events that derive from them are always meant to cause hilarity, not sexual arousal. Thus, sex is an important element around which a great part of *SATC*'s story lines revolve, but it is also the main source of comedy. I will now turn to the link between laughter and sex and the role played by humor in *SATC* as an important convention of romantic comedy.

The main story line in "The Big Journey" concerns Carrie's trip to San Francisco in order to have sex with Big. She does not want to go on her own, so she invites Samantha to come along. Carrie wants to go by train, and to persuade Samantha she appeals to those assumptions created by cinema about the fun and romance of train journeys: "Please, it'll be hilarious! Two gals on a train. Very *Some Like It Hot*." This allusion not only reinforces *SATC*'s cinematic connections but also its self-conscious play with romantic comedy conventions and its awareness of the spectator's familiarity with the genre. Indeed, much of the comedy in this episode derives from the viewer's acquaintance with Billy Wilder's classic film and other movies set in trains. Their journey to San Francisco serves, once more, to explore the different implications of women's recently acquired sexual independence:

> More and more single women of a certain age are looking for a certain thing. And that certain thing does not necessarily involve a certain ring. We may have traded the little black book for a little black dress, and replaced the Ferrari with a Fendi, but in view of certain evidence, I had to wonder . . . are we the new bachelors?

With this premise, we see Carrie and Samantha at the station, ready to board the train. They are smartly dressed. Carrie even wears an eyeshade and brings a highly impractical pink leather suitcase. Their confident strutting is underlined by jazz music, which evokes the mood of 1950s comedies, and specifically the equivalent scene in *Some Like It Hot*. Their excited anticipation of the journey's romantic/sexual possibilities is emphasized by Samantha's jokes: "I've always wanted to take a train. It's so sexy. You never know who's getting on and getting me off." Once they get on the train, the abrupt ending of the music marks the sudden subversion of their expectations. Their first-class sleeper is disappointingly small. However, their horror is not complete until they learn that their private restroom is so tiny one has to shower over the toilet. Suddenly, the romance of train journeys traditionally evoked by cinema disappears.

This is just the first of a series of ignominies that the two friends will have to endure along their trip. In the next scenes, they are thoroughly ridiculed by the text, as their expensive taste and aggressive sexuality are repeatedly mocked. Here, it must be pointed out that *SATC*'s articulation of its discourse about sex and sexuality is inextricably linked to socioeconomic issues. The show does not represent "women," or "female sexuality" as a whole. Rather, it depicts a particular class grouping: the so-called bourgeois bohemians, or bobos, a new petite bourgeoisie who replaced yuppies as the new culturally dominant class in the United States (Brooks). As Jane Arthurs has noted, this social group managed to reconcile the bourgeois and bohemian lifestyles:

> Sexual permissiveness, which in the bohemian movements of the 1960s was articulated with radical anti-capitalist political values, has been rearticulated to conform not only with the materialist priorities of consumer culture, but also with the emancipatory politics of the 1970s and 1980s. One effect has been to

free white, middle-class women from the sexual constraints required by bourgeois respectability. (*Television and Sexuality* 136)

For this group, sex is regarded as a source of hedonistic enjoyment closely
related to the contemporary consumerist ethos: it is an aesthetic, rather than
an ethic concern (Jancovich). *SATC*'s conception of female sexuality is highly dependent on signs of class. The liberated sexuality of the protagonists
derives from its bourgeois ascription and self-conscious rejection of charac-
teristics conceived as lower class. The "classiness" of female sexual activity
is thus a key element in its legitimation. The consumerist practices to which
this stylish approach to sex is linked renders sexuality an issue of taste or
aesthetics, rather than one of morality. All these meanings come into play in
the "New Woman" figure epitomized by *SATC*'s characters: an independent,
self-fashioned consumer whose sexuality is at once "stylish, a source of
physical pleasure, a means of creating identity, a form of body work, self-
expression, a quest of individual fulfillment" (Attwood 86). It is the mixture
of all these meanings that presents the characters' sexuality as a prominent—
and desirable—option for women at the turn of the century.

This depiction of female sexuality, which is generally considered as a
positive model by the series, shows its limitations in episodes like "The Big
Journey," as the following scenes suggest: a few hours later, Carrie and
Samantha have not yet lost hope in the success of their trip, and they decide
to go for a "classic train dinner in the club car." However, they are let down
again by what they find: instead of "white linen tablecloths and Bing Crosby
singing at a piano," the dining car is unglamorous, crowded, and small, and
they are evidently overdressed for the occasion. Carrie's accidental bump
into a man is not met by the flirtatious reaction she was expecting, which also
reinforces their unease. Their humiliation is complete when they are forced
to share a table with an Amish couple. Samantha's alarm at the turn their
adventure is taking is evident:

> **Samantha:** Are you aware every time we stop, good-looking people get
> off and more ugly people get on? I'm serious, this is the train to ugly.
> There isn't one man on this train I'd fuck. What about you?

> **Carrie:** Don't ask me. I'm horny and nine hours of train rocking hasn't
> helped.

This is the kind of conversation the girls are used to having in New York's
trendy restaurants, but the Amish couple's reactions not only provide an
effective comic counterpoint, but also underline their self-absorbed hedonism and oversexed lifestyle. Carrie's constant worry about the pimple that is
quickly developing on her face, thus rendering her less attractive to Big, also

emphasizes the vanity of their preoccupations. Their disdainful contempt toward the food served on the train—Samantha orders "a martini and an airplane"—makes it definitely clear that they do not fit in this scene.

Most episodes in *SATC* are meant for comic effect: even though the show's agenda is many sided, appealing to different areas of female experience, making the audience laugh is one of its primary targets. However, the reasons for hilarity are variable: sometimes viewers laugh with the girls and other times, they laugh at them. The first option is often preferred by the text. It is the girls' sexy, bold conversations that tend to provide the most memorable comic moments in the series, while empowering the characters at the same time and encouraging identification with their "liberated" moral positions. However, sometimes, the joke is on them, inviting the audience to laugh at the ludicrousness of some of their sexual romps. In this episode, for example, the complete mismatch between Carrie and Samantha's "bobo lifestyle," and the reality of life outside Manhattan's exclusive circles turns them into the butt of the joke. Their behavior on the train looks ridiculous, not only because of their unrealistic expectations of luxury and glamor, but also for the inadequacy of their sexual prospects, which, unlike in other cases, causes hilarity. It is evident that their "bobo" conduct looks utterly ludicrous outside New York, thus placing the girls in a new light and throwing into question their "sophisticated" ways.

According to T. G. A. Nelson, comedy encompasses two concepts: on the one hand, it evokes laughter and, on the other, a movement toward harmony, reconciliation and happiness (2). This coincides with Northrop Frye's view of the genre, which considers two main tendencies: one consisting "of comic irony, satire, realism, and studies of manners" and "the tendency of Shakespearean and other types of romantic comedy" (166–67). The former has a more social dimension, since laughter often implies the ridiculing of social mores. It requires an ironic distancing from something that is embarrassing and laughable. This kind of comedy can be traced back to Aristophanes's plays in fifth-century BC Athens. The reconciliatory potential of comedy implies a less social and more "utopian" dimension, and has been emphasized by Frye, who stresses the genre's impulse toward the harmony and joy inherent in the happy ending's potential for romantic fulfillment. The emphasis on the romantic reconciliation of the main couple is characteristic of the New Comedy tradition—the one followed by Shakespeare, among others—and it can be traced back to Aristophanes's quasi-peer, Menander (T. G. A. Nelson). These two dimensions of comedy have been "translated" into contemporary film criticism in the distinction between comedian and romantic comedy (Seidman, *Comedian Comedy*; Palmer; Neale and Krutnik; Horton; Jenkins; Karnick. The former is supposed to privilege laughter and satirical humor, while the latter gives prevalence to the happy ending's celebratory harmony. Both "types" of comedy have traditionally been regarded as incompatible notions, and only a few authors (T. G. A. Nelson; Deleyto) have argued for the contrary. In the case of *SATC*, the impulse toward laughter and the movement toward harmony can—and must—coexist: the satirical, more "social" dimension of humor is especially patent in Carrie and Samantha's antics on the train, while its more "utopian" side is later displayed through Carrie's meeting with Big. The integration of both dimensions confirms the ultimate feeling of mirth that *SATC* in particular, and romantic comedy in general, is supposed to transmit.

SATC's scorn of their protagonists in the first half of the episode clearly falls into the satirical tendency. So far, their sophisticated urban taste and sexual morality have made them look ridiculous in the context of the train. The next scene provides further evidence of how the girls' assumptions about sex are used to elicit laughter from the audience. The text keeps on poking fun at their protagonists when an excited and sloppy-looking Samantha rushes into the car to announce to Carrie that a group of men "not resembling the Elephant Man" got on the train and they are having a bachelor party in the bar car. However, the party turns out to be, once more, a complete disappointment. Carrie and Samantha's usually glamorous and sexy looks seem a little raunchy out of their "natural environment" and their predatory sexuality is definitely out of place. Samantha makes several passes at the dull-looking men in the car, which are repeatedly ignored, and Carrie makes a desperate attempt to talk the men into some flirtatious action, with no success either. The girls' over-the-top desperation to meet a man contrasts with their usual cool selves in New York, thus caricaturing their sex drive even further. In this way, *SATC* creates hilarity at the expense of its usually powerful and in-control characters. As this episode shows, the series never takes itself too seriously and it is always up for a measure of self-criticism. *SATC*'s playful combination of the two kinds of humor—both empowering and self-deflating—enmeshes the audience in a constant game of identification and ironic distancing from the text, implicitly sending an ambivalent message about the legitimacy of its protagonists' sexual behavior.

This scene, again, suggests that the text is making fun of a very specific type of "female sexuality": that of a particular social group that regards heterosexual relationships as an "aesthetic" rather than a "moral" issue. Samantha's teasing coquetry does not have any effect on the working-class men of the train, and her playful approach to sex looks clearly inappropriate in a lower-middle-class environment. When Carrie encourages the men to engage in some harmless flirtation with her friend, it becomes obvious that the girls' aesthetic view of socioerotic interplay collides with these men's, who are married and have promised to be "good." For them, sex is devoid of the hedonistic, stylish character of New York bobos' interactions, and it is more of an ethical question, as their indifference toward Samantha suggests. In this way, it is not only class differences that make the erotic game impossible: the text seems to imply that the girls' beliefs and assumptions about sexuality—as well as their worldviews as a whole—are not viable outside cosmopolitan circles like New York, thus satirizing the reductionism and classism of their life stance. This critique is made even more obvious in the next scene, which shows a drunken Samantha regretting the course of her life, thus providing a good example of the series' occasional mockery of its own shallowness.

Up to this moment, the text has put in play the social dimension of humor, since all of the comic moments have stemmed from ridiculing the girls in one way or another. However, once they arrive in San Francisco, the comic mood changes, and humor fulfills mainly a utopian function: laughter is still motivated by the girls' views of sex and sexuality, but the presence of Mr. Big brings about the possibility of romantic fulfillment, and Carrie's efforts to achieve this end become the main comic focus. As mentioned above, the social and the utopian dimensions of comedy coexist in this episode, and humor, far from being incompatible with narrative, plays an important role in the development of the romantic comedy plot.

Once in the San Francisco library where Carrie is going to do a reading of her book, she is disappointed to find that she is the opening act for Mr. Winkle, a famous puppet dog in children's fiction. Most of the people who crowd the place are there to see him, not her. However, Big's unexpected presence at the shop saves the day. The next scene shows Carrie, rushing into the hotel suite she shares with Samantha, who is taking a bath. She yells at her frantically, and urges her to vacate the room quickly. That is how desperate she is to have sex with Big. Carrie's agitation and hysterical preparation of their encounter accentuates the comic tone of the "seduction scene" that follows. Carrie opens the door coolly, as if nothing had happened, although Big has been stuck outside for half an hour. The intimate music, luxurious suite and Carrie's impeccable looks and soft voice form part of the "performance" she is staging for him to create a romantic mood. Instead of champagne, however, Big offers her some chewing gum. She takes it and, trying to seduce him, passes it on to him flirtatiously in quite a ridiculous manner. She does not keep her composed appearance for long, though. After a short verbal exchange, she suddenly leaps on Big, who, unprepared, swallows the gum. Carrie's attempts at seduction end in a ludicrous manner: what should be a passionate kiss winds up in Big's quasi-suffocation with the gum. This short gag constitutes a fairly uncommon example of physical comedy in the series. In *SATC*, laughter is usually dependent on verbal wit, and slapstick plays a very minor role. This is due to the show's adherence to the capitalist ethos: the commodified body of the characters is rarely ridiculed, and a more intellectual, "bourgeois" kind of "slapstick" is normally used (Arthurs, *Television and Sexuality* 139). Despite this, *SATC* does not shy away from the occasional pratfall to elicit laughter from the audience. The comic gag has often been regarded as a self-contained unit that stops the narrative (Neale and Krutnik). This scene shows this does not need to be the case, since the "chewing-gum incident" together with Carrie's other clumsy attempts at seduction, rather than distracting the viewer from the narrative, arguably contribute to its development by building the necessary tension and anticipation about the final sexual encounter, thus rendering it even more valuable.

Carrie wants to have sex right there and then, but Big insists on dining out. She maintains her flirtatious attitude, but soon it becomes clear that her sex plan is not going to be easily accomplished. Big has read her book and is concerned about the way he treated Carrie in the past. Back in the hotel room, she keeps trying to talk him into bed, but Big will not give up on his determination to clear up the past. In these scenes, laughter derives from Carrie's unsuccessful attempts to persuade Big to have sex with her, that is, hilarity stems from the reversal of gender roles, a typical comic device. These scenes show, once again, how laughter and narrative are not incompatible; Carrie's efforts to seduce Big elicit laughter but also move the action forward, building anticipation about its denouement. Apart from this, our privileged access to Carrie's consciousness by means of the voice-over allows for a great degree of identification with the character. We have accompanied Carrie through her difficult journey to San Francisco and we sympathize with her "needs." From this perspective, Carrie's ridiculous antics to captivate Big produce the kind of laughter that is not devoid of empathy, the sort of empathy necessary to accompany romantic comedy's characters through the winding path toward the fulfillment of desire. This idea is supported by Deleyto, who defends the inseparability of humor and narrative development: "Through humor, therefore, we indirectly acknowledge the humanity that is apparently being ridiculed as close to our own. In romantic comedy, this acknowledgement is crucial to understand our attitude towards the lovers' predicament but this predicament is precisely the subject of the narrative" (21–22).

The last scene between Carrie and Big takes place the morning after. It is evident that she has been unsuccessful in her campaign. However, in the light of day, Big seems to have forgotten all of his concerns and he is ready for sex. The sexual union is finally attained and the episode has its "happy ending." In seeing Carrie finally achieve her goal, the spectator is infected by her excitement with a kind of joy certainly different from the one produced by the satirical tone of the first half of the episode. The viewer's glee at the couple's final union is clearly related to the reconciliatory impulse of romantic comedy's happy ending, which is perceived as the "appropriate" outlet for Carrie's sexual frenzy.

Thus, this episode, which is representative of the way in which the show deploys a two-sided approach to comedy, contradicts the common assumption that both tendencies cannot coexist in the same text and exemplifies the way in which the series constructs an ambivalent image of contemporary female sexuality. Frequently associated with sex, comedy displays a double dimension in *SATC*. On the one hand, the spectator is sometimes placed in a superior moral ground, as he or she is invited to laugh at the characters' sexual attitudes and at the consequences of the sexual "freedom" proposed by the text: STDs, unwanted pregnancies, disappointing one-night stands, impotent husbands, and expensive shopping sprees to compensate for romantic disenchantments. The girls' sexual romps cue all kinds of "disasters" that are, nevertheless, always comically rendered. As has been shown, it is a specific social group represented by *SATC*'s protagonists—the bourgeois bohemians—that is usually the target of mockery: these people's values and approach to relationships—and life in general—are frequently made fun of. However at the same time, *SATC*'s comedy also features a "utopian" dimension, and not only in the sense of the text's relentless search for romantic reconciliation; sometimes, it levels a critique against the girls' lifestyles, but most of the time, it celebrates the climate of sexual freedom that characterizes the turn of the millennium, legitimating new models of sexual conduct for women. The most romantic or utopian perspective on sex introduces a more "traditional" way to channel female desire, helping make *SATC*'s daring discourses more palatable to a mainstream audience, while some of the most openly humorous moments provide a lighthearted mood that sometimes may level a critique against the kind of sexual conduct portrayed in the text, but also tends to disguise the real scope and "progressiveness" of some of *SATC*'s proposals.

At the same time, this twofold comic rendering of female sexuality (the mixture of the "comic" and "comedic" modes) provides a more complex representation of women's desire than audiences are generally used to seeing portrayed on the small screen, one that is not black or white, but highly contradictory and nuanced. The show's relentless self-questioning and spirit of contradiction has its limits, though, as it never seriously doubts the legitimacy of women's "right" to sexual fulfillment through a variety of means. Indeed, one of *SATC*'s main features is the joyous attitude it displays toward the emergence of a more pluralistic sexual culture, and more specifically, toward the growing openness of contemporary society's views on female sexuality. The text does show an ambiguous attitude toward myriad questions, thus reflecting the acute state of turmoil modern relationships find themselves in, but female entitlement to sexual satisfaction is never seriously questioned. *SATC*'s integration of a utopian or celebratory dimension with the more social or satirical function of comedy is symptomatic of the text's postfeminist ambivalence about the very discourses it puts forward. The apparent incompatibility between both dimensions suggests that *SATC* may find itself in the midst of a "gray area," culturally speaking. Due to the novelty of the discourses it proposed in its heyday, the text is not really sure about their convenience: sometimes it does not really know whether to celebrate them or to nervously laugh them off. As Carrie once said, the series is uncertain whether Samantha, the most "liberated" of the friends, represents "our future or our demise" ("Evolution," 2:11). For this reason, comedy's teasing mood proves to be the perfect means of representation for a number of discourses whose cultural validity is yet to be decided by the passing of time.[1]

PLASTIC SEXUALITY AND THE "DECLINE OF PERVERSION"

SATC's very title already announces the important role played by sex in the show. Even though the actual treatment of sex probably disappointed those viewers expecting a more titillating approach to the subject, it certainly fulfilled its promise: *SATC* contains a lot of sex, and a lot of city. Both appear to be inextricably linked. As the previous analysis has shown, New York presents itself as the only possible scenario not only for romance, but also for the sexual utopia represented in the series. The show's exploration of virtually every sexual practice (within certain parameters of acceptability) seemed to become *SATC*'s mission, especially during its first season, the most sex-loaded of all. This section will consider how, by acknowledging the multiple nuances of the meanings attached to sex today and by showing an open disposition toward its problematization, *SATC* has contributed to the expansion of media representations of female sexuality. With this purpose in mind, it will examine the text's conceptualization of Giddens's "plastic sexuality," as reflected by the series' engagement with the nonjudgmental representation of a great variety of sexual practices at the turn of the millennium, a representation which is always filtered through its comic approach.

Plastic sexuality is a fully autonomous kind of sexuality made possible by the advent of contraception and the separation between sex and pregnancy. Plastic sexuality is "malleable, open to being shaped in diverse ways, and a potential 'property' of the individual" (Giddens, *The Transformation of Intimacy* 27). This conception has led to the expansion in the variety of sexual activities and sexual identities (what Giddens calls the "decline of perversion"), as sexual traits formerly associated with perversions are today accepted as mere sexual diversity (*The Transformation of Intimacy* 32–34). This sexual diversity is faithfully represented in *SATC*. During its six seasons, all kinds of sexual experimentation are debated. Fellatio ("The Monogamists," 1:7), cunnilingus ("The Freak Show," 2:3), anal sex ("Valley of the Twenty-Something Guys," 1:4), rimming ("Baby, Talk Is Cheap," 4:6), masturbation ("The Turtle and the Hare," 1:9; "The Agony and the 'Ex'-tacy," 4:1), lesbian sex ("What's Sex Got to Do with It?," 4:4), straight men's desire to be penetrated ("The Awful Truth," 2:2), dirty talk in bed ("The Awful Truth," 2:2), sexual fetishes ("La Douleur Exquise!," 2:12), spanking

("Secret Sex," 1:6), golden showers ("Politically Erect," 3:2), phone sex ("All or Nothing," 3:10), sex toys ("The Turtle and the Hare," 1:9), or three-somes ("Three's a Crowd," 1:8; "A 'Vogue' Idea," 4:17). Apart from these activities, *SATC* also considers other questions related to the practice of sex, such as prostitution ("The Power of Female Sex," 1:5), frequency of inter-course ("The Drought," 1:11), sexual etiquette ("Secret Sex," 1:6), penis size ("Oh, Come All Ye Faithful," 1:12), circumcision ("Old Dogs, New Dicks," 2:9), fuck buddies ("The Fuck Buddy," 2:14), sexual expertise ("Was It Good for You?," 2:16), female orgasm ("My Motherboard, Myself," 4:8), sex addiction ("Was It Good for You?," 2:16), interracial sex ("No Ifs, Ands or Butts," 3:5), sex with younger men ("Valley of the Twenty-Something Guys," 1:4), tantric sex ("Was It Good for You?," 2:16), sex at the workplace ("Boy, Girl, Boy, Girl," 3:4; "Just Say Yes," 4:12), and even celibacy ("What's Sex Got to Do with It?," 4:4; "The Agony and the 'Ex'-tacy," 4:1). The show also devotes several episodes to the exploration of issues of sexual identity ("Evolution," 2:11; "Was It Good for You?," 2:16; "Boy, Girl, Boy, Girl," 3:4; "What's Sex Got to Do with It?," 4:4).

Of course, Samantha is the most sexually adventurous of the four charac-ters. She has tried virtually every sexual practice under the sun and she never rules out any possibility. Actually, she refers to herself as "try-sexual," be-cause she will "try anything once" ("Boy, Girl, Boy, Girl," 3:4). Despite the difficulty of matching Samantha's sexual exploits, the other characters do not fall much behind, regularly engaging in all kinds of sexual practices, which later become the object of close examination.[2] *SATC* dealt with myriad sex-related questions throughout its six seasons, so it would be impossible to comment on all of them. For this reason, I have chosen one episode that is representative of the show's interest in the exploration of "daring" sexual practices: "Three's a Crowd" (1:8).

"Three's a Crowd" focuses on threesomes. Charlotte's new boyfriend tells her he would like to do a three-way with her and another woman, an issue that is discussed in detail by the girls the following day. Far from being surprised, the characters seem to regard it as a fairly normal practice:

Samantha: Threesomes are huge right now. They're the blow job of the '90s.

Charlotte: What was the blow job of the '80s?

Samantha: Anal sex.

Carrie: Any sex, period.

This short exchange not only acknowledges the relative "normalcy" of invit-ing a third person into your bed nowadays, but also the quick social evolution of society's views of what "perverse" sexual behavior entails. The dialogue shows how "deviant" sexual practices become progressively normalized with the passing of time. Lillian Rubin's 1990 study of sexual behavior in U.S. society revealed a remarkable expansion in the variety of sexual activities generally deemed as "appropriate" by most people. As if to back Samantha's remark, an example of this is the results of Rubin's survey of people's views on oral sex, which was starting to be considered as a normal part of sexual behavior by younger generations in the late 1980s and early 1990s. Twenty years later, the Center for Sexual Health Promotion at Indiana University carried out the largest nationally representative study of sexual and sexual-health behaviors ever fielded, which showed how the degree of sexual experimentation in U.S. society had increased notably. The researchers were struck by the variety of ways in which the subjects engaged in sex: forty-one different combinations of sexual acts were identified, including vaginal and anal intercourse, oral sex, and partnered masturbation. This study confirmed, for instance, the full consolidation of oral sex as a "mainstream" sexual practice: more than 80 percent of women aged 20 through 49, and over 85 percent of men the same age reported engaging in it (Lopatto). The time span between Rubin's study and this more recent survey highlights the constructed nature of what "normal" sexual behavior actually means. People's views on sex change over the course of time as a consequence of their exposure to different cultural messages. In this sense, *SATC* episodes like "Three's a Crowd" have played a remarkable role in the normalization of certain practices and attitudes toward sex. The girls' conversation about threesomes, oral, and anal sex may not seem as groundbreaking today as it was in 1998, when this episode was first broadcast. The fact that this is so attests to the show's contribution to the increasing recognition of sexual diversity and to the decline of the very concept of "perversion."

In this way, the initial conversation about threesomes among the friends does not question the "adequacy" of this practice, but its possible effects on an intimate relationship. Charlotte is considering agreeing to do it in order to get closer to her boyfriend but according to Samantha, the only way to do a threesome is to be the "guest star." Otherwise, the relationship is spoiled. So, this is the question that the episode sets out to analyze—whether threesomes could be "the relationship of the future" or not, and not women's entitlement to this activity, which is taken for granted. As is frequently the case, different angles on the issue are explored through the perspectives of the four characters.

Even though the four story lines deal with threesomes in one way or another, Charlotte is the only one who actually gets to engage in this sexual practice in this episode. Encouraged by her boyfriend and by a steamy sex dream, she finally agrees to do it. The fact that even "conservative" Charlotte is willing to engage in such a practice could be regarded as a symptom of what McNair calls the "sexualization" of culture. People's increasing exposure to sexual messages has slowly modified our views about the practice of sex: as Charlotte's story line shows, "having sex" is no longer enough. It is expected to be "fulfilling, exciting and diverse" (Evans 120). This approach to sexuality is framed by those discourses that support a more malleable sexual model, freed from reproduction and from the "tyranny of the phallus." Giddens coined the term "plastic sexuality" in order to refer to a kind of decentered sexuality that became possible thanks to the advent of contraception. The separation of sex and reproduction allowed for the flourishing of a whole range of sexual practices whose only purpose was pleasure and self-fulfillment. The disconnection between sex and pregnancy was also the prerequisite for female sexual autonomy, and therefore, the sexual revolution. Practices like threesomes, whose motivation is wholly recreational, not reproductive, are an example of what Giddens understands by plastic sexuality, and *SATC*'s legitimization of this practice attests to the significance of his theory. The fact that a mainstream media product like *SATC* is able to present threesomes as a "normal" sexual activity at the end of the twentieth century corroborates what Giddens calls "the decline of perversion," that is, the incorporation of sexual activities and identities previously regarded as deviant into the everyday social world (32–34).

However, the show's positive attitude toward this activity does not mean it is necessarily advisable: Charlotte and her boyfriend meet an attractive woman at a party. After some flirtation, she follows them to a bedroom. Charlotte agrees to have a threesome, but when the action starts she is quickly left out. Feeling excluded, she leaves the room and we never get to see Charlotte's boyfriend again in the series. In this way, the show does not portray threesomes in a negative light because of their immorality, but it does suggest that they are incompatible with an intimate relationship.

As is usually the case, the issue of threesomes is further explored through the other characters' story lines. Samantha, for instance, is involved in another kind of triangle, since she is seeing a married man. Once again, the show does not level any kind of moral judgment against Samantha's behavior. In fact, Samantha's "libertine" sexuality is rarely condemned by the text. Her lack of boundaries in sexual experimentation is always a source of comic celebration. Her episodic approach to sexuality is actually positively regarded by Giddens as one more means of exploring the possibilities offered by plastic sexuality: "even in the shape of impersonal, fleeting contacts, episodic sexuality may be a positive form of everyday experiment. It reveals plastic sexuality for what it (implicitly) is: sex detached from its age-old subservience to differential power" (147).

When the wife of Samantha's lover learns about the affair, she contacts Samantha. This gives way to a very comic three-way conversation between Samantha, her lover, and his wife. Once again, sex is used as the main source of humor in the series while at the same time reflecting society's changing sexual mores. In this case, comedy stems from the subversion of generic expectations about cinematic sex triangles, as well as society's general assumptions about gender roles: contrary to the belief that a married man rarely leaves his wife for his lover, the man is eager to forsake his wife for Samantha. However, far from being glad, Samantha is horrified by the idea. The wife, for her part, calls Samantha to tell her she is willing to do a threesome with them if that is what it takes to keep her husband. In this way, the scene elicits the audience's laughter, subverting gender and genre conventions by having Samantha play the role of matchmaker between the two, while simultaneously contributing to the normalizing of a relatively unusual sexual practice.

In the third story line, Miranda feels left out in the threesome issue. When Charlotte says that she would rather do it with a friend, none of the other girls mention Miranda's name as a potential sexual partner. That makes her feel insecure, which prompts a series of visits to her psychiatrist. In the end, she finds reaffirmation by answering a classified ad. She meets a couple looking for a woman to do a threesome. However, once she confirms that the couple finds her attractive, she leaves. Miranda's story line is particularly telling about the anxieties and insecurities brought about by the quick changes undergone by sexual politics at the turn of the millennium. She does not actually want to have sex with her girlfriends, but she feels hurt because they do not even consider the possibility, reasoning "if your friends won't go down on you, who will?" Miranda's visits to her psychiatrist are, once again, especially reminiscent of the hyperreflective mood of Woody Allen's "nervous romances." The director's influence on the series is especially noticeable during the early seasons:[3] "Three's a Crowd," for instance, exhibits an anthropological interest and a self-conscious style that becomes progressively diluted later on in the series. As is usually the case during the first season, this episode includes a series of quick-cutting vox populi interviews, in which anonymous people express their preferences regarding threesomes. These interventions are actually a dramatization of Carrie's psyche, as she reads the newspaper contact ads. For instance, a threesome seeker speaks to the camera, saying: "Me, gorgeous with big boobs. You, a couple with class. Let's experience everything the city has to offer. I'm into museums, blow jobs, theater, and golden showers." Here, once again, sex is used as source of laughter. This particular line clearly shows Allen's influence on the show's screenplays in the juxtaposition of serious or high-culture elements with prosaic ones, a common device used in Allen's comedies (Wernblad 57). Apart from fulfilling comic purposes, these quick "interviews" also give an ethnographic feel to the series, thus expanding the text's scope in its exploration of contemporary sexual mores, while conveying a feeling of fragmentation that captures faithfully the mood of the city's hectic dating scene.

Carrie is experiencing another kind of three-way in her life: she not only discovers that Big was involved in a threesome once—it was with his former wife. Big's failure to mention that he was married prompts a series of very "Allenesque" neuroses in Carrie that drive her to meet his ex. She cannot decide whether she feels more disturbed by her good looks and general charm and talent, or by the discovery that Big cheated on her. The story line thus reflects on the issue of threesomes not from the sexual point of view, but in emotional terms: "So I guess you couldn't avoid a threesome because even if you're the only person in the bed, someone has always been there before you," Carrie reflects. When she shares her insecurities with Big, he tells her that the only reason why he had a threesome with his ex-wife was because they were both looking for somebody else. This confession seems to reassure Carrie, and extra-diegetic intimate jazz music is heard while they kiss. Meanwhile, we see Big's wife in the background—again, a projection of Carrie's conscience—walking away. This is accompanied by Carrie's final reflection: "And I realized the real appeal of the threesome: it was easy. It's intimacy that's the bitch."

The episode's closing scene has two implications: firstly, it confirms the girls' initial suspicion that threesomes are incompatible with relationships, since real intimacy can only be held between two people—not three—and it is far more complex than sex. Secondly, it implies that having a threesome is an indicator that a relationship does not really work, an idea that is backed by Charlotte's story. In this way, the episode offers a somewhat disappointingly "conservative" conclusion, which seems to undermine its initial celebration of plastic sexuality. *SATC*'s celebration of "more evolved," pleasure-seeking sexual activities for their own sake is hindered by the message that the diversity of sexual practices brought about by plastic sexuality may actually constitute an obstacle, rather than an enhancement, for satisfactory relationships. In spite of this, it should not be forgotten that *SATC*'s trademark ambivalence about the advisability of certain sexual activities—like threesomes—never amounts to their condemnation. Women's right to engage in virtually any kind of sexual practice is never really questioned or reproved. In this sense, despite the somewhat ambivalent readings of certain episodes, *SATC*'s generally open, nonjudgmental attitude toward sex constitutes one step forward in the path toward a less judgmental representation of female sexuality in the media.

LET'S TALK ABOUT SEX: *SEX AND THE CITY*'S CONFESSIONAL DISCOURSE

"Three's a Crowd" is a good example of how *SATC* self-consciously presented itself as the most sexually explicit U.S. television program ever. However, it also shows how actual sex action is relatively scarce and clearly overshadowed by sex talk. In these conversations, nothing is out of bounds: from vibrators to "funky tasting spunk." For the first time in TV history, female sexuality is presented as a "legitimate topic of public conversation" (Comella 109). In the show, sexuality is depicted as a social undertaking, not an individual one. It is the subject of never-ending analysis and shared female laughter. It also constitutes an invitation for the audience to participate in its social construction. The aim of this section is to consider the kinds of messages delivered by the series regarding sex and sexuality, and how this is articulated through a comic confessional discourse. With this purpose in mind, I will comment on two scenes from "Valley of the Twenty-Something Guys" (1:4) and "The Monogamists" (1:7), in which anal and oral sex are discussed, respectively. These scenes, which are very representative of the general tone of the series, will be connected with Foucault's ideas on the tradition of confession and how it shapes our modern concept of sexuality. This kind of scene may also be seen as a clear manifestation of what McNair calls "striptease culture," that is, today's culture of self-revelation and "public intimacy" that routinely disrupts the boundaries between private and public discourse. This tendency forms part of what McNair calls the "pornographication" of the public sphere, a larger process by which sex is becoming more and more visible and explicit everyday both in print and broadcast media (61).

"Striptease culture" is most commonly found in the confessional discourse of debate shows, documentaries, and "docusoaps," as well as in certain print media, like women's magazines (McNair). *SATC* is deeply connected to this confessional trend, which is partly explained by its participation in the conventions of some of these genres. Jonathan Bignell, for instance, has noticed *SATC*'s similarities with the dynamics of talk shows: both create a "structure of feeling" in which the audience is invited to participate. Through vicarious identification with the four types of women offered by *SATC*, viewers are invited to share in the discussion prompted by one character's "confession," just like in programs such as *The Oprah Winfrey Show*. Similarly, *SATC* is also influenced by the conventions of female glossy magazines, sharing with them not only the trope of confession characteristic of their advice columns, but also the centrality of sexuality as key to the expression of self-identity, and commodity fetishism. Like these magazines, *SATC* offers a utopian sense of sisterhood, both intra-diegetically, through the characters' friendship, and extra-diegetically, through the imagined community of fans gathered around the program (Bignell, "Sex, Confession and Witness"). Apart from this, *SATC* can also be said to take part in the conventions of docudramas or reality TV through its use of "real" dialogue (Gennaro).

The girls' discussion of oral sex in "The Monogamists" illustrates these points. Charlotte has a new boyfriend who keeps pushing her to perform oral sex on him. The series features a short scene between the couple that shows what Carrie's voice-over describes as "the blow job tug of war," followed by a much longer one in which the issue is analyzed by the girls. Charlotte confesses she never gives oral sex because she does not like it. Her friends are shocked. After the initial surprise, the group starts to dissect possible angles from which to tackle the situation. Different perspectives are offered: Samantha loves to do it, of course. For Miranda, "oral sex is like God's gift to women. You can get off without worrying about getting pregnant." Carrie is more moderate in her position, but she admits she enjoys it if she is with the right man. In this way, this activity is "democratically voted" as wholly acceptable and recommendable, and it is the more prudish Charlotte that is found to be the odd one out. Charlotte's dislike of fellatio has a further implication, though: "If you don't go down on him, how do you expect him to go down on you?" For Miranda the democratic character of contemporary sexual protocols is a given, which attests to the series' full engagement with the idea of "equal opportunity" sexual freedom. The double standard by which female sexuality was subordinated to that of men in the past is completely out of the question in the series: Miranda "only gives head to get head." However, Charlotte does not expect such a thing, a revelation that is received with shock again, thus implicitly reinforcing the show's taken-for-grantedness of women's entitlement to oral pleasure.

In any case, the whole scene revolves around Charlotte's confession: she does not give nor receive oral sex. According to Foucault, "the confession was, and still remains, the general standard governing the production of the true discourse on sex" (63). We have come to think of confession as a way of finding truth, one that makes us aware of our own subjecthood. This relationship between sexuality and self-identity was first unraveled by Freud in the early twentieth century. Since then this notion has progressively taken root, to the point that today, sex is regarded as a key element for the achievement of self-discovery and personal realization. In *The History of Sexuality*, Foucault traces the history of the discourses about sex and argues that the issue was brought into the spotlight for the first time in the seventeenth century by Christianity, which put previously repressed desires into discourse by means of the Christian confession. For Foucault, the tradition of confession—in combination with scientific discourse—shapes our modern concept of sexuality. The mixture of both discourses rendered sex as something "secret" that needed to be uncovered in order to find a hidden truth about ourselves that can be codified into knowledge. As such, sexuality is regarded as the key to understanding who we are. This centrality of public discourses in the shaping of our views on sexuality has not only continued into the present, but it has arguably intensified in recent decades:

It is no longer a question simply of saying what was done—the sexual act—
and how it was done; but of reconstructing, in and around the act, the thoughts
that recapitulated it, the obsessions that accompanied it, the images, desires,
modulations, and quality of the pleasure that animated it. For the first time no
doubt, a society has taken upon itself to solicit and hear the imparting of
individual pleasures. (Foucault 63)

Scenes like the one under consideration in *SATC* exhibit the kind of "pleasure of analysis" described by Foucault, which surpasses the pleasure derived
from the actual practice of sex. Rather than the titillation of the senses, *SATC*
seeks a more "intellectual" kind of stimulation as far as sex is concerned. To
put it in Foucauldian terms, *SATC* could be said to replace the *ars erotica*
with a kind of *scientia sexualis*, finding pleasure "in the truth of pleasure"
(71), in the thorough dissection of every single detail making up the sexual
experience, rather than in its actual practice. The show's fondness for revelation connects it with the "confessional comedy" genre (Levy, *Cinema of
Outsiders*; Deleyto). These films, which privilege talk over action and display an evident self-consciousness in their overanalytical approach to relationships, share with *SATC* "the pleasure of knowing that truth, of discovering and exposing it, the fascination of seeing it and telling it, of captivating
and capturing others by it, of confiding it in secret, of luring it out in the
open—the specific pleasure of the true discourse on pleasure" (Foucault 71).

All this sex talk in *SATC* is, of course, female talk. For Foucault, discourse is intimately linked to issues of knowledge and power: those who do
the speaking hold the power to shape society's views about sex. This theory
accounts for the sense of female empowerment that pervades the series.
Women's sex talk lifts the curtain on the "truth" of female desire and bodily
pleasures, thus putting women in the position of speaking subjects. The suspicion that this might entail a challenge to still-existing taboos about female
sexuality is confirmed by the hostile reception of the show by a sizeable
portion of critics. This hostility is not simply motivated by having women
talk about sex, but by the knowing, ironic attitude these women display about
the subject. The scene under analysis shows a humorous, lighthearted approach to oral sex, with the all-important phallus being compared with a
banana or a popsicle. The same attitude is found in the girls' conversation
about anal sex in "Valley of the Twenty-Something Guys" (1:4). Again,
Charlotte has been asked to engage in this practice and, appalled, she seeks
her friends' advice, getting a variety of viewpoints on the issue. The characters' opinions, albeit filtered by a comic perspective, offer different "blueprints" for sexual conduct, helping shape contemporary "sexual scripts."
Sexual scripts determine with whom to have sex, what acts to perform, when
and where sex will occur, and for what reasons (Atwood and Dershowitz).
The comic treatment given by *SATC* to these sexual "directions" does not

diminish their legitimacy or their influence. On the contrary, they are actually enhanced by the text's lighthearted approach: the protagonists' hilarity
over their sexual adventures allows them "to engage in a confirmation process that grants legitimacy to, and confers meaning on, each other's stories
and experiences" (Akass and McCabe, "Ms. Parker" 187).

Humor plays a remarkable role in this particular scene, since it is used to
demystify and turn on its head the meanings attached to a sexual practice
that, otherwise, could be seen as somewhat degrading for women. Once
again, the scene revolves around Charlotte's "confession": her current boyfriend wants to have anal sex with her but she has never done it and is not
sure that she wants to do it, mainly because this practice is incompatible with
her "good girl" image. Anal sex seems to be a trickier question than oral sex:
Charlotte is trying to explain her problem on the phone to a distracted Carrie,
who is late for her date with Big. However, when she learns about Charlotte's dilemma, Carrie drops what she is doing immediately. An emergency
meeting is quickly arranged in the backseat of a taxi. The formal organization
of the scene—with a new member of the group being gradually added—
emphasizes the polyphony of voices that is put at Charlotte's—and the viewer's—disposal. The fact that the whole conversation is overheard by the male
Indian driver has a double purpose: on the one hand, it adds to the scene's
comic effect. On the other, he can be said to stand for *SATC*'s potential male
audience. Unlike most of the girls' conversations, which are always private,
this time a man gets to witness what women talk about when they are on their
own. The driver's puzzlement at the conversation reveals the uneasiness a
sizeable part of the male audience may feel about the show, thus underlining
the threat that female sex talk still signifies for the male ego. However, the
fact that he eventually joins the girls in their laughter may point to the
positive effects female sexual liberation ultimately has for both sexes.

On their way to pick up Miranda, Carrie asks Charlotte to repeat the exact
words that have triggered the crisis: "We've been seeing each other for a
couple of weeks. I really like you. And tomorrow night after dinner . . . I
want us to have anal sex." The comic contrast between the formality and
correctness of the first part of the message and the prosaic character of the
second one is emphasized by Charlotte's visible bewilderment. Her confusion is actually described as a "state of abject blackness" by Carrie's voice-
over: a clear hyperbole that both legitimizes and pokes fun at the seriousness
of her problem. Here, it should be said that Carrie's voice-over is a device
constantly used by the series for comic effect, since it frequently offers an
ironic perspective on the visuals, and this scene is no exception. When Miranda joins the conversation, she offers a highly practical approach to the
situation:

Miranda: It all depends. How much do you like him?

Charlotte: A lot.

Miranda: "Dating a few months until somebody better comes along" a lot . . . or "marrying and moving to East Hampton" a lot?

Charlotte: I don't know. I'm not sure.

Miranda: Well, you better get sure real quick.

Charlotte: You're scaring me!

Carrie: Don't scare her!

Miranda: It's all about control. If he goes up there, there's gonna be a shift in power. Either he'll have the upper hand or you will. There's a certain camp that believes whoever holds the dick holds the power. . . . The question is . . . if he goes up your butt, will he respect you more or respect you less? That's the issue.

For Miranda anal sex is, therefore, not a more or less pleasurable sexual activity a woman chooses to engage in or not, but a negotiation tool able to tilt the power balance within the couple. This view of anal sex is, no doubt, comical, but it is also connected with Foucault's ideas about the intricate links between sexuality and social power relations. For Foucault, sexuality constitutes "an especially dense transfer point for relations of power . . . Sexuality is not the most intractable element in power relations, but rather one of those endowed with the greatest instrumentality: useful for the greatest number of maneuvers and capable of serving as a point of support, as a linchpin, for the most varied strategies" (103). This instrumental view of sex is corroborated by this scene; it is implied that a woman may agree to anal sex in exchange for a comfortable socioeconomic position. Sex, therefore, is a complex site of negotiation in which power relations are fluid; agreeing to a "submissive" practice does not necessarily imply being at a disadvantage in the relationship. This is confirmed by Samantha's views on oral sex in the previous scene: "The sense of power is such a turn-on. Maybe you're on your knees, but you got them by the balls." As in Foucault's conception, for Samantha, power is not something one "has," but something that flows through social relationships. [4]

When Samantha joins the conversation, she offers a less pragmatic and more "hedonistic" view on the subject. Miranda's perspective did not even consider the possibility that anal sex could be a pleasurable activity for women. Samantha, on the contrary, is all for it:

Samantha: Front, back, who cares? A hole is a hole.

Miranda: Can I quote you?

Samantha: Don't be so judgmental. You could use a little back door.

Charlotte: I'm not a hole!

Carrie: Honey, we know.

Samantha: All I'm saying is that this is a physical expression that the body was designed to experience. And P.S., it's fabulous.

Samantha's viewpoint provides comic relief to the somewhat "tense" mood of the scene so far. Even though the topic had been treated in a playful, tongue-in-cheek manner, it is Samantha's straightforward theory that "a hole is a hole" that provokes the release of laughter, while at the same time supporting women's entitlement to boundless, nonjudgmental forms of physical pleasure. Miranda's ironic remarks on Samantha's views and Charlotte's protests that she is "not a hole" exemplify *SATC*'s favorite strategy to create comic effect: in this kind of scene, one character's confession prompts the reactions of the others, which provide additional narratives to the main "confession." In the process, the characters poke fun at each other and even at themselves, while at the same time revealing truths about female desire traditionally hidden from view. In this way, humor is used in the series to enhance female solidarity, since the four women equally participate in the comic process through their sex talk, while at the same time undermining traditional power positions in sexual relationships between the sexes by opening up new possibilities for women's sexuality—in this particular scene sex is connected with female empowerment on the one hand, and guilt-free, boundless physical enjoyment on the other. Both views of female sexuality had been relatively unheard of on TV. It was thanks to its comic perspective that *SATC* was able to put forward this kind of discourse, breaking some taboos in the process.

SATC's sexual jokes are manifold: double entendre and play with language are central in the creation of humor. As previously mentioned, physical comedy is scarce in *SATC*, laughter being mainly elicited from witty verbal exchanges:

Charlotte: What are you talking about? I went to Smith!

Samantha: Look, I'm just saying, with the right guy and right lubricant . . .

Charlotte: What was that? [the taxi jams on its brakes]

Miranda and Samantha: A preview!

Despite Samantha's attempts to open Charlotte's mind, being a Smith graduate is incompatible with anal sex in her book. Her facial expression and tone of voice shows she is horrified by Samantha's advice: such raunchy practices are at odds with her eligibility as wife-to-be.

According to T. G. A. Nelson, sexual jokes are funny because of the sense of psychic release they provoke: "the child in us is defying the adult censor who normally forbids us to use threats, insults, or low words" (124). This is in line with Freud's theory on tendentious jokes, which are obscene, hostile and meant to give voice to the socially unacceptable wish. It could be argued that *SATC* breaks taboos and defies censorship thanks to its comic, playful approach to sex. It makes use of a humorous confessional discourse in order to convey messages about female sexuality that would be hard to express otherwise. Its characters' laughter intermingles with that of its female audience in a shared pact of mutual understanding. Despite the fact that many funny moments in the show emphasize the spectator's feeling of superiority toward the occasional silliness of the characters (as my previous analysis has shown), most of the comedy in *SATC* stems from identification, not detachment: we are aware of the traits we share with the protagonists, and we recognize ourselves in them. As Raymond Durgnat argues in a different context, in a way we know "that their weakness, rather than their immunity, is ours" (45), and this constitutes the ultimate cause of both hilarity and fan loyalty in the show. Indeed, although the series does habitually poke fun at its characters, it is the audience's empathy with them, and not a feeling of emotional superiority, that prompted its huge following all around the world. By laughing both at its characters and, more importantly, *with* its characters, *SATC* has managed to successfully integrate two dimensions of humor that do not frequently go hand in hand. In the process, it has succeeded in helping normalize a more daring and equalitarian view of female sexuality at the turn of the millennium. Despite accusations of anti-feminism and/or vulgarity and disengagement with the political side of the female struggle, the series' firm belief in women's entitlement to attitudes so far exclusively reserved for men reveals its commitment to the improvement of women's position not only in the bedroom, but in society as a whole.

IS HE A STRAIGHT GAY MAN, OR A GAY STRAIGHT MAN? SEXUALITY AS CONSTRUCTION

When Bill Clinton denied having had sexual relations with his intern in 1998, a great controversy arose around the definition of what *having sex* actually meant. The clarification of the term was relevant, since the honor of the U.S.

president was at stake. Independent of the results of such an investigation, three things became clear then: first, the heightened levels of sexual explicitness in the media at the threshold of the twenty-first century; second, sexuality's increasing theoretical elusiveness; and third, the power that the public confession of an individual's darkest sexual deeds still holds over society's imagination today.

We have seen how the trope of confession structures *SATC*'s dynamics. According to Foucault—and based on the Lewinsky scandal—it also shapes our modern concept of sexuality. Sex is regarded as something "hidden" that must be investigated and can only be accessed through confession. It is also seen as "container" of our true selves, the key to understanding who we really are (Foucault). Sexuality's mystifying power to unveil the truth about ourselves seems to be overestimated, though. For Foucault, our sexual desires, behaviors, and inclinations do not necessarily hold such deep truths about us. It is the discourses built around those desires, behaviors, and inclinations that reveal the greatest truths about our self-identity. The idea that our socially constructed beliefs about sex are more likely to reveal this "hidden truth" than the analysis of sex itself, reinforces once again the view of sex and sexuality as contingent social constructions. These discourses are everywhere in society: from prime-time television to *Cosmopolitan*'s advice columns, we are bombarded with messages that propose myriad attitudes toward the way in which sexuality should be lived. It is the analysis of those discourses and our relationship toward them that may prove most fruitful in our quest to find who we are.

SATC is evidently aware of this view of sexuality as the Holy Grail of personal identity and self-realization. However, like Foucault, it normally displays an open, nontaxonomic attitude toward the issue. The media usually propagates the idea that knowing one's sexual identity is crucial for the individual's happiness. *SATC*, on the contrary, offers a more fluid view of sexual labels. In the episode entitled "Evolution" (2:11), for instance, Charlotte dates a sensitive pastry chef from Chelsea, and she is confused about his sexual orientation:

Charlotte: I am so confused. Is he gay or is he straight?

Carrie: It's not that simple anymore. The real question is: Is he a straight gay man, or is he a gay straight man?

Carrie's voice-over: The gay straight man was a new strain of heterosexual male spawned in Manhattan as the result of overexposure to fashion, exotic cuisine, musical theater, and antique furniture.

Samantha: Hopefully, he's a gay straight man, meaning he's straight with great gay qualities. Whereas a straight gay guy is just a gay guy who plays sports and won't fuck you.

In the end, he turns out to actually like women but his feminine side is too "evolved" for Charlotte. She leaves him when she sees him squeaking like a little girl at the sight of a mouse in his kitchen. In "What's Sex Got to Do with It?" (4:4), Samantha has a relationship with a woman. Does that mean she is a lesbian now? Samantha does not like sexual categorizations: "It's just a label. Like Gucci, or Versace. . . . This is not about being gay or straight. Maria is an incredible woman."[5] The episode entitled "Boy, Girl, Boy, Girl" (3:4) also questions the fixity of gender identity. Charlotte's art gallery is holding a drag king exhibition, which makes her question her own identity as she poses for the artist dressed as a man. This allows for a temporary reversal of roles, as Charlotte takes the initiative in the seduction game. Carrie, on her part, is confused by her young boyfriend's sexuality: he claims to be bisexual, which prompts Carrie's reflections:

> Was sexual flipping the wave of the future? And if it was, could I play that game or was I over the hill? If women can transform into men and men can become women, and we can choose to sleep with everyone, then maybe gender doesn't even exist anymore. If we can take the best of the other sex and make it our own, has the opposite sex become obsolete?

Carrie goes with her boyfriend to a party where everybody seems to be bisexual or gay. They play "spin the bottle," and she is forced to kiss a woman. After that, she leaves, thinking she is "too old to play this game." In this way, the show exhibits a wide range of sexualities in this episode but they are not deemed appropriate for its protagonists—Charlotte quickly reverts to her feminine self after her "drag king experience," ashamed of her straightforward attitude. The series does not really condemn sexual "experimentation." It just pins it down to a generational gap: it is the new generations that are open to these options. This strategy allows the series to hold on to a normative heterosexuality while maintaining its "hip," open-minded spirit. The show has been frequently accused of sporting an apparent sexual tolerance when, in fact, it never aims at a serious destabilization of the heterosexual norm (Henry; Greven; Gill; Escudero-Alías). Charlotte's final rejection of her very "evolved" boyfriend and the quick failure of Samantha's lesbian relationship seem to support this view. However, despite its focus on heteronormative models of sexuality, it should be conceded that this was one of the first mainstream cultural texts to allow the inclusion of "peripheral" sexual identities and to explore the question of the elasticity of gender categories. It was thanks to this breakthrough that other, more "progressive" shows, like *Queer as Folk*, *The L Word*, or *Lip Service*, were able to see the light.

Despite *SATC*'s evident preference for heteronormativity, it displays a playful attitude toward sexual labels, openly acknowledging the performative character of gender. By doing this, the show recognizes that there is no such thing as a true "inner self." Rather, we are led to think that we have one, by means of repetition of the different discourses that make up gender roles. Of course, this idea was famously put forward by Judith Butler in *Gender Trouble*, which argues that the binary division of the sexes is a cultural construction meant to keep in place heteronormative identities and hierarchies.[6] As Samantha's lesbian affair shows, *SATC* supports the idea that, rather than a fixed attribute, gender identity is fluid and susceptible to change at given moments in a person's life trajectory. In Butler's words, gender is "a *relation* among socially constituted subjects in specifiable contexts" (*Gender Trouble* 10). It is also a performance, "a kind of imitation for which there is no original; in fact, it is a kind of imitation that produces the very notion of the original as an *effect* and consequence of the imitation itself " (Butler, "Imitation" 127). Despite its focus on heterosexual, upper-class, white identities, *SATC* is willing to acknowledge that no identity is more "real" than any other. If gender is simply a contingent category taken as truth by virtue of discursive repetition, then trendsetting cultural texts like this one, which are aware of gender's provisionality, play a key role in the legitimation and progressive acceptance of nonnormative sexual models.

The replacement of fixed sexual identities with a proliferation of "diverse eroticisms" (Bristow 219) was an innovative, yet well-received theory. However, Butler's contention that not only gender but also sex is a construction was far more controversial. Her theory was regarded as putting forward too idealistic a view of the possibilities for transformation in contemporary sexual politics. Even Butler herself "tamed" her radical opinions on the issue in her book *Bodies That Matter*. Despite this, she does have a point in her contingent view of sex, not so much as biological destiny, but as far as the actual performance of the sexual act is concerned. It can be argued that, in a less explicit way, *SATC* proposes not only that gender is fluid, but that sex itself is also a construction. The episode entitled, "Was It Good for You?" (2:16) questions, once again, the fixity of sexual categories. In this episode, Samantha is asked by a gay couple to join them in bed. Carrie's mild outrage is met by Samantha's more "progressive" views:

Samantha: Wake up. It's 2000. The new millennium won't be about sexual labels, it'll be about sexual expression. It won't matter if you're sleeping with men or women. It'll be about sleeping with individuals.

Carrie: Or in your case, twos or threes.

Samantha: Soon everyone will be pansexual. It won't matter if you're gay or straight.

Carrie: Just if you're good or bad in bed.

Samantha, therefore, does not believe in compartmentalizing people into sexual categories, only in their degree of sexual proficiency. However, who sets the standards for this? Who is entitled to decide if one is good or bad in bed? Throughout its six seasons, the show inadvertently gives a fairly clear definition of what "being good in bed" means, namely, being open to new experiences, uninhibited, and regarding sex as a democratic, recreational activity. What in other contexts might be regarded as shameless promiscuity is simply seen as a healthy sex life in *SATC*. Thanks to the display of a great variety of sexual practices and attitudes, and subsequent discussions about them, a certain view of what sex "is" at the fin de siècle is effectively conveyed. For instance, in "The Turtle and the Hare" (1:9) the girls talk about the "ultimate" sex toy: "the Rabbit." Charlotte does not like the idea of a vibrator replacing a man to obtain sexual gratification, but she agrees to give it a try. Despite her initial qualms, she soon becomes addicted to it, even canceling plans with her friends to stay home with "the Rabbit." This motivates an intervention: Carrie and Miranda storm into her apartment and confiscate the dangerous sex toy. Carrie's voice-over seals the scene thus: "with a little help from her friends, Charlotte decided that she wasn't going to settle for herself."

Despite *SATC*'s usually positive views on female masturbation, this episode makes clear that self-satisfaction may be fun, but it is not considered *real* sex, since it cannot compete with actual sexual intercourse. Masturbation is okay as a pastime, but not as a substitute for the "real thing." This is an example of how the series legitimizes some sexual practices, while leaving others out of the norm: rimming or golden showers are unmistakably rendered as unacceptable and even "deviant" activities. Other practices are also out of the scope of what sex encompasses, being simply characterized as "nonsexual." As we have seen, masturbation is not really taken seriously, and celibacy is considered to be unnatural.[7] However, the show is happy to incorporate oral sex, threesomes, or S/M practices into its repertoire of sexually accepted activities. The arbitrariness of its position toward different sexual practices shows that *SATC*'s discourse toward sex is historically specific, but it also reveals the very constructedness of their perceived legitimacy. It makes evident that no sexual practice is "normal" or "deviant"; they are rather what public discourses make of them. Just like sodomy or oral sex were considered to be aberrant behaviors by law—they were illegal not so long ago and still are in some states—other sexual practices like threesomes or S/M are progressively incorporated into the "norm"—or not—thanks partly to influential cultural texts like this one.

This idea, of course, dovetails with Foucault's conception of sex as a discursive form of entwined power, knowledge, and pleasure. According to Foucault, whoever determines what can be talked about also determines what can be known, that is, has control over sex. In the eighteenth century, medical discourse took on this "empowered" role. Today, the media may be viewed as the successor of science in the public dissemination of discourses about sex. In the eighteenth century, scientific interest in sexual "perversions" actually led to their multiplication. The very fact of labeling them, of paying attention to them, encouraged their expansion. In a similar vein, it can be said that by exposing different ways of understanding sex, programs like *SATC* are partly responsible for their expansion and, in some cases, their creation. Through its focus on sex, the series created a discourse, contributing to its diffusion in the form of new sexual practices, or a greater acceptance—or rejection—of already existing ones. Proof of its active role in the shaping of the way sex is currently perceived in the Western, industrialized world is that today the show does not look as shocking as it did in 1998, when it was first broadcast. Nowadays, representations of sex in popular culture have been taken up a notch in their degree of boldness. A good example of this is HBO's series *Girls*, which is a kind of *SATC* for the angst-ridden generation of "millennials." This show features much more nudity than *SATC* and far more explicit sex scenes. First broadcast in 2012, *Girls* has made a considerable splash in the public opinion, but nothing compared to *SATC*'s impact in its heyday. This shows how our conception of sex and sexuality has changed in roughly a decade or so and how it will, no doubt, continue to change, thanks in part to the media's influence. The media constitutes a cultural forum routinely used by individuals to learn about their social selves, which includes the shaping of expectations and beliefs about sex. Just as other cultural texts speak to different social concerns, shows like *Girls* and *SATC* provide a series of "sexual scripts" (Gagnon and Simon), or blueprints for sexual conduct that are unconsciously taken in by the dominant culture. In this way, these texts open a window to a new field of life politics referred to by Ken Plummer as "intimate citizenship," that is, a "new set of claims around the body, relationships and sexuality," a fourth realm of citizenship that would be added to concerns over civil, political, and social rights (38). *SATC* helped make sense of this realm, giving visibility to these new discourses and contributing to their creation and normalization. *SATC* may not be as "progressive" as some critics would like it to be, but its willingness to engage in the representation of nonnormative sexual identities and a more varied range of sexual practices than traditional vaginal intercourse between an active subject (man) and a passive object (woman) should be acknowledged as a bold step forward in the long road toward a more open-minded—and less phallocentric—culture.

In televisual terms, the show's racy, yet witty and intelligent, brand of humor infused new life into the sitcom genre, pushing its boundaries by allowing for unprecedented levels of explicitness in the treatment of female sexuality on the small screen. Arguably, *SATC*'s distinctiveness lay not only in its readiness to reflect shifting social mores, but in its will to lead the way in this task. This comedic approach to sex broadened the boundaries of what could be said—and seen—on TV, helping expand the range of "legitimate" sexual practices and identities in the process. Because of this, and despite the show's focus on different aspects of female experience, its most enduring legacy will probably be the landmark that it became in its approach to female sexuality. Artistic merits aside, the program set a true craze among women all over the world, and its effects do not seem to have waned more than fifteen years after it was first broadcast, as the enduring popularity of the franchise suggests. *SATC* was able to set sexual trends among women such as Brazilian waxing and remote-controlled sex toys, but more importantly, it revolutionized the way many women conceptualized sex and talked about it, helping them foster a sense of entitlement to more egalitarian sexual relationships at the turn of the millennium. Its protagonists have not only encouraged a new generation of women to find themselves a room of their own; it inspired them to set their sights on an Upper East Side apartment of their own, a high-flying professional career of their own, Manolo Blahniks of their own, and maybe more importantly, a sexuality of their own. I cannot help but wonder: How would Virginia Woolf have felt about Carrie, Samantha, Charlotte, and Miranda?

NOTES

1. A previous version of this section can be found in Beatriz Oria, "What's Love Got to Do with It? *Sex and the City*'s Comic Perspective on Sex," *Journal of Popular Culture* 47.2 (2014).

2. Throughout the six seasons, Samantha has forty-four sexual partners. Carrie is next with twenty. Miranda and Charlotte tie with eighteen (Avins).

3. SATC's creator, Darren Star, openly acknowledges his debt to Allen (Idato).

4. Samantha's views on the fluid relationships between sex, power, and economic status is better described by her thoughts on prostitution: "Money is power. Sex is power. Therefore, getting money for sex is simply an exchange of power" ("The Power of Female Sex," 1:5).

5. Samantha's equation of sexual labels with actual fashion labels reflects how the show's consumerist ethos extends to sexual intercourse as well. This seems to back some authors' claim that sex has been "commodified" today, enmeshed in a capitalist culture of spiraling consumerism. They establish a parallelism between consumerist patterns and contemporary sexual relationships: an individual's sexual desirability is constructed today in terms of ideals of consumption and set according to the parameters of marketable commodities (Evans). Moreover, sexual practices seem to be increasingly adapted to "shopping" habits. For Bauman, "[c]onsumerism is not about accumulating goods . . . but about *using* them and *disposing* of them after use to make room for other goods and their uses" (49). This author establishes the

similarity between this shopping practice and the proliferation of fleeting sexual encounters stripped from any kind of sentimental attachment or social meaning, thus highlighting the expansion of the capitalistic ethos to the realm of intimacy. It is evident that both activities are frequent occurrences in SATC, often becoming associated in the minds of the characters and, consequently, the spectators.

6. This idea has been subsequently discussed by numerous scholars from different fields. In the sociological field, the work of Jeffrey Weeks is especially salient, as he has written extensively about the contingency, diversity, and hybridization of human sexuality (*Sexuality and Its Discontents*; "Invented Moralities"; *Against Nature*; "The Sexual Citizen"; *Making Sexual History*; "Necessary Fictions").

7. Some authors like Sally Cline, Donna Marie Williams, or E. Kay Trimberger have complained about the contemporary stigmatization of celibacy. According to Trimberger, "celibacy does not have a place in the broader legacy of the twentieth century sexual revolution" (41), and she criticizes the idea that sex is necessary for personal happiness and health, as well as central for individual identity.

Chapter Five

With a Little Help from My Friends

New Family Models in Sex and the City

One of the most popular sitcoms of the 1980s was *The Golden Girls* , a show about four elderly women sharing the joys and pains of living without men by their side. These "elderly girls" were able to grapple with the vicissitudes of single life thanks to the security net provided by the family they had built for themselves. Personal problems and "adventures"—whether romantic or not—were routinely discussed in a humorous manner over defrosted cheese-cake around the kitchen table of the house they shared. The similarities between *The Golden Girls* and *SATC* are obvious (Schneider; Griffin and Bolonik; Flett; Macey; Jermyn, *Sex and the City*). The four "golden girls" could very well be Carrie, Samantha, Charlotte, and Miranda thirty years on. *SATC* 's universe gives the impression of being wide, but, like its predecessor, it is in fact a very small microcosm. Despite the great number of men the girls date and the considerable size of their social circle, the text is structured mostly around its four protagonists and their relationships with each other. Even though they do not live under the same roof, these women give the impression of always being together. The conspicuous absence of other meaningful friends in their close circle, as well as biological family members, presents the quartet as a cozy family, just as the *The Golden Girls* were.

The relationship between Carrie, Samantha, Charlotte, and Miranda clear-ly constitutes the show's basic pillar. A great deal of critical writing has revolved around this dimension of the show (Avins; Gerhard; Gennaro; Koh-li; Jermyn, "In Love with Sarah Jessica Parker"; Jermyn, *Sex and the City*; Winch) and some authors have emphasized the connection between female friendship and the program's feminist messages (Kim; Henry; Gerhard; Clark). However, as I have pointed out earlier, my aim is not to discuss the

135

nuances of *SATC*'s feminist allegiance. Rather, this book is more interested in the exploration of the discourses proposed by the show in the fields of intimacy and interpersonal relationships, which has led me so far to the analysis of its protagonists' relationships with the opposite sex. Issues like romance, intimacy, sex, and sexuality occupy a central position in the series and are explicitly addressed in every episode. However, the program also deals with another kind of intimacy that should be examined: same-sex friendship. Although it is rarely the object of direct interrogation in the series, this does not diminish its centrality, since it arguably constitutes the text's backbone. Albeit more implicitly dealt with, the relationship between the four female protagonists represents an overarching theme in the series, and its real leitmotif. Thus, this chapter aims to explore *SATC*'s treatment of friendship in connection with the conventions of the romantic comedy genre, showing how "families of choice" are presented as a viable alternative to the "family of fate," or biological family, and even to the heterosexual couple. With this purpose in mind, I will analyze the series' highly anticipated finale, "An American Girl in Paris: Part Une (6:19) and "An American Girl in Paris: Part Deux" (6:20). The first part of this chapter will provide an overview of the transformations that the institution of the family has undergone in the last decade and the role played by the increasing importance of friendship in this process. However, before doing so, I would like to comment briefly on the representation of the family in the U.S. sitcom before the appearance of *SATC*.

FAMILY MATTERS

Even though the family has always been a favorite topic of U.S. media, the sitcom genre has been particularly preoccupied with its representation. From the very beginnings of the genre, in the 1940s, the family has stood at the center of the genre's thematic concerns. The sitcoms of the 1950s and 1960s affirmed traditional American values in their depiction of nuclear families that portrayed a conservative image of daily life. Shows like *I Love Lucy, The Adventures of Ozzie and Harriet, Father Knows Best, Honeymooners, Leave It to Beaver, The Dick Van Dyke Show, The Brady Bunch,* and *The Partridge Family* depicted families that "appeared as the unquestioned bastion from which virtually all social interaction flowed. . . . The nuclear family was first and foremost the center of everyday life, the pillar of traditional gender relations and social order, a conduit of socialization processes" (Boggs 449). The social changes brought about by the 1970s and 1980s motivated new family scenarios, but not a loss of traditional family values, with "characters desperately trying to hold onto them under a tidal wave of societal change" (Crotty 10) in series like *Good Times, Chico and the Man, Welcome Back,*

Kotter, Who's the Boss?, Family Ties, The Cosby Show, Full House, Just the Ten of Us, and *Growing Pains.* The 1990s also featured a majority of sitcoms depicting "relatively stable, two-parent families" (Zoglin 33), like *Home Fires, The Wonder Years, Major Dad, Family Matters , The Fresh Prince of Bel-Air, Blossom, Step by Step, The Nanny,* and *Brooklyn Bridge.* However, more eccentric families also started to crop up on the small screen, like *Roseanne, The Simpsons, Married . . . with Children, Frasier,* and *Unhappily Ever After.* These shows offered different views of the meanings of family life in the last decade of the century. Some of them were even controversial, but they did not really represent an attack on the family in itself: the target was rather TV's sentimentalized depiction of it (Crotty). The 1990s also witnessed a proliferation of sitcoms depicting surrogate families, like *Ellen, Spin City, Just Shoot Me, Will & Grace, Seinfeld, Friends,* and *SATC.* The tendency toward the replacement of the biological family with a circle of friends or work colleagues goes back to shows like *The Mary Tyler Moore Show, Night Court,* or *Cheers,* but the unstable condition of the family in the 1990s encouraged the flourishing of this kind of sitcom, which symbolized its increasingly fragmented state (Mills, *Television Sitcom*). In the 2000s and early 2010s, surrogate families like those depicted in *Scrubs, The Office, How I Met Your Mother, 30 Rock, Entourage, The Big Bang Theory, Veep, Girls, Happy Endings, Two Broke Girls, Don't Trust the B*** in Apartment 23, Men at Work,* and *New Girl* tended to prevail over biological ones. However, this does not mean that the latter have altogether disappeared from the TV grid: shows like *Two and a Half Men, Family Guy, American Dad, Big Love, Californication, Modern Family, Shameless,* and *The New Normal* offer updated versions of the contemporary biological family, incorporating new discourses and family configurations. However, whether surrogate or biological, and despite these shows' various degrees of irony toward media depictions of the family, traditional values and beliefs remain fundamentally unchallenged. One such belief is the security and well-being it provides for the individual and its ultimate intrinsic value above everything else. As Carl Boggs argues, "the idealized notion that the family lives on as the moral, psychological, social, and of course material center of personal life remains probably as strong today as ever, despite vast challenges and changes that are visible for any interested observer to see" (449).[1]

Some writers have argued that TV has not been sufficiently adept at representing these changes so far. Vivien Burr and Christine Jarvis, for instance, think that TV images of the family are largely out of touch with the reality of family life for most people and they "fail to represent the diversity of living arrangements that actually exist today" (264). Yet this view does not account for the whole of the spectator's experience of sitcoms. As the previous lines show, television may have chosen to ignore certain social changes in the past—as was the case with the 1960s sitcoms, which continued to affirm traditional family values in the face of increasing divorce rates—but it is not so reluctant to reflect new social trends at the turn of the millennium as it may have been before. My analysis will hopefully show how some TV programs, like *SATC*, are more than willing to lead the way in the representation of alternative models to the traditional family that are more in tune with their context. With this purpose in mind, I will first sketch the state of this institution at the time *SATC* was broadcast.

WELCOME TO THE FAMILY: FROM "FAMILIES OF FATE" TO "FAMILIES OF CHOICE"

In episode 13 of the first season of *Modern Family*, Jay, the "patriarch," describes his family life thus: "I used to be just like one of those guys. Now look at me: I've got a house that looks like little Colombia, I've got a gay son, and a Chinese granddaughter." Jay is played by Ed O'Neill, the same actor who portrayed Al, the head of the family in *Married . . . with Children* twenty years earlier. Like *Modern Family*, *Married . . . with Children* also displayed a caustic view of the institution of family, but the differences between both series in terms of their basic configurations are obvious: while *Married . . . with Children* presented a relatively "traditional" two-parent home with biological children, in 2009 *Modern Family* includes a South American young wife and stepson, a gay couple, and an adopted Asian granddaughter.

The drive to depict the changing status of family life has been accompanied by a growing preoccupation with family issues in the field of social work theory. Debates about the state of the family have intensified at the end of the century without much agreement among social commentators. Broadly speaking, three main tendencies can be identified: those who perceive recent social changes as those portrayed in *Modern Family* as the end of the institution; those who argue that the traditional family is stronger than ever; and a more moderate position that speaks of pluralism in contemporary family configurations (Beck and Beck-Gernsheim, *Individualization*). The only thing critics seem to agree on is the fact that contemporary Western societies are undergoing sizeable changes that are having a remarkable impact on the family as social institution (Stacey; Burghes; Nicholson; Silva and Smart; Allan, *The Sociology of the Family*). The traditional family seems to be today more of an ideal than a reality, as an unprecedented diversity of family configurations become the norm rather than the exception in industrialized societies (Furlong and Cartmel; Cheal; Roseneil). These include the rise of single-parent homes, the increase in one-person households, or the heightened visibility and tolerance toward homosexual lifestyles. This "breakdown" of tradition is put down to multiple reasons, like women's economic independence, or the growing belief in greater sexual freedom, which has brought about the contemporary disconnection between sex and marriage (Ashbee). The tendency toward a more "democratic" kind of intimacy—which has already been discussed in this book—also prevents people from staying in unsatisfactory relationships: Giddens's "pure relationship" has probably contributed to the fleeting nature of the heterosexual union today. Actually, the high incidence of divorce is frequently blamed as the predominant factor in the reorganization of contemporary family life. The divorce rate rose steadily through the 1960s and 1970s in the United States, reaching a peak during the 1980s at just under 2.4 million per year (McLaren). During the 1990s, this rate declined slightly, but 50 percent of marriages were still "doomed" to end in divorce (MacCoby). The traditional family has not fared any better during the 2000s. The U.S. Census Bureau's figures show that married couples with children made up only 30 percent of all households in 2010. This means that what used to be the exception is becoming the new "normal": the seventy-four million single adults in the United States could soon define the new majority. This new panorama, which includes single parents, stepfamilies, cohabitation, gay partnerships, and a divorce rate of 50 percent, worries and alarms a sizeable sector of social commentators, who perceive these changes as a signal of moral decline (Popenoe; Dench; L. Ingraham, Scruton, "Becoming a Family"; Wilson; Tubbs and George; Hymowitz, "It's Morning After in America," "Gay Marriage vs. American Marriage," "I Wed Thee, and Thee, and Thee," "Marriage and Caste"). Other authors, however, believe that the family is not in decline, just changing (Gubrium and Holstein; Stacey; Skolnick; Coontz). Some argue that "change" does not necessarily mean "problem" (Smart and Neale; Featherstone) and warn us against the nostalgic idealization of a "blissful" past family life (Gillis; Smart and Neale).

Beck and Beck-Gernsheim disregard black-and-white approaches to the state of the contemporary family and point at individualization processes as one of the main reasons for the changes undergone by the institution. Individualization has not only affected the dynamics of the romantic couple; it has infiltrated family life too, giving way to an unprecedented multiplicity in the way people choose to organize their family life. The word "choose" is key here, as contemporary families are increasingly determined by choice rather than by biological destiny. The replacement of the "normal life history" with the "do-it-yourself" pattern in the life of the individual has run parallel to the evolution from a "community of need" in preindustrial societies to the "communities of choice" made possible by the welfare state. Beck and Beck-Gernsheim see individualization processes as a basic historical trend that "increasingly characterizes relations among members of the same family. A shorthand way of saying this is that a community of need is becoming an elective relationship. The family is not breaking up as a result; it is acquiring a new historical form" (*Individualization* 85). This new historical form is acknowledged by authors like Smart and Neale, and Featherstone, who argue in favor of expanding the meanings of the term "family," thus reflecting the wider range of relationships that are meaningful to people today. Among these relationships, friendship appears to have acquired an increasing importance.

For Allan Silver, friendship is being privileged over other types of relationships as the essence of modern personal life. He perceives it as "a continuous creation of personal will and choice . . . an ideal arena for that individualized conception of personal agency central to modern notions of personal freedom" (46). The increasingly important role of friendship as enabler of the individual's autonomy is intimately linked to the development of a sense of self. Friends become crucial agents in the process of discovering one's identity, providing a space for self-development. As Graham Little puts it, "friends are the great agents of self-discovery: they show us who we are when we are not at home" (245). This view is also supported by Watters's study of "urban tribes," which confirms that those individuals effectively engaged in the dynamics of friendship are able to become themselves not in spite of peer pressure, but as a result of it (72). In this way, there appears to be a growing tendency to replace traditional communities of fate with chosen social circles that seem to be displaying a high degree of competence, not only in allowing individuals to make sense of the world and helping them better develop a sense of self (Allan, "Personal Relationships"; Spencer and Pahl; Goodwin), but also in enhancing their self-respect and creating a safety net that diminishes one's level of anxiety when faced with important decisions or risks (Watters).

Although these changes have encountered a considerable degree of resistance in the last two decades,[2] the truth is that families of choice are not something new—they have been functioning for a long time now in the gay community. The tendency toward the valorization of friends as a substitute for families of fate started, as in the case of the "pure relationship," in the midst of the homosexual community. In the face of rejection from their biological families, gay people were the first to build a personal network of support for themselves that would play the roles usually fulfilled by the traditional family (Weston; Sullivan; Weeks, Heaphy, and Donovan; Allan, "Personal Relationships"; Watters). Allan argues that "family belonging is represented and achieved through the routine activities of doing family" ("Flexibility" 10). Being a family nowadays thus becomes something you "do" as opposed to the social configuration in which you are born. It becomes a construction, and, as in the case of gender, a performance: "how we perform 'family' is shaped by material as well as cultural practices that are often invisible to us" (Naples 33). In this way, it could be said that the homosexual community is way ahead of heterosexuals in the "performance of family." This understanding of the family as a cultural construction rather than a fixed entity allows for its constant reorganization in the face of changing living conditions. As we have seen, an egalitarian intimate model based on friendship—the "pure relationship"—is largely taken as the ideal in romantic interactions today. According to this, it makes sense that contemporary notions of the family are modified and adapted to new ideals of intimacy.

The increasing importance of the role played by friendship in the formation of contemporary families of choice in the heterosexual community[3] may be pinned down to changing social factors like growing rates of cohabitation and divorce, greater social and geographical mobility, increased female independence and integration in the labor market, and the growth of nonheterosexual living arrangements. As a result, the circle of significant people in one's life may no longer be restricted to the biological family (Pahl and Spencer). According to a survey carried out in the United States, 70 percent of people seemed to think that the best definition of family today is "people who love each other," as opposed to "people related by blood" or "people who live together" (Watters 131). This view provides an even ampler meaning of what the concept of "family" is able to encompass nowadays, placing friendship in a privileged position.

Spencer and Pahl use the term "personal community" in order to refer to this new situation of "suffusion" between family and friendship ties. They define personal communities as the "context of significant others who inhabit our micro-social worlds" (2). They give structure and meaning to individuals' lives, helping them to develop a sense of identity and belonging and providing a "biographical anchor" for the individual. In their analysis of the blurring of boundaries between friendship and kinship, Spencer and Pahl exhibit a cautious attitude toward clear-cut statements about the prevalence of one or the other, concluding instead that both "categories" have become inextricably mixed today in a complex dynamic characterized by a variety of possible permutations and combinations. Other writers are not as moderate in their opinions: Robert Goss and Jeffrey Weeks firmly believe in chosen communities as the preferred social organization of the future: "[w]e are witnessing the development and public affirmation of 'families of choice,'" Weeks, Heaphy, and Donovan conclude categorically (9). From a less empirical position, Watters defends a similar view, coining the term "urban tribe" to describe his own personal experience of this phenomenon. Unlike Spencer and Pahl's "personal communities," urban tribes constitute a more friendship-focused and urban approach to contemporary community formation. In urban environments, people are more involved with friends than kin. Studies show that, unlike popular belief, urbanism does not promote isolation. On the contrary, it makes a greater diversity of subcultures possible, since it provides increased opportunities to find like-minded others. These urban tribes are not just random collections of friends, but "functioning social entities" with differentiated and well-defined roles among their members (Watters 48). For Watters, the so-called loss of "community spirit" and "social capital" in American society mourned by authors like Robert D. Putnam has been recently resurrected thanks to urban tribes. Against the widespread view that the increasing number of singles is detrimental to this feeling of community, Watters thinks that urban tribes help foster community, and not just for their members, but for cities as a whole. Moreover, he argues that "social capital" is consistently integrated in the dynamic of the tribe. However, the fluid nature of urban tribes and their informal exchange of social capital make them highly fuzzy entities. Due to their freely chosen, elective nature, these groups are naturally formed and dissolved and have no clear limits or boundaries of belonging. As a result, they remain largely invisible to society as a whole. Unlike traditional family configurations, tribes lack a social narrative that validates the importance of their existence in present-day society.

As we shall see, the role played by popular media texts like *SATC* should not be underestimated in the process of acceptance, normalization, and expansion of "alternative" conceptions of social organizations to the traditional family. According to Barbara Caine, the general pessimism about friendship among social scientists that dominated the 1970s and 1980s contrasts powerfully with popular culture's celebration of friendship during the 1990s. TV shows like *thirtysomething, Friends, Will & Grace,* and *SATC* made friendship fashionable, so to speak. However, it was not just friendship that it was idealized. Female solidarity was especially singled out as the locus of personal satisfaction and well-being. For Caine, the 1990s made clear "the ways in which female friendships became even more central to popular as well as academic versions of ideal bonds" (319). This is even more obvious in cinema: on the big screen, there was a particularly successful cycle of films revolving around the pleasures of female friendship during the 1990s, with movies like *Thelma and Louise* (1991), *Bar Girls* (1994), *Boys on the Side* (1995), *Moonlight and Valentino* (1995), *How to Make an American Quilt* (1995), *Now and Then* (1995), *Waiting to Exhale* (1995), *The Baby-Sitters Club* (1995), and *The Incredibly True Adventures of Two Girls in Love* (1995) (Hollinger). In the 2000s, Alison Winch points out the preponderance of "girlfriend culture," which is now felt across a range of different media forms, such as film, TV, magazines, conduct books, and digital networking sites.[4] If television and film are a form of a "consensus narrative in which beliefs, values and characters are rehearsed, tested, challenged, confirmed and revised" (Caine 338), then the media's celebration of friendship—and more specifically, female friendship—at the turn of the century as a potential substitute for "obsolete" forms of intimacy must be taken into account in cultural analysis.

THE TIES THAT BIND: FEMALE FRIENDSHIP IN
SEX AND THE CITY

"I've never been friends with men. Women are for friendships, men are for fucking" ("Ex and the City," 2:18). In this succinct manner, Samantha summarizes the essence of her relationships with both sexes. In a way, this phrase constitutes a pretty accurate summary of *SATC*'s whole ethos: lovers and husbands may come and go, but the girls' bond is here to stay. This chapter aims to prove that, despite the centrality of "fucking" in *SATC*'s story lines, it is "friendships" that really structure the text. In a series that emphasizes the volatile state of relationships between the sexes, female bonding is presented as a safe haven, able to provide the individual with stability and satisfy his or her every need. As other TV shows did during the 1990s, the ensemble cast is unequivocally presented as a close-knit family, a self-sufficient unit of its own. My analysis focuses on the show's finale, but examples that illustrate the importance of female sisterhood in the series are manifold. For instance, when Miranda gets pregnant, her first instinct is to have an abortion, but she finally decides not to do it. When she tells the girls, Charlotte screams excitedly "We're going to have a baby!" ("Coulda, Woulda, Shoulda," 4:11). True to these words, it is Carrie that accompanies Miranda in the delivery room ("I Heart New York," 4:18) and she becomes the baby's godmother ("Unoriginal Sin," 5:2). As Watters pointed out, friends are constantly presented as a consistent safety net in times of crisis, fulfilling the role traditionally played by the biological family. This is constantly foregrounded by the series, and even made visually explicit in "The Catch" (6:8), which presents friends as a support system for scary situations.

The episode entitled "Shortcomings" (2:15) deals with "family issues" directly, contrasting families of fate and families of choice. Carrie is dating a writer, which gives her the opportunity to integrate herself into his "hip" biological family. When she realizes that she is more attracted to his wonderful family—and especially to his mother—than to him, she feels forced to break up with "them"[5] and go back to her friends, who are presented as Carrie's real family: "Wallis was right. The most important thing in life is your family. There are days you love them, and others you don't. But in the end, they're the people you always come home to. Sometimes it's the family you're born into. And sometimes it's the one you make for yourself."[6] Carrie's voice-over is foregrounded by the visuals: a very cozy scene of the four friends in a restaurant, laughing together merrily, evoking the traditional family we have just seen but without its tensions, in a much more relaxed atmosphere. This visual technique is frequently used in the series in order to underscore the group's "togetherness": at the end of many episodes, the camera usually focuses on the girls' "chat-and-chew" sessions, slowly pull-

Figure 5.1. Carrie's "safety net."

ing back to reveal the intimacy of the warm microcosm they form in the midst of Manhattan's hectic panorama of crowded restaurants and clubs.

This technique is also used in "Take Me Out to the Ball Game" (2:1). This episode highlights the importance of friends after a romantic breakup. Formally, this is conveyed in a climactic way by the episode's ending. Carrie's encounter with Big after their split upsets her a lot. She leaves her current date to make a phone call. The conversation is ambiguous: it looks like she is asking Big to meet her because she really needs to talk. When she arrives at the meeting place, suspense is built about the identity of Carrie's date. The camera pans, and hidden behind a waiter, we are surprised to find Miranda—with whom she had had a fight—not Big. Miranda apologizes for her behavior and offers her support to Carrie. The last shot shows the two women "framed" by the window, inhabiting the same space. It is raining, so the contrast between the terrible weather outside and the warmth of the coffee shop highlights the intimate atmosphere between the friends. This image is accompanied by Carrie's words, which stress the importance of her bond with Miranda above any man: "and finally, the most important breakup rule: no matter who broke your heart or how long it takes to heal . . . you'll never get through it without your friends." In this episode, Miranda takes the place of Big, subverting our expectations. Indeed, not only do friends serve

Figure 5.2. A cozy family.

as a substitute for the biological family in the series, they also frequently replace the roles normally filled by men. For instance, when Miranda's mother dies, the real tragedy in people's eyes seems to be her singleness. In this episode, Carrie takes on the role of a male partner by walking down the aisle with her ("My Motherboard, Myself," 4:8).

Similarly, when Carrie has financial difficulties, Big gives her a check, but unwilling to owe anything to a man, she prefers to accept Charlotte's help instead. In a moment rife with symbolism, Charlotte offers Carrie her beloved engagement ring to make the down payment for her flat. Carrie has just broken up with Aidan, and Charlotte has recently divorced Trey. The episode ends with a literal exchange of vows, with Charlotte asking if Carrie will accept the ring, and Carrie saying, "I do" ("Ring a Ding Ding," 4:16).

SATC repeatedly emphasizes the self-sufficiency of the group in coping with anything. In "Four Women and a Funeral" (2:5) it is Miranda who purchases her own apartment. Everybody around her is surprised that she is buying it on her own, which makes her paranoid about never finding a man and dying alone and eaten by her cat. In the end, the sense of security offered by her friends fills the gap of the "missing" partner, which is visually conveyed by having Miranda place a photo of the group on the chimney place—a spot usually reserved for family pictures. Many episodes, like this one,

Figure 5.3.   Carrie accompanies Miranda at her mother's funeral.

convey the idea that friendship compensates for the shortcomings of romantic relationships. Others, however, seem to go a step further, implying that
friendship is actually a more desirable state than heterosexual coupling. As
Carrie reflects in "Bay of Married Pigs" (1:3): "It'd be great to have that one
special person to walk home with . . . but sometimes there's nothing better
than meeting your single girlfriends for a night at the movies." As will be
seen, this view has relevant implications in the way the text conceptualizes
the "happy ending." The uncertainty of today's intimate panorama has sometimes led romantic comedy to eschew the traditional "happily ever after" for
the "happy right now" (Mernit; Deleyto; Azcona). This seems to be the case
in *SATC*: due to its serial form, provisional "happy endings" replace the
absolute "happily ever after" of traditional romantic comedy. However, as
my analysis hopes to show, *SATC* pushes the boundaries of the meanings
encompassed by this happy ending in order to incorporate friendship as the
primary reason for the genre's mirth. In "The Post-it Always Sticks Twice"
(6:7), once more, Carrie gets over a bad breakup thanks to her friends. The
provisional character of this happy ending of sorts is underlined by the voice-
over, which says: "I might never find the lesson in why Berger and I split.
But at least, for the moment, there was a banana split," referring to the ice
cream Carrie is gleefully enjoying in the company of her friends. It is the

merry moment shared with Charlotte, Miranda, and Samantha that wraps up the episode, conveying the feeling of fulfillment usually reserved for the heterosexual couple.

The issue of happy endings is explicitly addressed in "Don't Ask, Don't Tell" (3:12). Charlotte is about to get the "happily ever after" she always wanted, as she is about to marry Trey in a big, lavish wedding. For Samantha, marriage does not guarantee a happy ending, "just an ending." Her words prove to be prophetic as the episode unfolds: Charlotte sleeps with Trey for the first time the night before the wedding (she had been saving herself for him in a romantic gesture) and she is appalled at the realization that he is impotent, but she decides to go on with the ceremony. The wedding coincides with the breakup of Miranda's and Carrie's respective relationships. Thus, the girls are single again, and Charlotte is headed for a very difficult marriage that will end up in divorce. This makes the episode's "happily ever after" problematic, to say the least. However, the very last scene does provide a happy ending for this episode: despite their respective romantic disappointments, the four women pose together, smiling for a family picture, reassured in the knowledge that they still have each other. This is confirmed by Carrie's voice-over: "It's hard to find people who will love you no matter what. I was lucky enough to find three of them," thus implying that, unlike the heterosexual couple, friendship is the true locus of unconditional love these days.

In what follows I will try to show how the convention of the happy ending is affected by the important role played by friendship in the show. The issue of friendship will also be related to another important convention of the genre: the magic space of romantic comedy. With this purpose in mind, I will analyze the series' finale, which comprises two episodes ("An American Girl in Paris: Part Une," 6:19; "An American Girl in Paris: Part Deux," 6:20).

WHAT IF I HAD NEVER MET YOU?
FRIENDSHIP AND HAPPY ENDINGS

It seems appropriate to end a book with the ending of its object of analysis. Since this chapter aims to consider the convention of the happy ending, the choice of episodes seemed obvious. *SATC* ended in February of 2004. Followed by a record audience of 10.6 million viewers (Braxton, "'Sex,' Regis, and 'Fiance'"), the show's finale was a highly anticipated event. At this point in the series, Carrie seems to have found sentimental stability thanks to Aleksandr Petrovsky, an internationally known Russian artist. After innumerable breakups and reconciliations with Big, she decides it is time to settle with someone else. The problem comes when Petrovsky asks her to move to Paris with him. This happens in the previous episode ("Splat!" 6:18). Carrie

Figure 5.4.   Family portrait.

is hesitant at first. Besides, her friends—Miranda, especially—object strongly to the idea: basically, Petrovsky's offer, generous as it is, entails Carrie's
total dependence on him. She will be living in his apartment in a foreign city,
with no friends and no job. Since Carrie's work consists of chronicling New
York's sociosexual scene, it cannot be carried out anywhere else. Miranda's,
Charlotte's, and Samantha's endless questions about the possibility of her
moving to Paris bother Carrie. As always, they try to examine the question in
depth so that she can make an informed decision, but Carrie does not see it
that way this time, and becomes upset. Once alone, she reflects on the issue:

> They say the unexamined life is not worth living. But what if the examining
> becomes your life? Is that living or just procrastinating? And what if all those
> helpful lunches and late night phone calls to friends have made us all girl talk
> and no girl action? Is it time to stop questioning?

For the first time, the show throws into question the self-reflective ethos on
which it is based. It wonders whether it is time to stop thinking so much
about things and start to take action. This is what Carrie eventually does in
this episode. However, the end of the series proves that unreflective action is
not a good idea, since Carrie's impulsive behavior turns out to be deeply
mistaken. The show's conclusion will end up endorsing the self-analytical

ethos the series has maintained all along as a central component of contemporary intimate life, in which talk about relationships seems to be more meaningful than the relationships themselves.

Carrie has doubts, but her mind is suddenly made up after she attends a party with Petrovsky. There she meets Lexi (Kristen Johnston), an old friend of hers from her younger, wilder years. Lexi is the only single woman at the party and she is clearly out of place: loud, obnoxious, inappropriately dressed as if she were twenty, and doing cocaine to keep her spirits up, she paints a rather pathetic picture of singleness at forty. Her inadequacy is disproportionally "punished" by the text with death, as she falls out of a window while trying to smoke a cigarette—something nobody does anymore in New York in the 2000s. For a show that claims to celebrate single life, Lexi's character paints a shockingly negative picture of this particular single woman. It is a rather extreme way of suggesting what may happen to a woman if she is still single at forty. It seems as if the show is finally drawing the line in its celebration of singleness—the line being the forty-year-old barrier. The fact that such a tragic character was the "it" girl in the 1980s indicates that Carrie's mocking words at her funeral ("if you are single in New York, after a certain point, there is nowhere to go but down") may not be so tongue in cheek at the end of the series as they were at the beginning. Of course, it can be argued that this incident can be read as a narrative device to justify Carrie's sudden decision to leave her beloved New York behind in pursuit of the "happily ever after" she is running out of time to attain. On the other hand, the fact that her decision eventually proves to be wrong problematizes this episode's apparent demonization of singleness. Before the episode ends, Miranda and Carrie have a quarrel: Miranda tries to make her see that her life in New York is her real self and that she cannot leave it all behind to live her boyfriend's life, but Carrie does not come around. Miranda's diagnosis is clear: Carrie is living a fantasy, something that is visually confirmed by the last scene in the episode, a rather impossible image of Petrovsky and Carrie riding a horse-drawn sleigh through Central Park.

In tune with Miranda's words, *SATC*'s conclusion does feel like a fairytale fantasy, and can be read as such. The finale feels like a self-contained unit: its Parisian location, the longer running time of the last episode, and the explicit desire on the part of the text to present the last two episodes as a unique "whole" by means of their titles (Part Une and Part Deux) emphasizes its distinctiveness from the rest of the series. In fact, it could be said that the show's finale can almost be seen as a short film, an autonomous entity within the series. The abundant filming on location in the streets of Paris and the strong focus on Carrie's story to the detriment of the usual polyphonic structure reinforce these episodes' difference from the rest.

Now It's Different

The penultimate episode starts with Carrie's packing for Paris. While she packs, she listens to her phone messages. She has three: one from Petrovsky, who is already in Paris; one from Big, who is in town and wants to see her (which she deletes); and one from Miranda. Three weeks have gone by since their row and they seem to have made up, but Miranda has not changed her opinion about Carrie's decision and, as her message suggests, she has been trying to dissuade her during this time. As the previous episode had made clear, Miranda does not like Petrovsky. Her opposition to Carrie's decision to start a new life with him in Paris thus makes her decision even harder. Watters argues that the individual's integration in a "tribe" may reduce their possibilities of settling for a definitive partner. On the one hand, the comfortable safety and familiarity of the tribe renders romantic relationships lacking by comparison. The need to divide one's loyalty also prevents coupling: tribes create "an emotional life that in its fullness and scope would inevitably conflict with the beginnings of a serious romance. One might have the emotional energy to date casually while in the tribe, but investing in a serious relationship usually required a choice of where one's loyalty lay" (190). On the other hand, Watters points out that, today, friends have taken up the role of family in approving of or vetoing romantic partners. However, unlike parents, the tribe's reaction to a new mate is usually based on the perception of whether he or she is going to steal away the established member. Petrovsky is literally stealing Carrie away from her friends, and it is natural that Miranda feels negative about it. On the other hand, it is plain to see that the comfortable safety net that Carrie's friends had built for her so far may have prevented her from venturing into more complex romantic endeavors, such as the one she is about to take up. In this sense, Carrie's move away from the group represents a necessary step for the personal development of the individual in Watters's eyes, but not in the show's ethos, as its conclusion will reveal: for the series, the key to one's growth lies precisely in the integration within the tribe.

Carrie is rushing out of her apartment to have dinner for the last time with her friends before leaving for Paris that very night when she meets Big. His black limousine is parked at her door, and despite Carrie's qualms, he persuades her to get in. He wants to give their relationship another chance. The situation is all too familiar. Big and Carrie have discussed their relationship inside his limo countless times before. In fact, there is a clear similarity between this scene and the one previously analyzed in this book, when Carrie was about to accept Aidan's marriage proposal and Big "rescued" her from the New York traffic. As was the case then, Carrie is now about to take a very important step in her life. The parallelism between these two scenes serves to remind us that, no matter how many lovers Carrie has, Big is always there, popping up in the background. However, the difference between both scenes is that Big occupies a different position now. When Carrie was with Aidan, Big seemed to be the "wrong partner," as Aidan appeared to be a much more suitable option. This time, however, Big is placed in the position of the "right partner" (Neale, "The Big Romance"): he is "the One " for Carrie, but according to the codes of the romantic comedy genre, she does not know it yet. Something has to happen for her to realize this. In a traditional romantic comedy, characters usually have clearly assigned positions. The roles of right and wrong partners tend to be evident from the beginning. *SATC*'s formal structure, on the other hand, makes it necessary to complicate these roles. Big has alternated between both functions throughout the series, but his resilient presence during six seasons and Carrie's incapability to forget him makes clear that he represents her mythical "twin soul." Of course, the show's constant change of heart as far as Big's role is concerned is a symptom not only of the series' postfeminist ambivalence about Mr. Right's actual features, but also of the volatility and uncertainty that characterizes the contemporary romantic panorama: telling the heroes from the villains of the story is not as easy as it used to be, as both roles stand confusingly close to one another.

As the unfolding of Carrie's fairy tale will reveal, this time Big plays the role of the right partner. The ending will make clear that he is Carrie's real "knight in shining armor," with its white horse having been conveniently adapted to the consumerist spirit of the series. Big's black limo is one of the series' most recognizable props, encapsulating all of his economic might. As Cas Wouters argues, in popular culture texts it is power that makes men erotically appealing. In romance stories, "women need to look up to a man before they are willing to nestle in his arms" (200). All of the men presented as potential romantic partners for the girls meet this requirement: Richard Wright (James Remar), Trey, Aidan, or Petrovsky certainly occupied a superior position than the women they wooed. Those suitors who did not live up to the show's socioeconomic requirements were finally dismissed—as in the case of Jack Berger (Ron Livingston), Carrie's "unsuccessful" writer—or "upgraded" in their socioeconomic status, like Steve and Smith (Jason Lewis), who were suddenly transformed into bar owner and movie star, respectively, in order to qualify as Miranda's and Samantha's partners. According to this criterion, it is evident that Big is the most desirable of all the men that have cropped up in *SATC*'s ninety-four episodes. Petrovsky is a well-known artist and very well off financially, but as the very first episode in the series makes clear, Big is the wealthiest character in the show by far, having been described as "the next Donald Trump" in the pilot episode. He has the whole package. In sum, he is *SATC*'s Mr. Darcy.

At this point, Carrie is not aware of this yet. On the contrary, she feels upset by Big's declaration. Of course, as those familiar with the conventions of romantic comedy know, the "knight" will need to surmount certain obstacles in order to win the damsel's heart. However, the viewer's response to the all-too-familiar romantic plot is not so straightforward here. Having accompanied Carrie through the ups and downs of her relationship with Big and having witnessed his often inconsiderate behavior toward her, Big's status as right partner is in tension with the feeling of satisfaction that Carrie's rejection may provoke in the audience. His "now it's different" speech is met by Carrie's angry reproach. She yells at him, criticizing his constant "jerking her around." Every time she is in a successful relationship with someone, Big reappears in her life to spoil everything, and she is fed up with the situation. Enraged, she shouts in his face: "This is it, I am done! Don't call me, ever again! Forget you know my number! In fact, forget you know my name!" before walking away. This is the first time that Carrie shows such a self-assertive attitude with Big in the series. Seeing her set her boundaries in this way conveys a sense of empowerment that problematizes the viewer's allegiance to the traditional resolution of Big and Carrie's love story.

Still upset, Carrie meets her friends for their last dinner together. She discusses the incident with them, expressing her indignation with Big's attitude over the years: "Now that I'm with someone else, now that I'm leaving, it's different. . . . Fuck him! And you know I never say that." The girls' "chat and chew" sessions are usually devoted to the examination of some question or problem one of the characters has. In this case, there is no question to analyze: Carrie seems highly self-assured in her position, and all she wants is to release her frustration with the whole situation. The group of friends is thus able to fulfill different functions, all of them aimed at helping the individual in the development of her self-identity, fulfilling a therapeutic role and serving as a form of self-help (Kohli). The friendship network helps its members make decisions about their lifestyle choices and provides emotional support once these decisions have been made. Friendship in the series functions as a vehicle for self-knowledge, not only for the character who does the talking, as is the case with Carrie this time, but also for her listeners. In the dynamics established between fictional female friends, a mirroring relationship is usually established: "[b]y trying to know and understand her female friends, a woman comes to know herself, and through this self-knowledge she can begin to understand not only her friend's situation, but her own. In other words, identification in female friendship is a means of mutual recognition and interpretation" (Hollinger 15). Friendship thus becomes a self-reflexive process that contributes to the shaping of the identities of all the members in the group, and—in the case of *SATC*—the audience's as well, as they are invited to feel as part of the conversation.

It has been suggested that fictional representations of female friendships, such as *SATC*'s, are able to powerfully engage their female audience in their own quest for self-development (Gardiner). *SATC*'s viewer is invited to join the characters in their bonding experience. By means of identification with the different subject positions offered by the text, the audience is able to engage in its own process of self-understanding. This theory would partly account for the show's unexpected success. The huge fan following it earned may be somehow explained by the program's efficient provision of a vicarious bonding experience to its audience that assisted them in their own processes of self-definition. In this sense, the show would have a positive effect on its audience: for Hollinger, representations of fictional female friendships "validate their female audience, instilling in them the self-confidence they need to interact more productively with other women and to cultivate more involvement in both private and public spheres" (245). Moreover, she thinks that viewers "are encouraged to alter their identities in accord with the identity transformations enacted by the characters" (21). According to this, Carrie's assertive attitude in this scene, which is backed by the group's validation, would constitute a positive model of female self-affirmation that could serve as an inspiring example for some members of its audience. This idea is actually supported by Jermyn's small-scale audience reception study of the show. Her research shows how the female fans of the series actually got together to watch it, mirroring the bonding experience taking place on screen. The study confirmed that these fans regarded the show as a potential source of empowerment, as they put the emphasis on female sisterhood rather than on romantic entanglements ("In Love with Sarah Jessica Parker"). The scene under analysis is a case in point of the kind of empowerment usually provided by the series to its female viewers: it promotes female independence and self-assertion in a context of female solidarity. However, as will be later discussed, this empowering message will necessarily stand in tension with the text's resolution, problematizing the traditional take on the "happy ending."

Goodbye New York . . . Bonjour Paris

Once the "therapy" is over, Carrie begins with her formal goodbye words. The mood of the scene changes drastically, as Carrie, shot in a close-up and accompanied by sentimental piano music, says: "Today, I had a thought. What if I . . . what if I had never met you?" Carrie's rhetorical question prompts individual reaction shots of the girls, which show their teary-eyed faces. This is a highly emotional moment only matched by other interactions between the women in the series, such as the scene in which Carrie accompanies Miranda in her son's birth or in her mother's funeral. Few moments involving a love interest have reached the same level of intensity in the show. As this scene shows, *SATC* 's friendships have a degree of devotion and commitment largely unmatched by any romantic attachment. In her study of "female friendship films," Hollinger identifies five types of friendships: sentimental, erotic, manipulative, political, and social. Even though Carrie's, Charlotte's, Samantha's, and Miranda's friendship has an important social component, as the previous lines have shown,[7] the intensity of their bond makes it rather a "sentimental" kind of friendship:

> Sentimental friendships are close, emotionally effusive, dyadic same-sex unions. They are conventionally presented as nurturing and psychologically enriching partnerships that also exhibit a fervent passion that is reminiscent of heterosexual romantic love. Sentimental female friends cry and confide, protest and embrace, and relate so intensely that their friendship acquires many of the signs of the love affair. (Hollinger 7)

Indeed, the emotional satisfaction that friendship provides in the series clearly surpasses any heterosexual encounter, which has led some authors to see a queer element in the show (Greven; Gill; Buckley and Ott; Jermyn, *Sex and the City*). Jane Gerhard, for instance, argues that the family of choice presented by *SATC* gives the women an alternative to the heterosexual norm. Without marking them as gay, the show is structured around its protagonists' nonheterosexual desires, and it features a view of friendship akin to the nineteenth-century "passionate" concept of same-sex friendship. For Gerhard, *SATC*'s unapologetic portrayal of a homosocial world set it apart from other shows, contributing to the normalization of "alternative" lifestyles: "[w]hat made *SATC* different was that it regularly suggested that this family of four could be enough to make up a life, a life still worth living without the husband and baby, a life led outside the historic feminine and feminist script" (45).

The next scene shows Carrie leaving her home. The last thing she takes with her is the necklace with her name she has been wearing since the beginning of the series. Before she leaves, she takes a last look at her beloved apartment from the cab. A point of view shot tilts from the steps where she has kissed goodnight dozens of lovers, to the window from which we have seen her write her column week after week. As the taxi moves away, the camera stays put, focusing on its "New York" license plate as it recedes into the shadows to the sound of a melancholic soundtrack.

The sadness of Carrie's departure from New York contrasts with her optimistic arrival in Paris. The French capital's magnificent beauty welcomes her as she arrives at the Hotel Plaza Athénée, Petrovsky's provisional residence while his apartment is being refurbished. Confident and elegantly dressed, Carrie sets foot on Parisian soil as the attentive staff of the luxurious five-star hotel picks up her designer suitcases and informs her that Petrovsky is at the salon. Carrie is visibly excited, joyously practicing the few words she knows in French. However, her glee is somewhat subdued as she enters the fancy salon to find Petrovsky cuddling a young girl. She is relieved to find out that she is his daughter, but her relief does not last long, since the girl turns out to be cold and distant. From the very beginning she refuses to bond with Carrie, ridiculing her tacky American taste and lack of worldliness. Carrie's first meeting with a Parisian already hints that her ignorance of the French language is going to be a major problem, as it will basically cut her off from the social world she used to master in New York.

Petrovsky announces that he will not be able to meet Carrie till later. He has an early dinner with the people of the museum, but he promises to meet her after that. Carrie is not discouraged by this, and she rejoices at Petrovsky's luxurious suite. The room's lavish interior pales in comparison with its views, though: Carrie screams with joy as she contemplates the Eiffel Tower from her balcony.

As Kristen Hohenadel says, "the dream of Paris is so ingrained in the world's romantic imagination that one simple shot of the Eiffel Tower shouts romance." Paris is depicted as a clichéd signifier of the romantic and the picturesque. Just like New York, it is a place of the imagination, a city conjured up in the collective unconscious by means of popular culture's fictional constructions. When Petrovsky's daughter asks Carrie if this is her first visit to Paris, she replies: "not if you include movies." For Carrie, as for many Americans, Paris represents the epitome of glamor and romance. She expects it to be the romantic playground New York has been for her so far,

Figure 5.5.   The dream of Paris.

with the added touch of worldly sophistication provided by the European heritage. The glorious image of the Eiffel Tower flooded by daylight gives way to a more serene night image. Ten hours have gone by and Petrovsky has not shown up, leaving Carrie secluded in her luxury suite, all dressed up for dinner. Prince Charming finally appears, although much too late, waking her from her sleep. The fairy-tale vibe is underscored by the mise-en-scène, which presents Carrie as a modern—and expensively dressed—Sleeping Beauty. Despite her disappointment, Petrovsky still manages to make her laugh. At this point, he is still the romantic hero of Carrie's tale.

Carrie's bitter first night in Paris is a preview of what is to come. Her expectations about the city are steadily crushed as it reveals itself as an increasingly hostile place. A week after her arrival, she goes shopping. This is Carrie's favorite pastime, her most pleasurable source of enjoyment in New York. However, what used to be a fun activity at home becomes a painful experience here, as she makes a fool of herself by falling down in the middle of Dior, becoming the focus of everyone's looks. When she arrives at the hotel, she realizes she has lost her "Carrie" necklace—an evident meta-phor for the progressive loss of her identity. She is so upset and homesick that she phones Miranda. She tells her how much she misses them and how lonely she feels in Paris. She also tells her about the loss of her necklace and we learn that the reason why she is so attached to it is that it reminds her of her friends. She also admits that she feels lost and she still thinks about Big, who, compared with aloof Petrovsky, is starting to look like the "right part-ner" in her eyes.

Meanwhile, back in New York, we see Charlotte going to Carrie's apart-ment to pick up her mail. She realizes she has left behind her laptop, another basic prop in the series that epitomizes Carrie's identity as a writer. By chance, she overhears the phone message Big is leaving on her answering machine. Just after he utters the words "I love you," Charlotte picks up the phone. The next scene shows us Big meeting the girls. He is received with hostile looks by Samantha and Miranda, but Charlotte, the hopeless roman-tic, encourages him to talk. He says:

> Well, God knows I've made a lot of mistakes with Carrie. I fucked it up. Many times. I know that. Look, I need your advice. You three know her better than anyone. You're the loves of her life. And a guy's just lucky to come in fourth. But I do love her. And if you think I have the slightest chance, I'll be on the next plane to Paris, I'll roam the streets until I find her. I'll do anything. But if you think that she really is happy, well, I wouldn't want to wreck that for her. And I'll be history.

The scene replicates Carrie's, Samantha's, Miranda's and Charlotte's endless "therapeutic" sessions, but this time the "subject" under analysis is not Car-rie, but Big, who seeks the "experts'" advice. Big's speech shows that he is a changed man now. He seems to have learned the value of what he has lost, and more importantly, he is willing to give it up for the sake of Carrie's happiness. Big's sudden change of heart in not explained by the text, but his newly attained self-knowledge and unselfish spirit is at odds with his former self, and reveals he has finally completed the romantic transformation that romantic comedy's heroes must undergo in order to be deserving of their "happily ever after." However, despite the importance of Big's transformation, the focus of the scene is not on him, but on the women, and more specifically, on Miranda. Big is the first to recognize that they are "the loves of her life," thus emphasizing the "sentimental" and quasi-romantic nature of their friendship. In spite of Big's determination to do what it takes to win Carrie back, it is not his doing, but her friends' that is finally responsible for the "happy ending." Miranda is torn between her dislike of Big and the knowledge that Carrie is not really happy in Paris. In the end, she turns out to be the enabler of the romantic union, as she admonishes Big to bring her back. In a way, this scene can be read as the dramatization of social theorists' idea that female friendship is crucial for the success of their heterosexual relationships (Caine). There are social theories that argue that the support of a close group of friends make women's relationships with men easier. In this scene, it is Carrie's friends' direct intervention that literally makes the romantic union possible. However, friendship is important to heterosexual coupling in a less tangible way throughout the series. The show does provide abundant examples of how female solidarity is never at odds with romantic partnerships. Quite the contrary—the group of friends always encourages romantic unions in an active manner. Although the working classes are more likely to perceive the spare time spent with friends as detrimental to their partnerships, friendship is regarded as a complement for heterosexual coupling among middle-class women, who see friends as a source of support in the maintenance of their heterosexual relationships (Jamieson). *SATC* supports the basic compatibility between friendship and love, as this scene shows, but this does not necessarily take the spotlight away from the former. It is significant that the moment of the romantic hero's "conversion" is eclipsed by the agency of the heroine's friends: Big's decision to go to Paris lies, after all, in Miranda's hands. This is not the first time the girls take the roles usually played by the male romantic lead. As we have seen, it is Samantha who picks Carrie's engagement ring when she is about to marry Aidan, for instance, and it is the choice of the right ring that impels Carrie to accept his proposal. *SATC*'s emphasis on the importance of the group of friends over the heterosexual couple is not an exception in the film and television panorama in which the series was born, though. Apart from the "female friendship" films of the 1990s identified by Hollinger, the 1990s also witnessed a significant tendency of romantic comedy to subordinate the traditional couple to the group. These films acknowledge the fact that, since romantic relationships are no longer a stable source of security, it may be safer to rely on friendship as a more dependable "safety net" for the individual. This tendency is depicted in movies like *Singles* (1992), *Beautiful Girls* (1996), *Denise Calls Up* (1996), *Walking and Talking* (1996), *The Brothers McMullen* (1995), *American Pie* (1999), and *The Sidewalks of New York* (2001), to name just a few. In this respect, texts with a multi-protagonist structure, like some of the aforementioned examples, are especially prone to take away the spotlight from the couple in favor of the social group of friends (Azcona).

Diamonds Are Not Forever

After the climactic moment of Big's decision to go after Carrie, the episode's ending brings us back to Paris, where Carrie and Petrovsky are finally enjoying an evening alone. He gives her an expensive diamond necklace to replace the lost one and promises to devote all of his time to her once the exhibition opens. However, as soon as he utters these words, the couple is surrounded again by his French-speaking friends, leaving Carrie out of the conversation. Isolated, she plays with her new necklace, missing her old self. The first part of *SATC*'s finale ends on a low note for Carrie, thus pointing to her bleak future in Paris.

If this episode hinted at the possibility that Paris might not be the dream city Carrie had imagined, *SATC*'s final episode reveals it to be an openly hostile place. She is supposed to have lunch with Petrovsky and his classy ex-wife, Juliet (Carole Bouquet), but he does not show up due to some last-minute "emergency" at the museum. Juliet confirms Carrie's suspicions: work always comes first for him. Petrovsky agrees to spend the next morning together, but she is left to her own devices again. She wanders the streets of Paris which, unlike New York, turns out to be an overtly unfriendly city through a series of small, but significant, unpleasant occurrences: a child hits her on the head and makes fun of her. Still mystified by this, she steps on dog's excrement. Trying to clean her expensive shoes in a fountain, she is repeatedly addressed by natives, who tell her incomprehensible things in French. Most of Carrie's misfortunes are shown in long shot, which underscores her loneliness. It is cold in Paris and the streets are quite empty, which makes a strong contrast with Manhattan's crowded sidewalks. Carrie ends up sitting by herself by the Seine, chewing on a baguette. At this point, it becomes clear that Paris has dispossessed her of her identity. Her flirtatious and lively old self is nowhere to be found, which becomes evident when a handsome tourist waves at her from a *bateau mouche*, and she waves back shyly. Back at the hotel, a close-up of Carrie, who pretends to be asleep when Petrovsky comes, shows that her affection for him is cooling off.

As previously mentioned, Paris lives in the popular imagination as the capital city of romance. Cinema has played a major part in the construction of this image: since its beginnings, Paris has been the romantic scenario par excellence thanks to films such as *Casablanca* (1942), *An American in Paris* (1951), *Sabrina* (1954), *Gigi* (1958), *Paris When It Sizzles* (1964), *Last Tango in Paris* (1972), *French Kiss* (1995), *Forget Paris* (1995), *Everyone Says I Love You* (1996), *Chocolat* (2000), *Le fabuleux destin d'Amélie Poulain* (2001), *Moulin Rouge* (2001), and *Before Sunset* (2004), to name just a few. However, as Ernst Lubitsch once said: "I've been to Paris, France, and I've been to Paris, Paramount. Paris, Paramount, is better" (Hohenadel). Indeed, Carrie's dreamed Paris turns out to be much more glamorous and welcoming than the real one is. In New York, Carrie used to master the city. She strolled its streets confidently, and Manhattan was consistently presented as a magic space fraught with possibilities for romantic transformation and personal pleasure. However, her lifestyle proves to be impossible anywhere else. Every time she ventures out of Manhattan in the show, she is let down by her surroundings: the suburbs, the countryside, the Hamptons, Los Angeles, San Francisco, and even Brooklyn are explicitly presented as the "Other" to Manhattan, unable to compete with it in all respects. Paris is not only unable to live up to New York's virtues; it is an openly hostile place: Manhattan is a safe haven for single women, where Carrie is free to shape her own identity. Paris, on the other hand, has deprived her of her real self, which is symbolized not only by the loss of her "Carrie" necklace but also by the absence of the voice-over. The French capital has literally taken away Carrie's voice. The lack of the text's main structuring device effectively conveys Carrie's feeling of aimlessness and lack of direction in this city. It also presents Paris as a truly foreign city: without the guidance of the voice-over, the viewer feels as lost as Carrie is in the navigation of the urban space. This desolate depiction of Paris not only makes it unfit as a space of romantic transformation; it underlines New York's unmatched status as romantic playground and site of self-realization and personal fulfillment. Thus, Carrie's disappointing stay in Paris emphasizes that, in *SATC*, "it is far more difficult and heartbreaking to change your city than it is your partner" (Handyside 407). Despite Carrie's incipient longing for Big, what is really killing her is the loss of her beloved New York—and everything this involves.

In one of her walks Carrie stops at a bookshop window. She is surprised to see her book and she walks in. There, she meets two excited fans of her column, who insist on throwing a party for her. Very happy at the prospect of possibly reconstructing her social life, she tells Petrovsky, who will not be able to accompany her to the event: that is the night he unveils his work to the museum's curator. That night comes and Petrovsky feels very anxious. He begs Carrie to come with him. Carrie hesitates, unwilling to cut off the only social connections she has made so far, but, seeing the state he is in, she agrees to go. When they get there, he forgets about Carrie as soon as they set foot in the exhibition room. Carrie is sitting by herself in the museum, which is codified as an empty, cold place—the only place in Paris where smoking is forbidden. It is there, in her darkest hour, that Carrie seems to find herself again: she realizes her handbag's lining is broken. She had been carrying her "Carrie" necklace with her in her handbag the whole time. This discovery impels her to run to her party, in pursue of her social, lively, true self. Ever since she put on Petrovsky's necklace it is as if she has been bereft of her identity: she left behind her independent, vivacious self to become a needy, isolated woman. The contrast between Petrovsky's diamond necklace and Carrie's inexpensive one points, once more, to the show's "democratic" notion of "the real." Carrie starts a frantic race through the streets of Paris to get to her party. Lost, she looks for a free taxi. Right next to her, in a car, we see Big. This scene replicates a typical situation in *SATC*: during its six seasons, Big has "rescued" Carrie from the city traffic with his limousine many times. However, they do not see each other this time. Any romantic comedy fan knows the important role played by fate or chance in the genre: luck can make or break a couple. It was by chance that Charlotte was able to overhear Big's phone message, thus making the romantic reunion possible. However, fate is now preventing the couple from getting together, thus building up the anticipation about the happy ending.

When she gets to the restaurant the party is over. Disappointed, she goes back to the hotel, where she finally confronts Petrovsky, reproaching his attitude: "I had a life in New York. I had a job and friends and I didn't give all of that up to come here and wander the streets of Paris alone!" At this point, Petrovksy is clearly presented as Carrie's wrong partner. In the heat of the argument, he slaps her and breaks her necklace. It is an accident, but this is clearly the last straw: physical violence is the ultimate offense Carrie suffers in Paris. The disintegration of both relationship and necklace allow for the flourishing of Carrie's true identity, that is, the same old Carrie, but with a newly acquired insight about herself:

> Maybe it's time to be clear about who I am. I am someone who is looking for love. Real love. Ridiculous, inconvenient, consuming "can't live without each other" love. And I don't think that love is here in this expensive suite and this lovely hotel in Paris.

On the one hand, Carrie's words confirm Giddens's view of romantic love as a quest for self-identity. Carrie's identification between "who she is" and her longing for love makes the connection clear. On the other hand, her argument for a passionate, all-consuming type of love seems to answer the text's perpetual dilemma between a rational, friendship-like approach to relationships and a more "romanticized" view of love. As we have seen, the series has shown a constant hesitation between these two models, wanting to believe in the latter but usually closer to the self-reflective character of the former. However, the show's finale, as most happy endings do, chooses to endorse the exaltation of intensely romantic, tumultuous, "can't live without each other" love . . . in sum, the kind of tempestuous relationship Carrie has with Big. The show's finale seems to support a romanticized view of relationships, thus "wiping away" the argument put forward by "Splat!" (6:18), the episode that motivated Carrie's decision to go to Paris and supported the idea of settling down before it is too late. The finale shows that Carrie is willing to settle down, but this does not mean that she is ready to settle: she wants the whole package. Carrie's speech also reassures the text in its "democratic" spirit: the fact that the glamor of Paris's expensive suites and diamond necklaces are not necessarily synonymous with romantic love reinforces *SATC*'s "nonconsumerist" view of romance while pointing to the genre's need to rework its conventions and imagery. The show does this by subverting the image of Paris as the quintessential setting for romance. Its depiction as a cold, hostile environment renders *SATC*'s conception of New York as an even warmer space for romantic transformation and self-realization, implicitly supporting the genuineness of "American" values over European artifice. The text's endorsement of popular versus high culture, authenticity versus pretentious sophistication, and expensive taste versus "nonconsumerist" pleasures render New York the world's definite romantic capital for the twenty-first century, a view that is framed by a wider cinematic tendency to choose New York as romantic scenario.

Picking Up the Pieces

After breaking up with Petrovsky, Carrie seems to recover her old self again. We see her at the reception desk, asking for a single room. At this moment Big comes to the rescue, making his grand entrance: Carrie is trying to clumsily pick up the diamonds from her broken necklace from the floor. She raises her head and sees Big, which starts her crying. Between sobs, she explains her misfortunes to him. When she tells him she got slapped by Petrovksy he is scandalized and determined to "avenge" her honor. This changes the mood of the scene, as Big's frantic pursue of Petrovsky gives way to a comic sequence in which Carrie chases him frantically through the hotel. She claims she does not need to be rescued—at least, not in this sense—before tripping him up. The couple falls down, laughing hysterically. In this scene we see Carrie laugh louder than she has ever done with Petrovsky. In the world of romantic comedy, the couple who laughs together is meant to be together. Fun, games, and laughter are an indispensable element of love and an unmistakable sign of the couple's compatibility (Neale and

Krutnik). With this scene, *SATC* makes it clear that Carrie and Big are meant for each other.

Laughter continues in the next scene: Carrie and Big are strolling the streets of Paris—something we have never seen Carrie do with Petrovsky. Under the lens of their newly formed alliance, Carrie's tragedy looks funny and Paris is no longer threatening, but beautiful and serene. Carrie's face glows with happiness. When she asks him how he got there, Big replies: "It took me a really long time to get here. But I'm here. Carrie, you're the One." The couple then fuses in a kiss. The climactic moment is underlined by the uplifting music and by the charming beauty of the mise-en-scène, thus fully enforcing romantic comedy's potential for magic transformation. Big has finally uttered the words Carrie has longed to hear all this time. His sudden transformation goes largely unexplained, but it is not questioned: Carrie is "the One" with a capital letter. The almost impossible reunion of two twin souls repeatedly thrown into doubt by the text has been miraculously achieved. For once, the show leaves reason aside and abandons itself to the sheer joy of romantic fulfillment, without wondering what tomorrow may bring. The fairy-tale ending is sealed with Carrie's petition to Big to take her home. Once in New York, we see Big leaving Carrie at home in his limo, as he has done countless times before. When she asks him if he wants to come up, he replies "abso-fucking-lutely." This was Big's answer to Carrie's question— "Have you ever been in love?"—in the very first episode. The text thus "brackets" their love story by means of this parallelism, providing a nice sense of closure to their relationship.

In this way, *SATC* seems to reward its final couple with an unambiguous "happily ever after" in the most traditional sense of the term. However, this "absolute" happy ending is problematic. For Robert Lapsley and Michael Westlake, contemporary culture's obsession with the myth of romance—of which *SATC* is a perfect example—is an attempt to fill the intrinsic absence in human sexuality pointed out by Freud and Lacan. Basically, Lacan says that it is only in the imaginary realm that this lack can be made good. The imaginary consists in the forever elusive objects that the subject believes would make good the lack. What is missing is what Lacan terms the *objet a*—the discordance between one's ideal image of him- or herself and his or her real self. The subject's search for the *objet a* always fails because the Other is always found to be lacking. That is why "the sexual relation exists therefore only in the imaginary and only insofar as each pretends to be what will make up the lack in the Other" (Lapsley and Westlake 32). In this way, the individual searches incessantly for what Lacan terms *la chose*. This is interpreted by Lapsley and Westlake as "the promise of an absolute plenitude" which, when encountered, gives way to the experience of lack. Thus, *la chose* is "the void around which the subject is structured" (32–33). When one gets too close to it, it becomes obvious that it cannot fill his or her lack, and plenitude becomes loss. This psychological mechanism described by Lacan shapes *SATC*: it features a "lacking" protagonist—her constant self-interrogation emphasizes this "lack"—engaged in a never-ending quest for happiness, which is assumed to reside in a suitable partner. However, all of Carrie's relationships are bound to fail, as every time things get serious, something goes wrong. What usually happens is some "flaw" appears in the relationship. Whether Carrie's partners are too unavailable or too available, too loving or too detached, there is always some problem with them, and Big is no exception. Every time Carrie gets "too close" to the object of her desire—and to what it represents for her: total happiness and self-fulfillment—the illusion vanishes. Thanks to its serial form, *SATC* is better equipped than cinematic romantic comedies to enact the subject's relentless search for unity described by Lacan: week after week, Carrie is faced with the impossibility of making good her lack, and the search is resumed. However, despite their longevity, TV series have to end. Like most Hollywood films, *SATC* refuses to acknowledge the impossibility of the "sexual relationship." It also wants to contribute to the perpetuation of the myth of romance, as most popular culture texts do. To this end, Hollywood deploys two basic strategies. One is the "establishment of figures that function to mask the lack in the Other" (Lapsley and Westlake 34). In the case of male characters, it is common to find strong, autonomous heroes who are seemingly "complete" and provide the illusion that unity between subject and object is possible. As previously discussed, Big's very name already indicates his self-sufficiency. He is the most powerful, charismatic, and wealthy of all of Carrie's suitors, giving the impression she could be happy "if only" he changed his mind. His positive qualities and his partial unavailability mask his shortcomings when it comes to fulfilling Carrie's lack, because he is always kept at a distance, personifying the text's romantic ideals and providing the illusion that he actually is *la chose*. The narrative between Carrie and Big keeps the viewer on tenterhooks because Carrie can never get close enough, and therefore the "enigma" of Big is never fully resolved.

Another strategy to create the illusion that romance is possible is the use of a certain narrative structure. Despite the great emphasis placed on romantic comedy's happy ending, the truth is that it only lasts a few minutes, even seconds. What has engaged the spectator's attention until that point are the obstacles the couple has had to overcome along the way. Spectatorial pleasure does not lie in the "suspense" of the story's denouement, which is known in advance, but in the unraveling of the familiar plot. Romantic comedy's focus on the obstacles is a means of enhancing desire: obstacles keep the object at a distance, "lending enchantment to the object, guarding against exposure of the void behind it" and "preventing its exposure as nothing" (Lapsley and Westlake 40). This is something most romantic comedies do: they defer fulfillment because it means the end of desire, but it is a much more obvious pattern in the case of a TV series like *SATC*. Being a text whose very premise is based on the constant pursuance of fulfillment—in all senses—complete satisfaction must be forever delayed to create the illusion that such fulfillment is actually possible. For this reason, obstacles are the essence of the text; they mask the lack in the Other, keeping desire alive and trying to hide the evidence that there is no ultimate satisfaction, that *la chose* does not really exist. This is something *SATC*, like most TV series, does episode after episode, but when the end comes, it is obliged to provide a sense of closure for its main couple. Instead of acknowledging what its structure has been conveying all along, the show settles for a conventional happy ending using one of Hollywood's favorite strategies to represent the "unrepresentable": the "happily ever after" is placed outside the text. Since the *objet a* is impossible to attain—the final encounter between subject and object means the end of the illusion—romantic bliss must be left in the imaginary. As most romantic comedies do, Carrie and Big's "happily ever after" is set in the future, left in the hands of the viewer's imagination. It is, therefore, just an *illusion*.

As James MacDowell argues, the final heterosexual union does not necessarily guarantee closure: Big's sudden "transformation" goes unexplained. Besides, during ninety-four episodes we have accompanied Carrie and Big in myriad breakups and reconciliations. This past experience suggests that this is just one more of the text's climaxes, not an absolute "happily ever after." If anything, it could be read as a "happy right now" (Mernit 116). Unlike cinematic romantic comedy, which tends to present a more "monolithic" view of happy endings, television series lend themselves better to a more tentative reading of their conclusions. Seen in the light of everything that has happened before, the "happily ever after" of *SATC*'s protagonist couple is much more conspicuously revealed to be a delusion of the text. In this way, television proves to be a more suitable medium to reflect the reality of people's romantic experience. The uncertainty and volatility that characterizes the contemporary intimate panorama coupled with the human being's inherent state of psychological unrest produced by a lack impossible to fulfill, paints a much more complex and less idealistic picture of today's romantic relationships than Hollywood's endings frequently make us believe.[8]

And She Lived Happily Ever After

This does not mean that *SATC* does not have a "real," unambiguous happy ending, but this ending is to be found in a less conventional place. As the last few scenes suggest, the show's actual "happily ever after" lies in Carrie's reunion with her beloved New York and with Miranda, Charlotte, and Samantha, her "family of choice." Carrie and Big's union may not be built on very solid ground, but the series has provided enough evidence so far to attest to the resilience of Carrie's bonds with her city and her friends.

Even though *SATC*'s finale focuses mainly on Carrie, the other characters' stories are also provided with a sense of closure. Samantha is successfully recovering from cancer, but she has lost her sex drive with the chemo. She encourages her young boyfriend, Smith, to have sex with other girls, but then she realizes that she does not really want that. By the end of the series Samantha seems to finally have become monogamous with a man who, according to her words, means more to her than any other lover ever has. Charlotte is in the process of adopting a baby with her husband. They are disappointed when the couple who was going to give them their baby backs down but, in the end, Charlotte's efforts to become a mother are rewarded with a Chinese baby girl. Lastly, Miranda, who now lives in Brooklyn, has to face a bleaker reality: Steve's mother has Alzheimer's disease. Miranda takes care of her, taking her into their home. In an emotive scene Magda (Lynn Cohen), the housekeeper, tells her: "What you did. That is love. You love." Miranda is the character who undergoes the greatest transformation: at the start of the series she was presented as a fiercely independent, wary single woman. By its conclusion, she has become finally capable of giving herself to others unselfishly, building a home for her newly extended family, which now includes Steve, her son, Magda, Steve's mother, and two pets.

Carrie's romantic vicissitudes take most of the spotlight in the final episode. However, the series does not conclude with her climactic union with Big. On the contrary, this all-important narrative position is reserved for Carrie's joyful reunion with her friends. She makes her triumphant entrance at the cafe where they usually meet. They scream cheerfully, incapable of restraining their joy. After that, we see them walking out of the café together, and it is this image of the group that sticks in the mind of the viewer. This is the series' real "happily ever after."

Although at the end of the narrative the four women are in more or less stable heterosexual relationships, *SATC*'s six seasons have made it sufficiently clear that their protagonists can never be completely sure about the solidity of such liaisons, but the veracity of the surrogate family they have built for themselves is not to be doubted. The closing images are accompanied by Carrie's final words:

> Later that day, I got to thinking about relationships. There are those that open you up to something new and exotic. Those that are old and familiar. Those that bring up lots of questions. Those that bring you somewhere unexpected. Those that bring you far from where you started. And those that bring you back. . . . But the most exciting, challenging, and significant relationship of all is the one you have with yourself.

Figure 5.6.   Together again.

Back in New York, Carrie has recovered her "voice." We hear her reflections over a montage sequence that encapsulates the characters' evolution: Samantha has finally given in to romance and monogamy with a wonderful man, Charlotte is happily married and about to have the offspring she always wanted, and Miranda has learned the meaning of selfless love thanks to her extended family. Apparently, Carrie is the one who has changed the least: we see her happily strolling the streets of New York, with a Manolo Blahnik bag in her hand. This image serves to "bracket" the text, as it recalls the opening credit sequence. The final message is clear: "the most exciting, challenging, and significant relationship of all is the one you have with yourself." As this analysis has shown, there are two preconditions for this conclusion: Carrie can only be her true self at home in New York and surrounded by her family of choice. As her own words confirm, a romantic partnership is desirable, but not indispensable to be happy ("and if you find someone to love the 'you,' you love . . . Well, that's just fabulous"). Being in a romantic relationship is preferable, but being true to oneself is the main prerequisite for personal happiness. This idea is visually conveyed by having Carrie walk down the crowded Manhattan streets on her own while talking to Big on the phone: she remains her old independent self, but still connected to him in a non-stifling way. After ninety-four episodes, the viewer finally learns his real name:

John. This narrative detail points to his final "opening up" to Carrie and also to the permanent presence he is presumably going to have in her life from now on: their conversation reveals that he is moving back to New York. However, the fact that we can only see Carrie in the closing scene, instead of the traditional couple, points to the text's privileging of women's autonomy and right to decide how they want to shape their lives: either in conventional families like Miranda and Charlotte, or in less traditional ways, like Samantha and Carrie. As we watch Carrie become one with the city, getting lost in the Manhattan crowd, the camera stays put, letting her go in her endless ambling along the streets of New York. The scene conveys the feeling that the walk will never end, and the fact that she is on the phone with Big while walking away from us signals the "provisional" character of the romantic closure.

This image is accompanied by Candi Staton's uplifting pop melody that keeps repeating, "You've got the love." Such lines from the song as "you've got the love I need to see me through" and "I know I can count on you" convey a feeling of optimism, but we are not really sure who this "you" is. It may refer to Big, to Carrie's friends, or to Carrie herself. *SATC*'s final postfeminist desire to "have it all" suggests that this "you" may be referring to "the whole package": at the turn of the millennium women's complete real-

Figure 5.7.   Carrie walks away . . . "happy for now."

ization entails a romantic partnership, the security provided by family—biological or surrogate—and, most importantly, being happy with oneself regardless of the lifestyle choices one makes. While traditional romantic comedy tends to offer a somewhat limited ideal of romantic wish-fulfillment with its almost exclusive focus on the couple,[9] *SATC* provides a more complex postfeminist fantasy of self-realization: it privileges the wish to be independent and happy on one's own terms, but this does not mean having to relinquish the desire for intimate relationships with the opposite sex.[10] Without excluding romance, *SATC* assigns a more significant role to friendship, which is presented in the show as the key to individual female autonomy and self-identity.

To conclude, it can be safely argued that despite the controversy surrounding the show's finale and the accusations of "conservatism," generically speaking, after a more balanced exploration, the series remains committed to the examination of social changes in the realm of interpersonal relationships. Its ambiguous and multifaceted ending involves the expansion of the definition of what a "happy ending" means for romantic comedy today, thanks to the slight displacement of the spotlight from the heterosexual couple to other issues like personal autonomy and female sisterhood. In this way, the sheltering influence that the space of romantic comedy traditionally exercises on its characters is here preeminently connected with friendship, rather than with romantic entanglements. The show's equation of female solidarity with New York thus tweaks the meanings traditionally attached to this city in contemporary romantic comedy, expanding its cultural significance to include a broader range of connotations.

The decentering of the couple in favor of a positive, nonsimplistic portrayal of friendship serves to empower its female audience, encouraging their involvement in both the private and the public sphere. Apart from this, the proliferation of culturally relevant texts like *SATC*, which put forward the possibility of alternative lifestyles, constitutes a step forward in the creation of public narratives that contribute to the normalization of nontraditional life options.[11] In a way, it could be said that here lies *SATC*'s most innovative, controversial, and contested stand, not in the display of nudity nor in debates about "funky-tasting spunk" and the like. *SATC*'s main transgression has been to consider the possibility that women could create a self-sufficient homosocial universe able to satisfy the individual's need for intimacy without excluding heterosexual romance. Viewed in this light, *SATC*'s most provocative statement may have gone largely unnoticed, having been uttered by Charlotte, the most "traditional" of its characters: "maybe we could be each other's soul mates. And then we could let men just be these great, nice guys to have fun with" ("The Agony and the Ex-tacy," 4:1). In *SATC*'s world, this is not a possibility, it is a reality.

NOTES

1. The cinema has always shown more diversity and variety in the depiction of families than has TV (Levy, "The American Dream"). The 1980s and 1990s, for instance, witnessed the rise of a tendency toward dystopian views of the family, which turned increasingly mordant, and even violent, in films like *Fatal Attraction* (1987), *War of the Roses* (1989), *Thelma and Louise* (1991), *Reversal of Fortune* (1990), *Mortal Thoughts* (1991), *Sleeping with the Enemy* (1991), *Cape Fear* (1991), and *The Hand That Rocks the Cradle* (1992). Less violent, but equally disturbing images of the family were popular at the end of the decade in films like *The Opposite of Sex* (1998), *Very Bad Things* (1998), *Your Friends and Neighbors* (1998), *American Beauty* (1999), and *Erin Brockovich* (2000). Apart from this, postmodern cinema has also been concerned with the representation of a more culturally diverse family structure, with films like *The Joy Luck Club* (1993), *Mississippi Masala* (1991), *Mo' Better Blues* (1990), and *Boyz N the Hood* (1991) (Boggs).

2. Many authors still support the prevalence of the family of fate over any other option (Etzioni; Davies), arguing that "[t]he traditional family is the best incubator of our future" (L. Ingraham 29). Others think that friends are not able to perform the needs traditionally met by the biological family (Park and Roberts; Allan, "Flexibility").

3. For more information on the increasing importance of friendship in contemporary family configurations, see Pahl; Cameron; Watters; Pahl and Spencer; Tyre; Caine; Goodwin.

4. For Winch, the connotations of female friendship in this decade are slightly different, though, as it becomes less idealistic and more "strategic."

5. The mother of Carrie's boyfriend is played by Valerie Harper, who played the protagonist of *Rhoda*, a feminist icon during the 1970s. The fact that she is playing such a cool character, someone Carrie looks up to, says a lot about the series' feminist allegiance.

6. As this quote shows, it is worth noting that the families of choice presented in *SATC* and other media texts do not really constitute such a radical break with tradition (Weeks, Heaphy, and Donovan; Weston; Holmes); albeit in a slightly modified form, new ways of life have in common with the old ones the search for a consistent mechanism to fulfill the individual's needs for intimacy. However, evolving social circumstances have made certain changes imperative, and the consequence is that intimacy frequently needs to be sought in different places.

7. For Hollinger, in social female friendship portrayals women "aid and sustain each other, perhaps by promoting a friend's heterosexual romance or by easing her pain at the loss of her male lover. Although social female friendship does not in any way attack patriarchal society, and even works to facilitate women's integration into the existing social structure, it challenges articulations of conventional femininity in two ways: by portraying female friendship as an alternative to women's complete dependence on men and by qualifying traditional concepts of feminine passivity" (8).

8. I am aware that there are exceptions to romantic comedy's general tendency toward "monolithic" happy endings. Contemporary multi-protagonist romantic comedies, for instance, exhibit a preference for less definite endings that acknowledge the ephemeral nature of today's relationships. As Azcona argues, films like *Singles* (1992), *Sidewalks of New York* (2001), *Beautiful Girls* (1996), *The Real Blonde* (1997), *He's Just Not That into You* (2009), and *Valentine's Day* (2010) portray love as something that comes and goes, "a force that fades and eventually disappears," rather than as an immutable, all-powerful frenzy (103).

9. The equation between the "happy ending" and the constitution of the heterosexual couple is a common assumption in film studies (Lapsley and Westlake; Mellencamp; Strinati; Jeffers McDonald, *Romantic Comedy*).

10. Despite romantic comedy's traditional focus on the formation of the couple, the existence of a trend in the genre that is currently redefining the meaning of the happy ending should be acknowledged. As Manuela Ruiz-Pardos points out, this convention is being reformulated thanks to "plot resolutions in which the social and cultural relevance of individual autonomy, extended family ties or friendship relations is more or less explicitly emphasized over that of romantic commitment" (116). These "innovations" are, in fact, more frequent in contemporary romantic comedy than most critics are willing to concede. Deleyto, for instance, goes against the grain by arguing that such variety and ambiguity in the happy ending is "even part of the

convention itself" (127). Films like *Clueless* (1995), *The Brothers McMullen* (1995), *The Truth about Cats and Dogs* (1996), *Walking and Talking* (1997), *My Best Friend's Wedding* (1997), *The Object of my Affection* (1998), *Shakespeare in Love* (1998), *Prime* (2005), *The Break-Up* (2006), *Once* (2006), *Becoming Jane* (2007), and *(500) Days of Summer* (2009) do not comply with the traditional romantic comedy ending for one reason or another.

11. Contemporary social changes like the increasing importance of families of choice or the legitimacy of female singleness are progressively normalized thanks to their growing visibility in the media. As Watters says, "shared social narratives influence our conceptions of our own lives and happiness . . . important things in our own lives can go unseen or misunderstood if we lack the story template in our cultural vocabulary to describe them" (10). The concepts of marriage and family are deeply embedded in our cultural vocabulary, in the fabrics of everyday life and the way society is organized. On the other hand, concepts like "urban tribe" or "family of choice" have not fully taken root yet, which means that their importance goes largely unnoticed. Even the members of these groups may not be fully aware of their belonging to a system of social organization which started to gain momentum at the turn of the millennium and which can be as fulfilling as the traditional family model. Watters complains that "the small things we did with and for our friends lacked the moral meaning those same acts might have in the context of a family" (38). Since this way of life is not a full part of public narratives about how "normal" individuals should lead their lives, many people miss the opportunity to consider the possibility that being a part of an interrelated network of chosen friends instead of a traditional family unit may be as satisfying, and as legitimate a way of life as traditional living arrangements are. Arguably, popular culture texts like *SATC* have contributed to legitimizing alternative lifestyles.

Conclusion

Pushing Boundaries

SATC's final episode was a long-awaited event. Before its broadcasting, it raised a great deal of expectation: Would Carrie end up with Petrovksy? With Big? Or alone? Would she stay in Paris or would she return to New York? On February 22, 2004, 10.6 million viewers gathered in front of their television sets to find out. The rolling of the final credits was quickly followed by a media frenzy of farewells, tributes, and behind-the-scenes features. The series' finale also brought a considerable amount of controversy. The discrepancies among the fans' opinions about the conclusion were evident in an online poll run by HBO, which asked its participants: "When it's all said and done, who do you think Carrie will end up with?" Forty-nine percent chose Big, followed by "herself" at 20 percent; Charlotte, Miranda, and Samantha (17 percent); Petrovsky (7 percent); Aidan (5 percent); and Jack Berger with the remaining 1 percent (Frey). This suggests that most fans were pleased to see their heroine finally coupled with the show's "Mr. Darcy." However, others were disappointed by what they perceived to be a conservative ending. Some people thought that the show's feminist spirit was somehow "betrayed" by Carrie's final decision.

The media frenzy produced by the program's finale is indicative of its relevance as a cultural media product. It still lingers in people's minds a decade after its conclusion. The *SATC* Hotspots Bus Tour organized by On Location Tours in New York is still the most popular of all. The series is still regularly broadcast in syndication all over the world, with good audience ratings. However, the most tangible proof of the show's relevance at the turn of the 2000s is the success of its two cinematic sequels: with a $65 million budget, *Sex and the City* (2008) grossed more than $415 million worldwide, becoming the eleventh-highest-grossing film of the year. *Sex and the City 2* (2010) was not so successful—it "only" grossed $288 million worldwide—but still managed to make an ample profit on its $100 million budget, showing that fans all around the world had not forgotten Carrie, Samantha, Charlotte, and Miranda. At the time of this writing, the *SATC* franchise is still somehow present in the small screen, as its "prequel" series, *The Carrie Diaries,* is being broadcast by The CW.

SATC's enduring popularity surpassed the boundaries of a regular TV program to become a cultural landmark, and its influence is still felt in a TV grid greatly indebted to this show's pushing of generic and cultural boundaries. Far from detrimental, the controversy that has always accompanied the series arguably helped it achieve this status. Apart from being a hot topic at the workplace watercooler, it spurred endless discussions both in the media and the academy about its stance toward issues like feminism, consumption, and sexuality, which usually took the form of highly polarized debates between those who perceived the show as a step forward in the feminist struggle and those who regarded it as a backward-looking representation of women.

This book has not been concerned with elucidating whether *SATC* is an ideologically conservative or progressive text. That is a dead end. The answer depends on numerous factors, one of them being the speaker's own personal stance—most opinions about *SATC*'s ideological messages say more about the person who does the speaking than about the text itself. Apart from this, the series never offers a monolithic reading. The contradictory spirit inherent in its postfeminist sensibility ensures that no definitive answers are given to the myriad questions posed in the show throughout its ninety-four episodes. In a way, much of *SATC*'s ability to capture the imagination of such a large audience lies in its plurality. The series offers a variety of opinions for the viewer to choose from. The same "pick and choose" ethos that the text exhibits toward shoes or romantic conquests is applied to its internal narrative dynamics: the audience is free to choose the ideological position that suits them best out of the polyphonic panorama of voices offered by each episode.

Instead, this book has explored the discourses put forward by the show about intimacy and interpersonal relationships at the turn of the millennium from a generic perspective. Despite its mixture of elements from different genres and media, romantic comedy constitutes its most obvious generic point of reference. One of the text's greatest innovations lies in its reworking of a series of conventions traditionally associated to a different format—the feature film. This book has been concerned with, among other things, the exploration of the ways in which *SATC*'s formal structure interacts with the conventions of a genre usually linked to the big screen.

The program's formal structure has a double effect, simultaneously constraining and liberating the text in its relationship with the romantic comedy genre. On the one hand, the need for the weekly continuation of the plot restricts the characters' evolution, trapping them in an endless personal quest with no end in sight. The sitcom format limits the characters' options, since its basic configuration cannot be altered: *SATC*'s world is formed by its four protagonists. The rest of characters come and go; they have "peripheral" roles. The inherent fixity of this premise makes romantic attachments necessarily transitory. The sitcom's structure may be seen as a narrative straitjacket, but in the particular case of *SATC*, this limitation works in its favor. Since the show's premise is based on the exhaustive interrogation of the individual's life trajectory, its formal structure is particularly apt to convey the never-ending nature of this task; the show captures faithfully the individual's sense of uncertainty and restlessness in the postmodern, postindustrial world she inhabits. The endless cycle of self-interrogation that ensues from *SATC*'s episodic structure accurately reflects the process of introspection and self-examination required by today's individualistic society.

Since the show is preoccupied with the representation of the complex nature of intimate relationships at the turn of the century, its "circular" structure also constitutes an appropriate vehicle to express the serial nature of today's dating panorama. The characters' forever incomplete romantic quests may be determined by extra-textual factors, but the serial structure turns out to be the most logical way to convey the provisionality, volatility, and fragmentation characteristic of contemporary romantic liaisons. In this way, *SATC* takes advantage of its "seriality" in order to offer a quasi-ethnographic view of those topics routinely dealt with by romantic comedy in a necessarily more "restricted" manner. New living conditions have created a social context in which the "Big Love" narratives of yore have been replaced by a succession of fragile, anxiety-fraught affairs, and "till death do us part" vows give way to "till further notice" engagements. In this context, the absolute "happily ever afters" of cinematic romantic comedy are perceived as less appropriate for representing the climate of uncertainty pervading today's intimate panorama than *SATC*'s "happy for now" endings.

The influence of *SATC*'s serial structure on its representation of love is also felt in the text's chronic ambivalence about it. Unlike conventional romantic comedies, which tend to exhibit a more clear-cut attitude toward love—usually a hopeful, starry-eyed one—one of the show's main conflicts lies in the permanent struggle between its wish to believe in the possibility of "true romance" and the necessary acknowledgment of a bleaker, more cynical reality. The optimistic romantic climaxes offered at the end of some episodes betray the series' longing for the former, but its serial structure forces it to acknowledge the need for a more rational and analytical approach to relationships, which lies arguably closer to the reality of people's experi-

88ces. Unable to draw the curtain after the final kiss, *SATC* shows what happens between the couple the morning after, depriving it of the "happily ever after" that can only exist in the audience's imagination and in Hollywood's happy endings. As previously mentioned, the outcomes of *SATC*'s overanalytical spirit are often ambiguous. However, one thing is clear: despite the show's internal conflict between its romantic longings and its tendency toward rationality, it always comes to the same conclusion—whether single or in a couple, the individual's priority is to maintain an honest relationship with herself. This idea is not only endorsed by the series' resolution, but is a recurrent concept in the series, which depicts a sentimental order solely based on one's duty to oneself. In *SATC*, personal fulfillment and self-realization are perceived as the prerequisites for happiness within the couple. When these conditions are not met, singleness is preferred. This means a remarkable departure with respect to the basic ethos of romantic comedy which, constrained by a more limited running time, is forced to focus almost exclusively on the romantic union, disregarding other aspects.

SATC's formal structure also interacts with romantic comedy in other ways. Its serial form "frees" the text from some of the conventions of the genre, allowing it to push its boundaries and contributing to the reinvention and development of the genre as a whole. An example of *SATC*'s reshaping of romantic comedy's conventions is its desire to expand the meanings of the happy ending: the text's conclusion includes heterosexual coupling, but the serial structure has routinely privileged female friendship over romantic attachments. So, by placing the emphasis on personal autonomy and female sisterhood, not only at the end but throughout the series, *SATC* contributes to the reworking of the genre's conventions while also helping normalize alternative lifestyles and living arrangements. *SATC*'s postfeminist final aspiration "to have it all" thus contributes to the redefinition of romantic comedy's conception of the happy ending, which is rendered as a more complex, nuanced cluster of meanings in the light of its serial structure.

SATC's "tweaking" of the happy ending's connotations is linked to the expansion of the meanings traditionally attached to New York as romantic comedy's space of transformation. From the late 1970s, the Big Apple has been used as shorthand for romance. *SATC* offers a much more culturally specific depiction of the city than traditional romantic comedy has done, but it still presents it as the space for romantic regeneration par excellence. The important role played by the city in the show undoubtedly helps foster this image of New York, but also redefines the meanings attached to it in romantic comedy's imaginary by expanding its scope: *SATC* extends the city's benevolent mantle beyond love and desire to include friendship and personal autonomy. New York thus becomes not only the place "where love happens," but the place where complete individual realization can be attained, thus pushing the boundaries of what this benevolent space is able to encompass.

Another convention of romantic comedy that is redrawn by *SATC*, so to speak, is its use of humor. Normally, the main function of humor in the genre is to facilitate the romantic union. It tends to have a "utopian" dimension and—with some exceptions, often of the gross-out kind—is not so concerned with eliciting laughter from the audience. In *SATC* comedy does serve "sentimental" purposes: laughter and fun within the couple is an indispensable ingredient of the romantic union and an unmistakable sign of their compatibility. However, humor in *SATC* is more conspicuously linked to the discussion of sex and female sexuality: the centrality of sex in the series constitutes an evident innovation in a somewhat "coy" genre. Apart from its comic function, the girls' unashamed sex talk serves two purposes: First, it empowers women through the open acknowledgment of their physical urges and enjoyment of sex, displaying a nonjudgmental attitude toward female sexuality. Secondly, it is not only female desire that is legitimized—the show's liberal approach to sexuality as a whole also contributes to the normalization of a wide array of sexual practices and identities, which are presented as contingent cultural constructions. In this sense, the program's episodic format constitutes an asset in terms of the "ethnographic" documentation of a wide range of sexual preferences, and also of the depiction and legitimation of a new kind of sexuality, characterized by "casualness" and "seriality," that forms part of the "plastic sexuality" blueprint. *SATC*'s deployment of sex as its main source of humor proved to be a successful formula among its viewers. Unlike conventional romantic comedy, which has traditionally shied away from the explicit representation of sex—both in visual and verbal terms—*SATC* turned it into its basic comic pillar.

As happened with the object of my analysis, it is difficult to find satisfying closure for this book. The show deals with a wide range of issues, many of which have not been addressed here. Having chosen a generic perspective, this book has attempted to elucidate one particular aspect of the text that has gone relatively unnoticed in the existing literature about the series, namely, the flexibility of one particular genre, romantic comedy, to adapt itself not only to the sociocultural context in which it is inscribed, but to a medium different from its usual "home ground." The result is a welcome revamping of the genre that strengthens its connection with its sociocultural context. Aided by its formal structure, *SATC* updates romantic comedy in order to attune it to new social conditions. These innovations do not constitute radical breaks with tradition. They are, rather, significant additions that contribute to the evolution of the genre in new and exciting directions. Due precisely to the fluid, intangible, and somehow "mysterious" nature of generic development, *SATC*'s contributions have largely gone unnoticed. The "buzz" it generated in its heyday focused on different issues, such as its controversial views of sexuality, gender identity, and female representation. However, since form and content are inextricably linked, it can be said that the show's generic innovations have played a preeminent role in the attainment of its landmark status, a status that has been reached thanks to its ability to speak directly to contemporary women's fantasies and to strike a massive cultural chord with the audience. *SATC* may not offer straightforward answers to the myriad questions it poses, but it has surely helped millions of women feel that they are not on their own in their daily struggle, making them feel "less alone, more thoughtful and more bold" (Sayeau, "Carrying On"). The unanimity of this collective feeling among women all around the world opens the door to the possibility that this show may be more than its glossy surface suggests. It may be the answer to Virginia Woolf's question: What would women do if they became free? According to the series, they would act like men do. They would fuck a lot. But they would also buy fabulous footwear. They need it, though, because as *SATC* has taught us, it is an arduous task to walk in a single woman's shoes.

Works Cited

Abbot, Stacey, and Deborah Jermyn, eds. *Falling in Love Again: Romantic Comedy in Contemporary Cinema*. London and New York: I. B. Tauris, 2009.

Akass, Kim, and Janet McCabe. "Ms. Parker and the Vicious Circle: Female Narrative and Humour in *Sex and the City*." Akass and McCabe 177–98.

Akass, Kim, and Janet McCabe, eds. *Reading Sex and the City*. London and New York: I. B. Tauris, 2004.

Alksnis, Christine, Serge Desmarais, and Eileen Wood. "Gender Differences in Scripts for Different Types of Dates." *Sex Roles* 34.5/6 (1996): 321–36.

Allan, Graham. "Flexibility, Friendship, and Family." *Personal Relationships* 15 (2008): 1–16.

———. "Personal Relationships in Late Modernity." *Personal Relationships* 8 (2001): 325–39.

———. *The Sociology of the Family: A Reader*. Oxford: Blackwell, 2000.

Altman, Rick. *Film/Genre*. London: BFI, 1999.

Andersen, Kurt. "I Want My HBO." *New York* 24 July 2005. http://nymag.com/nymetro/news/columns/imperialcity/12199/ (accessed 8 February 2010).

Anderson, Christopher. "Producing an Aristocracy of Culture in American Television." Edgerton and Jones 23–41.

Arthurs, Jane. "*Sex and the City* and Consumer Culture: Remediating Postfeminist Drama." *Feminist Media Studies* 3.1 (2003): 83–98.

———. *Television and Sexuality: Regulations and the Politcs of Taste*. New York: Open University Press, 2004.

Ashbee, Edward. *American Society Today*. Manchester and New York: Manchester University Press, 2002.

Associated Press. "HBO's 'Sex and the City' Draws Record Ratings for Its Series Finale." *Augusta Chronicle* 25 February 2004. http://chronicle.augusta.com/stories/2004/02/25/tel_405825.shtml (accessed 30 September 2013).

Attwood, Fiona. "Sexed Up: Theorizing the Sexualization of Culture." *Sexualities* 9.1 (2006): 77–94.

Atwood, Joan D., and Susan Dershowitz. "Constructing a Sex and Marital Therapy Frame: Ways to Help Couples Deconstruct Sexual Problems." *Journal of Sex and Marital Therapy* 18.3 (1992): 196–218.

Avins, Mimi. "Let's Talk about 'Sex'—They Sure Do." *Los Angeles Times* 5 June 1999. http://articles.latimes.com/1999/jun/05/entertainment/ca-44282 (accessed 18 January 2014).

Azcona, María del Mar. *The Multi-Protagonist Film*. Oxford and Malden, MA: Wiley Blackwell, 2010.

Babington, Bruce, and Peter Evans. *Affairs to Remember: The Hollywood Comedy of the Sexes*. Manchester: Manchester University Press, 1989.

Baird, Julia. "Girls Gone Mild." *Newsweek* 16 May 2008. http://www.newsweek.com/id/ 137300/page/2 (accessed 1 June 2009).

Barrick, Lucy. "True Confessions." *Guardian* 9 January 2001: 17.

Bart, Peter. " Sexual Politics: Ifs, Ands, Butts." *Variety* 4 December–10 December 2000: 1, 4.

Bauman, Zygmunt. *Liquid Love: On the Frailty of Human Bonds.* Cambridge and Malden, MA: Polity Press, 2003.

Bawin-Legros, Bernadette. "Intimacy and the New Sentimental Order." *Current Sociology* 52.2 (2004): 241–50.

Beck, Ulrich, and Elisabeth Beck-Gernsheim. *Individualization.* London: Sage Publications, 2002.

———. *The Normal Chaos of Love.* 1995. Cambridge, Oxford, Malden: Polity Press, 2004.

Behrendt, Greg, and Liz Tuccillo. *He's Just Not That Into You: The No-Excuses Truth to Understanding Guys.* New York, London, Toronto and Sidney: Simon Spotlight Entertainment, 2004.

Bellah, Robert N., Richard Madsen, William M. Sullivan, Ann Swidler, and Steven T. Tipton. *Habits of the Heart: Individualism and Commitment in American Life* . 1985. Berkeley, Los Angeles, London: University of California Press, 1996.

Ben-Ze'ev, Aaron. *Love Online: Emotions on the Internet.* Cambridge: Cambridge University Press, 2004.

Berman, Marc. "HBO's Midlife Crisis." *MediaWeek* 12 June 2006: 38.

Bignell, Jonathan. *An Introduction to Television Studies.* London and New York: Routledge, 2008.

———. "Sex, Confession, and Witness." Akass and McCabe 161–76.

Billen, Andrew. "Why I Love American TV." *The Observer* 28 July 2002. http://www. guardian.co.uk/theobserver/2002/jul/28/features.review27 (accessed 23 January 2010).

Blum, Virginia L. "Love Studies: Or, Liberating Love." *American Literary History* 17.2 (2005): 335–48.

Boggs, Carl. "Postmodern Cinema and the Demise of the Family." *The Journal of American Culture* 26.4 (2003): 445–63.

Bourdieu, Pierre. *The Field of Cultural Production.* New York: Columbia University Press, 1993.

———. *Outline of a Theory of Practice.* Trans. R. Nice. Cambridge: Cambridge University Press, 1977.

Brasfield, Rebeeca. "Rereading: Sex and the City: Exposing the Hegemonic Feminist Narrative." *Journal of Popular Film and Television* 34.3 (2006): 130–39.

Braxton, Greg. "*Sex and the City* Gets Set to Call It a Night." *Los Angeles Times* 9 January 2003. http://articles.latimes.com/2003/jan/09/news/wk-braxton9 (accessed 14 August 2009).

———. "'Sex,' Regis, and 'Fiance' Are Big Hits." *Los Angeles Times* 25 February 2004. http:/ /articles.latimes.com/2004/feb/25/entertainment/et-tvratingstext25 (accessed 14 August 2009).

Bristow, Joseph. *Sexuality.* London and New York: Routledge, 1997.

Brooks, David. *Bobos in Pardise: The New Upper Class and How They Got There.* New York: Simon and Schuster, 2000.

Brown, Helen Gurley. *Sex and the Single Girl.* New York: Random House, 1962.

Brownsfield, Paul. "When Characters Talk about Sex, Do Women Have More Fun?" *Los Angeles Times* 23 November 2001. http://articles.latimes.com/2001/nov/23/entertainment/ ca-7309(accessed 19 August 2009).

Buckley, Cara Louise, and Brian L. Ott. "Fashion (able/ing) Selves: Consumption, Identity, and *Sex and the City.*" Leverette, Ott, and Buckley 209–26.

Bunting, Madeleine. "Loadsasex and Shopping: A Woman's Lot." *The Guardian* 9 February 2001. http://www.guardian.co.uk/media/2001/feb/09/comment.broadcasting (accessed 6 August 2009).

Burghes, Louie. *Lone Parenthood and Family Disruption: The Outcomes for Children.* London: Family Policy Studies Center, 1994.

Burr, Vivien, and Christine Jarvis. "Imagining the Family. Representations of Alternative Lifestyles in *Buffy the Vampire Slayer.*" *Qualitative Social Work* 6 (2007): 263–80.

Butler, Judith. *Bodies That Matter: On the Discursive Limits of "Sex."* New York: Routledge, 1993.

———. *Gender Trouble*: *Feminism and the Subversion of Identity.* New York and London: Routledge, 1990.

———. "Imitation and Gender Insubordination." *The Judith Butler Reader.* Ed. Sara Salih. Malden, MA: Blackwell Publishing, 2004. 119–37.

Caine, Barbara. *Friendship: A History.* London, Oakville: Equinox Pub, 2009.

Cameron, Amy. "Kindred Spirits Instead of Kin." *Maclean's* 13 January 2003. http://business. highbeam.com/4341/article-1G1-96254253/kindred-spirits-instead-kin-many-adults-notes-amy-cameron (accessed 22 January 2011).

Carter, Bill. "If Media Is Really AOL's Oyster, Its Biggest Pearl Is Clearly HBO." *New York Times* 20 July 2002. http://www.nytimes.com/2002/07/20/business/if-media-is-really-aol-s-oyster-its-biggest-pearl-is-clearly-hbo.html?pagewanted=1 (accessed 8 February 2010).

Casas, Quim. "Series de Televisión de la Última Década: un Lenguaje Renovado." *Dirigido* 39 (2010): 44–51.

Chang, Yahlin, and Veronica Chambers. "Sex and the Single Girl." *Newsweek* 2 August 1999. http://www.newsweek.com/id/89175 (accessed 6 August 2009).

Chaplin, Julia. "I'm Stylish, I'm Single and I'm Not Carrie Bradshaw." *The New York Times* 26 August 2001. http://www.nytimes.com/2001/08/26/style/view-i-m-stylish-i-m-single-and-i-m-not-carrie-bradshaw.html (accessed 14 August 2009).

Chauncey, George. *Gay New York: Gender, Urban Culture, and the Making of the Gay Male World, 1890–1940.* New York: Basic Books, 1994.

Cheal, David. "The One and the Many: Modernity and Postmodernity." *The Sociology of the Family: A Reader.* Ed. Graham Allan. Oxford: Blackwell, 2000. 56–86.

Clark, Dana. *Not Just a Guilty Pleasure: A Feminist Analysis of "Sex and the City."* Ann Arbor, MI: Proquest, 2008.

Cline, Sally. *Women, Passion, and Celibacy.* New York: Carol Southern Books, 1993.

Comella, Lynn. "(Safe) *Sex and the City:* On Vibrators, Masturbation and the Myth of 'Real' Sex." *Feminist Media Studies* 3.1 (2003): 109–12.

Coontz, Stephanie. *The Way We Never Were: American Families and the Nostalgia Trap .* New York: Basic Books, 1992.

Coren, Victoria. "*Sex and the City* Has Betrayed Us Single Women." *Evening Standard* 3 January 2003: 11.

Cramer, Janet M. "Discourses of Sexual Morality in *Sex and the City* and *Queer as Folk.* " *Journal of Popular Culture* 40.3 (2007): 409–32.

Crittenden, Danielle. *What Our Mothers Didn't Tell Us: Why Happiness Eludes the Modern Woman.* New York: Simon & Schuster, 1999.

Crotty, Mark. "Murphy Would Probably Also Win the Election: The Effect of Television as Related to the Portrayal of the Family in Situation Comedies." *Journal of Popular Culture* 29.3 (1995): 1–15.

Davidson, Max. "Television." *Sunday Telegraph* 7 February 1999: 8.

Davies, Jon. *The Family: Is It Just Another Lifestyle Choice?* London: Institute of Economic Affairs, 1993.

Davis, Flora. *Moving the Mountain: The Women's Movement in America since 1960.* 1991. Urbana and Chicago: University of Illinois Press, 1999.

Deleyto, Celestino. *The Secret Life of Romantic Comedy.* Manchester and New York: Manchester University Press, 2009.

D'Emilio, John, and Estelle Freedman. *Intimate Matters: A History of Sexuality in America.* Chicago: The University of Chicago Press, 1998.

Dench, Geoff. "Nearing Full Circle in the Sexual Revolution." *Rewriting the Sexual Contract.* Ed. Geoff Dench. London: Institute of Community Studies, 1997. 40–54.

D'Erasmo, Stacey. "The Way We Live Now: 8-29-99; Single File." *The New York Times Magazine* 29 August 1999. http://www.nytimes.com/1999/08/29/magazine/the-way-we-live-now-8-29-99-single-file.html?scp=4&sq=stacey+d%27erasmo&st=nyt (accessed 13 January 2014).

di Mattia, Joanna. "What's the Harm in Believing? Mr. Big, Mr. Perfect and the Romantic Quest for *Sex and the City*'s Mr. Right." Akass and McCabe 17–32.

Douglas, Ann. "Soft-Porn Culture." *The New Republic* 30 August 1980: 25–29.

Durgnat, Raymond. *The Crazy Mirror: Hollywood Comedy and the American Image*. New York: Horizon Press, 1970.

Echart, Pablo. "La Última Comedia Romántica Estadounidense (2000–2007): Panorámica de un Género Ensimismado." *Comunicación y Sociedad* 22.1 (2009): 161–95.

Edgerton, Gary R., and Jeffrey P. Jones, eds. *The Essential HBO Reader*. Lexington: The University Press of Kentucky, 2008.

———. "HBO's Ongoing Legacy." In Edgerton and Jones 315–30.

Ellwood, Mark. "*Sex and the City* Ruined My Love Life." *Red* February 2003: 65.

Elster, Jon. *Making Sense of Marx*. New York: Cambridge University Press, 1985.

Epstein, Michael M., Jimmy L. Reeves, and Marc C. Rogers. "Surviving 'The Hit': Will *The Sopranos* Still Sing for HBO?" *Reading The Sopranos: Hit TV from HBO*. Ed. David Lavery. London: I. B. Tauris, 2006. 15–25.

Escudero-Alías, Maite. *Long Live the King: A Genealogy of Performative Genders*. Newcastle, UK: Cambridge Scholars Publishing, 2009.

Etzioni, Amitai. *The Parenting Deficit*. London: Demos, 1993.

Evans, Mary. *Love: An Unromantic Discussion*. Cambridge: Polity Press, 2003.

Faderman, Lillian. *Twilight Girls and Odd Loves: A History of Lesbian Life in Twentieth-Century America*. New York and London: Penguin, 1992.

Faludi, Susan. *Backlash: The Undeclared War against Women*. London: Vintage, 1992.

Featherstone, Brid. "Rethinking Family Support in the Current Policy Context." *British Journal of Social Work* 36.1 (2006): 5–19.

Fielding, Helen. *Bridget Jones's Diary*. London: Picador, 1996.

Firestone, Shulamith. *The Dialectic of Sex: The Case for a Female Revolution*. London: Jonathan Cape, 1971.

Fiske, John. *Media Matters: Race and Gender in U.S. Politics*. Minneapolis: University of Minnesota Press, 1996.

Flett, Kathryn. "I'm Still Wild about Carrie." *The Observer* 27 July 2003. http://www.guardian.co.uk/theobserver/2003/jul/27/features.review37 (accessed 9 August 2009).

Flint, Joe. "As Critics Carp HBO Confronts Ratings Slump." *Wall Street Journal* 8 June 2005: B1.

Foucault, Michel. *The History of Sexuality, Volume 1: An Introduction*. 1978. New York: Random House, 1990.

Freud, Sigmund. *Jokes and Their Relation to the Unconscious*. 1905. Harmondsworth: Pelican, 1976.

Frey, Jennifer. "Just One Last Fling." *The Washington Post* 21 February 2004. http://www.washingtonpost.com/ac2/wp-dyn/A59329-2004Feb20?language=printer (accessed 12 February 2011).

Frith, Hannah, and Celia Kitzinger. "Reformulating Sexual Script Theory: Developing a Discursive Psychology of Sexual Negotiation." *Theory of Psychology* 11.2 (2001): 209–32.

Frye, Northrop. *Anatomy of Criticism: Four Essays*. 1957. Princeton, NJ: Princeton University Press, 1973.

Furlong, Andy, and Fred Cartmel. *Young People and Social Change: Individualization and Risk in Late Modernity*. Buckingham: Open University Press, 1997.

Gagnon, John H., and William Simon. *Sexual Conduct: The Social Sources of Human Sexuality*. Chicago: Aldine, 1973.

Gardiner, Judith Kegan. "The (US)es of (I)dentity: A Response to Abel on '(E)merging Identities.'" *Signs* 6.3 (1981): 436–42.

Gennaro, Stephen. "*Sex and the City*: Perpetual Adolescence Gendered Feminine?" *Nebula* 4.1 (2007). http://www.nobleworld.biz/images/Gennaro.pdf (accessed 1 August 2009).

Gerhard , Jane. "Sex and the City : Carrie Bradshaw's Queer Postfeminism." *Feminist Media Studies* 5.1 (2005): 37–49.

Giddens, Anthony. *The Transformation of Intimacy: Sexuality, Love and Eroticism in Modern Societies*. Cambridge: Polity Press, 1992.

Gill, Rosalind. *Gender and the Media.* Cambridge: Polity Press, 2007.

Gillis, John R. *A World of Their Own Making: A History of Myth and Ritual in Family Life.* Oxford: Oxford University Press, 1996.

Goodwin, Robin. *Changing Relations: Achieving Intimacy in a Time of Social Transition.* Cambridge and New York: Cambridge University Press, 2009.

Goss, Robert E. "Queering Procreative Privilege: Coming Out as Families." *Our Families, Our Values: Snapshots of Queer Kinship.* Eds. John Dececco, Robert E. Goss, and Amy A. Squire. New York: The Harrington Park Press, 1997. 3–20.

Gottlieb, Lori. "Marry Him!" *Atlantic Monthly* March 2008. http://www.theatlantic.com/doc/200803/single-marry (accessed 2 November 2010).

Greer, Germaine. *The Female Eunuch.* London: McGibbon and Kay, 1970.

Greven, David. "The Museum of Unnatural History: Male Freaks and Sex." Akass and McCabe 33–47.

Griffin, Jennifer, and Kera Bolonik. "The Prequel, and Sequel, to *Sex and the City.*" *New York Times* 22 June 2003. http://www.nytimes.com/2003/06/22/arts/television-the-prequel-and-sequel-to-sex-and-the-city.html?pagewanted=1 (accessed 9 February 2010).

Grigoriadis, Vanessa. "Baby Panic." *New York Magazine* 20 May 2002. http://nymag.com/nymetro/urban/family/features/6030/ (accessed 15 October 2013).

Grindon, Leger. The Hollywood Romantic Comedy: Conventions, History and Controversies. Chichester, West Sussex: Wiley-Blackwell, 2011.

Grochowski, Tom. "Neurotic in New York: The Woody Allen Touches in *Sex and the City.*" Akass and McCabe 149–60.

Gubrium, Jaber F., and James A. Holstein. *What Is Family?* Mountain View, CA: Mayfield, 1990.

Handyside, Fiona. "It's Either Fake or Foreign: The Cityscape in *Sex and the City.*" *Continuum: Journal of Media and Cultural Studies* 21.3 (2007): 405–18.

Hanks, Robert. *Independent* 4 February 1999: 18.

Hayes, Dade. "'Sex' and the City of Tabloids." *Variety* 22–28 October 2007: 8.

Henderson, Brian. "Romantic Comedy Today: Semi-Tough or Impossible?" *Film Quarterly* 31.4 (1978): 11–23.

Henry, Astrid. "Orgasms and Empowerment: *Sex and the City* and the Third Wave Feminism." Akass and McCabe 65–82.

Hetherington, E. Mavis, and John Kelly. *For Better or for Worse: Divorce Reconsidered.* New York: Norton, 2002.

Hewlett, Sylvia Ann. *Creating a Life: Professional Women and the Quest for Children.* New York: Hyperion, 2002.

Hohenadel, Kristen. "Paris for Real vs. Paris on Film: We'll Always Have the Movies." *New York Times* 25 November 2001. http://query.nytimes.com/gst/fullpage.html?res=9E0CE4D91F3BF936A15752C1A9679C8B63 (accessed 22 January 2011).

Hollinger, Karen. *In the Company of Women: Contemporary Female Friendship Films.* Minneapolis: University of Minnesota Press, 1998.

Holmes, Mary. "The Precariousness of Choice in the New Sentimental Order: A Response to Bawin-Legros." *Current Sociology* 52.2 (2004): 251–57.

Holston, Noel. "*Sex and the City*: The 'City' Women's Clueless Search for the Perfect Man Continues with Six Bonus Episodes." *Newsday* 6 January 2002: Section D.

Horton, Andrew. "Introduction." *Comedy/Cinema/Theory.* Ed. Andrew Horton. Berkeley: University of California Press, 1991. 1–21.

Hösle, Vittorio. "Why Do We Laugh at and with Woody Allen?" *Special Issue on Woody Allen.* Special edition of *Film and Philosophy* (2000): 7–50.

Hymowitz, Kay S. "Gay Marriage vs. American Marriage." *City Journal* Summer 2004. http://www.city-journal.org/html/14_3_gay_marriage.html (accessed 7 July 2010).

———. "I Wed Thee, and Thee, and Thee." *City Journal* Autumn 2004. http://www.city-journal.org/html/14_4_sndgs04.html (accessed 7 July 2010).

———. "It's Morning After in America." *City Journal* Spring 2004. http://www.city-journal.org/html/14_2_its_morning.html (accessed 7 July 2010).

————. "Marriage and Caste." *City Journal* Winter 2006. http://www.city-journal.org/html/ 16_1_marriage_gap.html (accessed 7 July 2010).

————. "The New Girl Order." *City Journal* Autumn 2007. http://www.city-journal.org/html/ 17_4_new_girl_order.html (accessed 16 July 2009).

Idato, Michael. "Are You Old Enough?" *Sydney Morning Herald* 4 June 2001: 6.

Illouz, Eva. *Consuming the Romantic Utopia: Love and the Cultural Contradictions of Capitalism.* Berkeley, Los Angeles, London: University of California Press, 1997.

Ingraham, Chrys. *White Weddings: Romancing Heterosexuality in Popular Culture.* 1999. New York and London: Routledge, 2008.

Ingraham, Laura. *Power to the People.* Washington: Regnery Publishing, 2007.

Jamieson, Lynn. *Intimacy: Personal Relationships in Modern Society.* Cambridge and Malden, MA: Polity Press, 1998.

Jancovich, Mark. "Naked Ambitions: Pornography, Taste and the Problem of the Middlebrow." *Scope* June 2001. http://www.scope.nottingham.ac.uk/article.php?issue=jun2001&id=274& section=article&q=jancovich (accessed 20 December 2010).

Jeffers McDonald, Tamar. "Homme-Com: Engendering Change in Contemporary Romantic Comedy." Abbot and Jermyn, 146–59.

————. *Romantic Comedy: Boy Meets Girl, Meets Genre.* London and New York: Wallflower, 2007.

Jenkins, Henry. *What Made Pistachio Nuts? Early Sound Comedy and the Vaudeville Aesthetic.* New York: Columbia University Press, 1992.

Jensen, Robin E., and Jakob D. Jensen. "Entertainment Media and Sexual Health: A Content Analysis of Sexual Talk, Behaviour, and Risks in a Popular Television Series." *Sex Roles* 56 (2007): 275–84.

Jermyn, Deborah. "In Love with Sarah Jessica Parker: Celebrating Female Fandom and Friendship in *Sex and the City.*" Akass and McCabe, 201–17.

————. *Sex and the City.* Detroit: Wayne State Press, 2009.

Jones, Arthur. "Pirates Zero In on Small-Screen Hits." *Variety* 2–8 June 2003: 21.

Joyard, Olivier, and Loïc Prigent, dirs. *Hollywood: Le Règne des séries.* Agat Films & Cie and ARTE France, 2005. Documentary.

Kantrowitz, Barbara, and Pat Wingert. "Unmarried, with Children." *Newsweek* 28 May 2001: 46–55.

Karnick, Kristine Brunovska. "Commitment and Reaffirmation in Hollywood Romantic Comedy." *Classical Hollywood Comedy.* Eds. Kristine Brunovska Karnick and Henry Jenkins. New York and London: Routledge, 1995. 123–46.

Kelso, Tony. "And Now No Word from Our Sponsor: How HBO Puts the Risk Back into Television." Leverette, Ott, and Buckley 46–64.

Kim, L. S. "'Sex and the Single Girl' in Postfeminism." *Television and New Media* 2.4 (2001): 319–34.

King, Jennifer. "Sluts in the City." *The American Partisan* 18 March 2004. http://www. american-partisan.com/cols/2004/king/qtr1/0318.htm (accessed 9 October 2009).

Kipnis, Laura. *Against Love: A Polemic.* New York: Pantheon Press, 2003.

Kirkland, Ewan. "Romantic Comedy and the Construction of Heterosexuality." *Scope: An Online Journal of Film and TV Studies* 9 (2007).http://www.scope.nottingham.ac.uk/article. php?issue=9&id=957(accessed 23 February 2010).

Kohli, Joy. *Governing Women's Sexuality in "Sex and the City": Pleasure, Relationships, and Reproduction.* Ann Arbor, MI: Proquest, 2008.

Kotlowitz, Alex. "Let's Get Married." *Frontline.* PBS. 14 November 2002.

Kristjánsson, Kristian. "Parents and Children as Friends." *Journal of Social Philosophy* 37.2 (2006): 250–65.

Krutnik, Frank. "Conforming Passions? Contemporary Romantic Comedy." *Genre and Contemporary Hollywood.* Ed. Steve Neale. London: BFI, 2002. 130–47.

————. "The Faint Aroma of Performing Seals: The 'Nervous' Romance and the Comedy of the Sexes." *The Velvet Light Trap* 26 (Fall 1990): 57–72.

————. "Love Lies: Romantic Fabrication in Contemporary Romantic Comedy." *Terms of Endearment: Hollywood Romantic Comedy in the 1980s and 1990s.* Eds. Peter Evans and Celestino Deleyto. Edinburgh: Edinburgh University Press, 1998. 15–36.

Kumbier, Alana. "Wedding Bells and Welfare Bucks." *The W Effect: Bush's War on Women.* Ed. Laura Flanders. New York: The Feminist Press at CUNY, 2004. 70–78.

Lamanna, Mary Ann, and Agnes Riedmann. *Marriages and Families: Making Choices in a Diverse Society.* 2006. Belmont: Wadsworth, 2009.

Langford, Wendy. *Revolutions of the Heart: Gender, Power, and the Delusions of Love.* London and New York: Routledge, 1999.

Lapsley, Robert, and Michael Westlake. "From *Casablanca* to *Pretty Woman*: The Politics of Romance." *Screen* 33.1 (1992): 27–49.

Leonard, John. "Carried Away." *New York Magazine* 7 January 2002. http://nymag.com/nymetro/arts/tv/reviews/5556/ (accessed 5 October 2009).

Leverette, Marc. "Cocksucker, Motherfucker, Tits." Leverette, Ott, and Buckley 123–51.

Leverette, Marc, Brian L. Ott, and Cara Louise Buckley, eds. *It's Not TV: Watching HBO in the Post-Television Era.* New York and Oxon: Routledge, 2008.

Levinas, Emmanuel. "Philosophy, Justice and Love." *On Thinking of the Other Entre Nous.* Eds. Michael B. Smith and Barbara Harshav. London: The Athelone Press, 1998. 103–21.

Levy, Emanuel. "The American Dream of Family in Film: From Decline to a Comeback." *Journal of Comparative Family Studies* 22.2 (1991): 187–204.

————. *Cinema of Outsiders: The Rise of American Independent Film.* New York and London: New York University Press, 1999.

Lewis-Smith, Victor. "The World of Hump It and Hop It." *Evening Standard* 4 February 1999. http://www.encyclopedia.com/doc/1P2-1647566.html (accessed 10 September 2009).

Limbaugh, Rush. "Why Men Hate *Sex and the City.*" *The Rush Limbaugh Show* 9 June 2008. http://www.rushlimbaugh.com/home/daily/site_060908/content/01125112.guest.html (accessed 5 October 2009).

Lindholm, Charles. "Love and Structure." *Theory, Culture and Society* 15.3–4 (1998): 243–64.

Lipka, Sara. "The Case for Mr. Not-Quite-Right." *The Atlantic* 19 February 2008. http://www.theatlantic.com/magazine/archive/2008/03/the-case-for-mr-not-quite-right/306678/ (accessed 15 October 2013).

Little, Graham. *Friendship: Being Ourselves with Others.* Melbourne: Text, 1993.

Lopatto, Elizabeth. "Experimental Sex Practiced More Often by Americans." *Bloomberg* 4 June 2010. http://www.bloomberg.com/news/2010-10-04/experimental-sex-practiced-more-often-by-americans-study-finds.html (accessed 24 December 2010).

Lotz, Amanda. *Redesigning Women: Television after the Network Era.* Urbana and Chicago: University of Illinois Press, 2006.

Luckett, Moya. "A Moral Crisis in Prime Time: *Peyton Place* and the Rise of the Single Girl." *Television, History and American Culture: Feminist Critical Essays.* Eds. Mary Beth Harlovich, and Lauren Rabinovitz. Durham, NC: Duke University Press, 1999. 75–95.

Luhmann, Niklas. *Love as Passion: The Codification of Intimacy.* Cambridge, MA: Harvard University Press, 1986.

MacCoby, Eleanor E. *The Two Sexes: Growing Up Apart, Coming Together.* Cambridge and London: Harvard University Press, 1998.

MacDowell, James. "The Final Couple: Happy Endings in Hollywood Cinema." Diss. University of Warwick, Department of Film and Television Studies, 2011.

Macey, Deborah Ann. *Ancient Archetypes in Modern Media: A Comparative Analysis of "Golden Girls," "Living Single," and "Sex and the City."* Ann Arbor, MI: Proquest, 2008.

Maglin, Nan Bauer, and Donna Perry, eds. *"Bad Girls"/"Good Girls": Women, Sex, and Power in the Nineties.* New Brunswick, NJ: Rutgers University Press, 1996.

Marikar, Sheila. "*Sex and the City* Fiend: Show Turned Me into Samantha." *ABC News* 21 May 2008. http://abcnews.go.com/Entertainment/Story?id=4895398 (accessed 5 October 2009).

Markle, Gail. "Can Women Have Sex Like a Man? Sexual Scripts in *Sex and the City.*" *Sexuality and Culture* 12 (2008): 45–57.

Martin, Denise. "It's TV, Not HBO, on Sunday Nights." *Variety* 10–16 October 2005: 18.

Martínez Roig, Alex. "La Caja Tonta Es Más Lista." *El País* 5 October 2008. http://www. elpais.com/articulo/portada/caja/tonta/lista/elpepusoceps/20081005elpepspor_7/Tes (accessed 23 January 2010).

Mauss, Marcel. *The Gift: Forms and Functions of Exchange in Archaic Society.* Trans. I. Cunnison. 1954. New York: W. W. Norton, 1967.

McCabe, Janet, and Kim Akass. "Introduction: Debating Quality." McCabe and Akass 1–11.

———. "It's Not TV, It's HBO's Original Programming." Leverette, Ott, and Buckley 83–93.

———. "Sex, Swearing and Respectability: Courting Controversy, HBO's Original Programming and Producing Quality TV." McCabe and Akass 62–76.

McCabe, Janet, and Kim Akass, eds. *Quality TV: Contemporary American Television and Beyond.* London and New York: I. B. Tauris, 2007.

McGrath, Ben. "The Talk of the Town: Neighborhood Watch/Shakedown Street." *The New Yorker* 29 August 2005: 29–30.

McLaren, Angus. *Twentieth Century Sexuality: A History.* Oxford and Malden: Blackwell Press, 1999.

McNair, Brian. *Striptease Culture: Sex, Media and the Democratization of Desire* . London and New York: Routledge, 2002.

Mellencamp, Patricia. *A Fine Romance: Five Ages of Feminism.* Philadelphia: Temple University Press, 1995.

Merck, Mandy. "Sexuality in the City." Akass and McCabe 48–62.

Mernit, Billy. *Writing the Romantic Comedy.* New York: HarperCollins, 2000.

Miller, Toby. "Foreword: It's Television. It's HBO." Leverette, Ott, and Buckley ix–xii.

Millett, Kate. *Sexual Politics.* London: Virago, 1977.

Mills, Brett. "I Love Lucy." *Fifty Key Television Programs.* Ed. Glenn Creeber. London: Arnold, 2007. 105–9.

———. *Television Sitcom.* London: BFI, 2005.

Modleski, Tania. *Loving with a Vengeance: Mass-Produced Fantasies for Women.* New York: Routledge, 1982.

Moore, Thomas. *Soul Mates: Honoring the Mysteries of Love and Relationship.* New York: Harper Perennial, 1994.

Moss, Linda. "Original Shows Add Fuel to Cable's Syndie Fire." *Multichannel News* 29 May 2006. http://www.multichannel.com/content/original-shows-add-fuel-cable%E2%80%99s-syndie-fire/113803 (accessed 13 January 2014).

Naples, N. A. "A Member of the Funeral: An Introspective Ethnograpy." *Queer Families, Queer Politics: Challenging Culture and the State.* Eds. Mary Bernstein and Renate Reinmann. New York: Columbia University Press, 2001. 21–43.

Neale, Steve. "The Big Romance or Something Wild? Romantic Comedy Today." *Screen* 33.3 (1992): 284–99.

———. *Genre and Hollywood.* London and New York: Routledge, 2000.

Neale, Steve, and Frank Krutnik. *Popular Film and Television Comedy.* London: Routledge, 1990.

Nehring, Cristina. *A Vindication of Love: Reclaiming Romance for the Twenty-First Century.* New York: HarperCollins, 2009.

Nelson, Ashley. "Miss Bradshaw Goes to Washington." *PopPolitics* 14 July 2002. http://www. poppolitics.com/archives/2002/07/Miss-Bradshaw-Goes-to-Washington (accessed 1 July 2009).

———. "Sister Carrie Meets Carrie Bradshaw: Exploring Progress, Politics and the Single Woman in SATC and Beyond." Akass and McCabe 83–95.

Nelson, Robin. "Quality TV Drama: Estimations and Influences through Time and Space." McCabe and Akass 38–51.

Nelson, T. G. A. *The Theory of Comedy in Literature, Drama, and Cinema.* Oxford and New York: Routledge, 1990.

Nicholson, Linda. "The Myth of the Traditional Family." *Feminism and Families.* Ed. Hilde L Nelson. New York and London: Routledge, 1997. 27–42.

Orenstein, Catherine. "What Carrie Could Learn from Mary." *The New York Times* 5 September 2003. http://www.nytimes.com/2003/09/05/opinion/what-carrie-could-learn-from-mary.html (accessed 1 July 2009).

Pahl, Ray. *On Friendship.* Cambridge: Polity Press, 2000.

Pahl, Ray, and Liz Spencer. "Personal Communities: Not Simply Families of 'Fate' or 'Choice.'" *Current Sociology* 52.2 (2004): 199–221.

Palmer, Jerry. *The Logic of the Absurd: On Film and Television Comedy.* London: BFI Publishing, 1987.

Park, Alison, and Ceridwen Roberts. "The Ties That Bind." *British Social Attitudes: The 19th Report.* Eds. Alison Park et al. Aldershot, UK: Ashgate, 2002. 185–207.

Parker, Ian. "Ageless, Clueless and Strapless." *Observer Review.* 7 February 1999. http://www.guardian.co.uk/theobserver/1999/feb/07/featuresreview.review12 (accessed 7 October 2009).

Parks, Steve. *"Sex and the City* Is Simply Insipid." *Newsday* 31 May–16 June 1998: 3.

Pasha, Shaheen. " Showtime: Trying to Sing 'Soprano.' " *CNN/Money* 26 August 2005 . http://money.cnn.com/2005/08/26/news/fortune500/hbo_showtime/ (accessed 8 February 2010).

Pearson, Roberta. "*Lost* in Transition: From Post-Network to Post-Television." McCabe and Akass 239–56.

Person, E. S. *Love and Fateful Encounters: The Power of Romantic Passion.* London: Bloomsbury, 1990.

Piore, Adam. "'Sex' and the Single Guy." *Newsweek* 29 October 2007. http://www.newsweek.com/id/63417/page/3 (accessed 4 August 2009).

Plummer, Ken. "Intimate Citizenship and the Culture of Sexual Story Telling." *Sexualities and Society: A Reader.* Eds. Jeffrey Weeks, Janet Holland, and Matthew Waites. Cambridge, Oxford and Malden: Polity Press, 2003. 33–41.

Pollard, Michael, and Kathleen Mullan Harris. "Cohabitation and Marriage Intensity: Consolidation, Intimacy, and Commitment." *RAND Corporation* 2013. http://www.rand.org/pubs/working_papers/WR1001.html (accessed 15 October 2013).

Popenoe, David. "Family Decline, 1960–1990: A Review and Appraisal." *Journal of Marriage and Family* 55.3 (1993): 527–42.

Preston, Catherine L. "Hanging on a Star: The Resurrection of the Romance Film in the 1990s." *Film Genre 2000: New Critical Essays.* Ed. Wheeler Winston Dixon. New York: State University of New York Press, 2000. 227–43.

Putnam, Robert D. *Bowling Alone: The Collapse and Revival of American Community.* New York: Simon & Schuster, 2000.

Radway, Janice. *Reading the Romance: Women, Patriarchy and Popular Literature.* New York: Verso, 1984.

Raven, Charlotte. "All Men Are Bastards. Discuss . . ." *Guardian* 9 February 1999. http://www.guardian.co.uk/Columnists/Column/0,,238284,00.html (accessed 5 August 2009).

Ream, Amanda Osterhaus. *Only the Lonely: A Rhetorical Analysis of "Sex and the City."* Ann Arbor, MI: Proquest, 2003.

Regis, Pamela. *A Natural History of the Romance Novel.* Philadelphia: University of Pennsylvania Press, 2003.

Roberts, Yvonne. "There's More to Sex Than the Facts of Life." *The Observer* 5 May 2002: 30.

Rogers, Mark, Michael Epstein, and Jimmie L. Reeves. "*The Sopranos* as HBO Brand Equity: The Art of Commerce in the Age of Digital Reproduction." *This Thing of Ours: Investigating the Sopranos.* Ed. David Lavery. New York: Columbia University Press, 2002. 42–57.

Rosen, Ruth. *The World Split Open: How the Modern Women's Movement Changed America.* New York: Viking Penguin, 2000.

Roseneil, Sasha. "Towards a More Friendly Society?" *The Edge* 15 (2004): 12–14.

Rubin, Lillian B. *Erotic Wars: What Happened to the Sexual Revolution?* New York: Farrar, Straus & Giroux, 1990.

Ruiz-Pardos, Manuela. "'Not Quite the End': The Boundaries of Narrative Closure in Hollywood Romantic Comedy." *Happy Endings and Films.* Eds. Armelle Parey, Isabelle Roblin, and Dominique Sipière. Paris: Houdiard, 2010. 115–23.

Sayeau, Ashley. "As Seen on TV: Women's Rights and Quality TV." McCabe and Akass 52–61.

————. "Carrying On: Where We Got by Walking in Their Manolos." *The Washington Post* 18 May 2008. http://www.washingtonpost.com/wp-dyn/content/article/2008/05/16/ AR2008051603616.html (accessed 1 June 2009).

Schneider, Michael. "Girls' Night Out on Cable: 'Sex' Sells, but Old Sitcom Still Golden." *Variety* 25 February–3 March 2002: 3, 386.

Scitovsky, Tibor. *The Joyless Economy.* New York: Oxford University Press, 1976.

Scruton, Roger. "Becoming a Family." *City Journal* Spring 2001. http://www.city-journal.org/ html/11_2_urbanities-becoming.html (accessed 7 July 2010).

————. "Sex in the Commodity Culture." *Rewriting the Sexual Contract.* Ed. Geoff Dench. London: Institute of Community Studies, 1997. 57–63.

Seidman, Steve. *Comedian Comedy: A Tradition in Hollywood Film.* Ann Arbor: UMI Research Press, 1981.

————. *Embattled Eros: Sexual Politics and Ethics in Contemporary America.* New York and London: Routledge, 1992.

————. *Romantic Longings: Love in America, 1830–1980.* New York and London: Routledge, 1991.

Setoodeh, Ramin. "Sexism and the City." *Newsweek Web Exclusive* 3 June 2008. http://www. newsweek.com/id/139889(accessed 2 August 2009).

Shalit, Wendy. "Sex, Sadness, and the City." *Urbanites* 9.4 (1999). http://www.city-journal. org/html/9_4_a4.html (accessed 15 November 2008).

Shumway, David R. *Modern Love: Romance, Intimacy and the Marriage Crisis.* New York and London: New York University Press, 2003.

Silva, Elizabeth B., and Smart, Carol. *The New Family?* London: Sage, 1999.

Silver, Allan. "'Two Different Sorts of Commerce': Friendship and Strangership in Civil Society." *Public and Private in Thought and Practice on the Grand Dichotomy.* Eds. Jeff Weintraub and Krishan Kumar. Chicago and London: University of Chicago Press, 1997. 43–74.

Skolnick, Arlene S. *Embattled Paradise: The American Family in an Age of Uncertainty.* New York: Basic Books, 1991.

Skov Anderson, Marie Louise, Vibeke Arildsen, Kohl Louise Gade, Tatiana Mastilo, and Christopher Christian Johan von Hedemann. "Blurred Sex and the City: An Analysis of Language and Gender in "Sex and the City." *Roskilde University Digital Archive* 2005. http://diggy.ruc.dk/bitstream/1800/1653/1/Blurred%20Sex%20and%20the%20City.pdf (accessed 9 August 2009).

Smart, Carol, and Bren Neale. *Family Fragments?* Cambridge: Polity, 1999.

Smith, Corless. "Sex and Genre on Prime Time." *Journal of Homosexuality* 21.1/2 (1991): 119–38.

Sohn, Amy. *Sex and the City: Kiss and Tell.* Basingstoke: Boxtree, 2004.

Spencer, Liz, and Ray Pahl. *Rethinking Friendship: Hidden Solidarities Today.* Princeton, NJ: Princeton University Press, 2006.

Stacey, Judith. *Brave New Families: Stories of Domestic Upheaval in Late-Twentieth-Century America.* New York: Basic Books, 1991.

Strinati, Dominic. *An Introduction to Studying Popular Culture.* London: Routledge, 2000.

Sullivan, Andrew. *Love Undetectable: Notes on Friendship, Sex, and Survival.* New York: Alfred A. Knopf, 1998 .

Swidler, Ann. *Talk of Love: How Culture Matters.* Chicago and London: University of Chicago Press, 2003.

Tang, Alissa. "*Sex and the City* Sells Well in Asia." *Associated Press* 20 September 2002. http:/ /www2.ljworld.com/news/2002/sep/20/sex_sells_well/ (accessed 8 September 2009).

Thompson, Robert J. *Television's Second Golden Age: From* Hill Street Blues *to* ER. New York: Continuum, 1996.

Trimberger, E. Kay. *The New Single Woman.* Boston: Beacon Press, 2005.

Tubbs, David L., and Robert P. George. "Redefining Marriage Away." *City Journal* Summer 2004. http://www.city-journal.org/html/14_3_redefining_marriage.html (accessed 7 July 2010).

Tyre, Peg. "Poker Buddies for Life." *Newsweek* 20 February 2006: 61.

van Calcar, E. *Gelukkig—ofschoon getrouwd. Een boek voor gehuwden en ongehuwden.* Haarlem: Bohn, 1886.

Waite, Linda J., and Maggie Gallagher. *The Case for Marriage: Why Married People Are Happier, Healthier, and Better Off Financially.* New York: Doubleday, 2000.

Wallerstein, Judith S., Julia M. Lewis, and Sandra Blakeslee. *The Unexpected Legacy of Divorce.* New York: Hyperion, 2000.

Watters, Ethan. *Urban Tribes: Are Friends the New Family?* London: Bloomsbury, 2004.

Weeks, Jeffrey. *Against Nature: Essays on History, Sexuality and Identity.* London: Rivers Oram Press, 1991.

———. "Invented Moralities." *History Workshop* 32 (Autumn 1991): 151–66.

———. *Making Sexual History.* Cambridge, Oxford and Malden: Polity Press, 2000.

———. "Necessary Fictions: Sexual Identities and the Politics of Diversity." *Sexualities and Society: A Reader.* Eds. Jeffrey Weeks, Janet Holland, and Matthew Waites. Cambridge, Oxford and Malden: Polity, 2003. 122–31.

———. "The Sexual Citizen." *Theory, Culture and Society* 15.3/4 (1998): 35–52.

———. *Sexuality and Its Discontents: Meanings, Myths, and Modern Sexualities.* London and New York: Routledge, 1985.

———. *The World We Have Won: The Remaking of Erotic and Intimate Life.* London and New York: Routledge, 2007.

Weeks, Jeffrey, Brian Heaphy, and Catherine Donovan. *Same Sex Intimacies: Families of Choice and Other Life Experiments.* London: Routledge, 2001.

Weinman, Jaime J. "Is It Time to Declare HBOver?" *Macleans* 31 March 2006. http://www.macleans.ca/article.jsp?content=20060403_124355_124355 (accessed 8 February 2010).

———. "The Macleans.ca Interview: Darren Star." *Macleans.ca* 17 April 2008. http://www.macleans.ca/article.jsp?content=20080417_105150_5988 (accessed 15 January 2014).

Wentworth, Marjory. "Remembering Joseph Brodsky." *The Post Courier* 1 June 2008. http://www.postandcourier.com/news/2008/jun/01/remembering_joseph_brodsky42841/(accessed 1 October 2013).

Wernblad, Annette. *Brooklyn Is Not Expanding: Woody Allen's Comic Universe.* London and Toronto: Associated University Press, 1992.

Weston, Kath. *Families We Choose: Lesbians, Gays, Kinship.* New York: Columbia University Press, 1991.

Whelehan, Imelda. *Overloaded. Popular Culture and the Future of Feminism.* London: The Women's Press, 2000.

Williams, Donna Marie. *Sensual Celibacy.* New York: Fireside Books, 1999.

Wilson, James Q. "Why We Don't Marry." *City Journal* Winter 2002. http://www.city-journal.org/html/12_1_why_we.html (accessed 7 July 2010).

Winch, Alison. *Girlfriends and Postfeminist Sisterhood.* Basingstoke and New York: Palgrave Macmillan, 2013.

Wolcott, James. "Twinkle, Twinkle, Darren Star." *Vanity Fair* January 2001: 64–66, 69, 72.

Wolf, Naomi. "Cover Story: Sex and the Sisters." *The Sunday Times* 20 July 2003. http://www.timesonline.co.uk/tol/news/article845276.ece (accessed 15 July 2009).

Wolfe, Tom. *Mauve Gloves and Madmen, Clutter and Vine.* New York: Farrar, Strauss and Giroux, 1976.

Wouters, Cas. "Balancing Sex and Love since the 1960s Sexual Revolution." *Theory, Culture and Society* 15.3/4 (1998): 187–214.

Zoglin, Richard. "Where Fathers and Mothers Know Best." *Time* 1 June 1992: 33.

Index

About the Author

Beatriz Oria, PhD, is lecturer in the English Department, University of Zaragoza (Spain), where she teaches film analysis. Her primary areas of interest include film, television, and cultural studies. Her current research focuses on globalization and comedy, and she has published articles on *Sex and the City*, Woody Allen, and romantic comedy. She is the coeditor of *Intimate Explorations*: *Readings across Disciplines* (2009).